I0605479

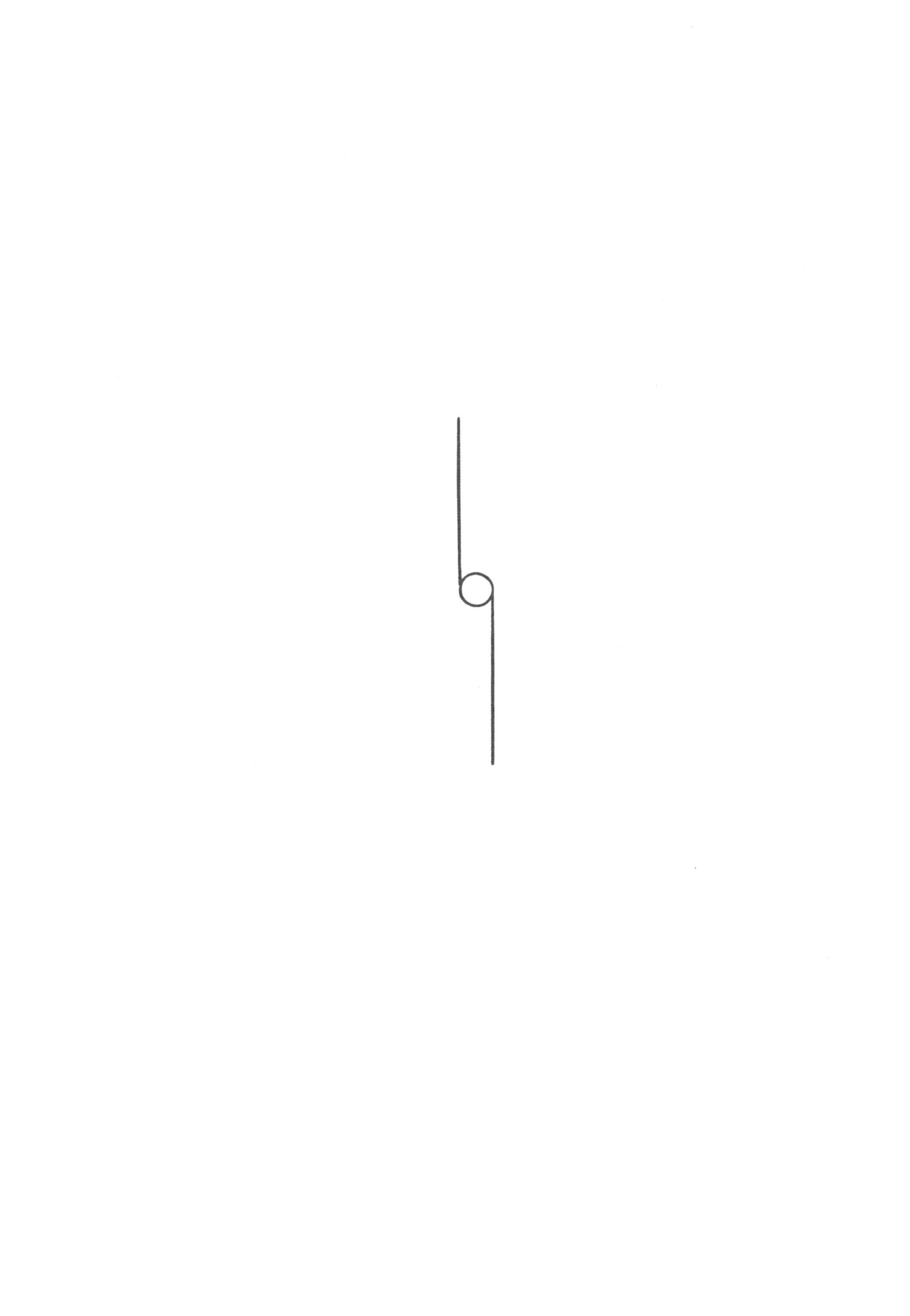

BRUCE GOFF MATERIAL WORLDS

EDITED BY ALISON FISHER AND CRAIG LEE

With contributions by Lawrence Chua, David G. De Long, Penelope Dean, Alison Fisher, Scott Herring, Janna Ireland, Hadley Jerman Bruss, Kelly Keegan, Craig Lee, Paula Lupkin, and Nolan Vallier

The Art Institute of Chicago | Distributed by Yale University Press, New Haven and London

Contents

FIG. 1 Bruce Goff outside the Eleanor and John Garvey House during construction, Urbana, Illinois, 1954 or 1955. Photographer unknown. Bruce A. Goff Archive.

Major support for *Bruce Goff: Material Worlds* is provided by Jack Butler and John VanderLinden, Margot Levin Schiff and the Harold Schiff Foundation, and Kathleen Nagle and Ralph Johnson.

Additional support is provided by the Graham Foundation for Advanced Studies in the Fine Arts and Dirk Denison and David Salkin.

Graham Foundation

Members of the Luminary Trust provide annual leadership support for the museum's operations, including exhibition development, conservation and collection care, and educational programming. The Luminary Trust includes an anonymous donor, Karen Gray-Krehbiel and John Krehbiel, Jr., Kenneth C. Griffin, the Harris Family Foundation in memory of Bette and Neison Harris, Josef and Margot Lakonishok, Liz and Eric Lefkofsky, Ann and Samuel M. Mencoff, Sylvia Neil and Dan Fischel, Cari and Michael J. Sacks, and the Earl and Brenda Shapiro Foundation.

Foreword

Bruce Goff (1904–1982) is known for a groundbreaking approach to modern architecture that is as rigorous in method as it is idiosyncratic in material effects. Departing from the minimalist, European-inspired approach that dominated elite circles in the United States after the 1930s, his work is often seen as successor to an independent strain of American architecture forged by Louis Sullivan and Frank Lloyd Wright in the early decades of the twentieth century. Goff also charted new paths with a celebration of postwar culture and consumer goods that aligned his practice with the diverse art and media of the 1950s and 1960s. *Bruce Goff: Material Worlds*—the first major retrospective of the architect's work in thirty years—explores the many facets of Goff's expansive career to establish his role as a unique chronicler of twentieth-century America.

Over six decades, Goff designed more than five hundred projects and realized nearly one hundred fifty buildings across fifteen states. Although much of this work is grounded in the Great Plains—Kansas, Oklahoma, Texas—he also had significant ties to Chicago, starting in 1920, when he first made contact with future mentors and local moderns Sullivan and Wright. Goff spent nine years in the city beginning in 1934, after the Great Depression forced the closure of the Tulsa architecture firm Rush, Endacott and Goff, where he had risen from apprentice at age twelve to partner at age twenty-six. In Chicago he immersed himself in the arts, teaching design, working with sculptor and designer Alfonso Iannelli, and finding opportunities to paint and compose music. This period had a seismic effect on his career, broadening Goff's worldview and feeding into the great mix of natural and artificial, high and low, organic and geometric that would define his mature work after World War II.

The Bruce A. Goff Archive came to the Art Institute of Chicago after Goff's death in 1982 as a major gift from the Shin'enKan Foundation, led by art collectors Etsuko and Joe Price, Goff's longtime patrons. This broad collection and archive is now held across multiple curatorial departments and the Ryerson and Burnham Art and Architecture Archives. It includes vivid architectural drawings, personal and professional correspondence and photographs, more than four hundred of Goff's abstract paintings, a large cache of Japanese prints, works by contemporary Native American painters, and rare pieces by Gustav Klimt and the Wiener Werkstätte, as well as, most exceptionally, a selection of humble yet intriguing objects he kept in his home, including crystals, feathers, and jewelry.

Embracing the diverse and multidisciplinary nature of this collection, *Bruce Goff: Material Worlds* charts new narratives that build on the museum's 1995 exhibition *The Architecture of Bruce Goff, 1904–1982: Design for the Continuous Present*. Addressing a wide range of subjects—from queer modernisms, questions of appropriation, and diverse influences to issues of abstraction and materiality—this publication and exhibition offer an expansive understanding of the architect's life and work. Representing a major intervention in the history of Goff scholarship, and of modern architecture writ large, this bold reinterpretation of Goff's work was inspired by the unconventional and expansive nature of his archive and collection in Chicago, making it a story that is uniquely possible to tell at the Art Institute.

For their inspired work on this exhibition and publication, I am grateful to co-curators Alison Fisher, Harold and Margot Schiff Curator of Architecture and Design; and Craig Lee, Assistant Curator of Architecture and Design. Loans of important works from the Los Angeles County Museum of Art; Museum of Modern Art, New York; and other institutional and private lenders enhanced the exhibition's narrative about Goff and his circle of clients, peers, and students. I extend a special thanks to David G. De Long, whose dedication to the architect's legacy began when he first catalogued the museum's Goff collection in the late 1980s and continues with our current project, for which he offered invaluable advice and contributed a poignant preface to the publication. The catalogue authors have my sincere appreciation for contextualizing and examining the nuances of Goff's wide-ranging productions and influences. Annual support for Art Institute exhibitions is provided by the Luminary Trust, and I am thankful for the generous funding for this project from Jack Butler and John VanderLinden, Margot Levin Schiff and the Harold Schiff Foundation, and Kathleen Nagle and Ralph Johnson. Additional support is provided by the Graham Foundation for Advanced Studies in the Fine Arts and Dirk Denison and David Salkin. Members of the Luminary Trust provide annual leadership support for the museum's operations, including exhibition development, conservation and collection care, and educational programming. The Luminary Trust includes an anonymous donor, Karen Gray-Krehbiel and John Krehbiel, Jr., Kenneth C. Griffin, the Harris Family Foundation in memory of Bette and Neison Harris, Josef and Margot Lakonishok, Liz and Eric Lefkofsky, Ann and Samuel M. Mencoff, Sylvia Neil and Dan Fischel, Cari and Michael J. Sacks, and the Earl and Brenda Shapiro Foundation.

In the 1960s Goff recalled his attraction to the Midwest, which he viewed, in contrast to the more established East Coast, as being always in the process of reinventing itself. This dynamic quality is part of Chicago's modern architecture history, an important legacy that is reflected in the holdings of the Art Institute. Goff never stopped exploring. He reached the height of his international influence in the decade before his death, when his practice was celebrated in Paris, London, and Tokyo. With this project, Goff's life and work is now too in the process of reinvention, ready to be discovered by another generation of museum visitors, artists, and architects.

JAMES RONDEAU
President and Eloise W. Martin Director
The Art Institute of Chicago

Acknowledgments

This critical reappraisal of Bruce Goff's life and work is framed by current concerns, yet many of our guiding questions emerged from the dense material traces of Goff's long and vibrant career. Reanimating this legacy for contemporary audiences relied on the expertise and knowledge of our colleagues and on the memories of Goff's own colleagues, friends, and clients. Since we began developing this project more than five years ago, we have found generous partners across the United States and beyond. These connections enabled us to realize the publication and exhibition *Bruce Goff: Material Worlds*, which together represent a significant new chapter in the long history of Goff scholarship.

We are indebted to our predecessors at the Art Institute of Chicago, including founding curator of architecture John Zukowsky and archivist Mary Woolever, whose inclusive approach to preserving Goff's archive was a catalyst for our project. Woolever, along with Art Institute curator Pauline Saliga and professor Sidney K. Robinson, co-curated the museum's 1995 exhibition *The Architecture of Bruce Goff, 1904–1982: Design for the Continuous Present* and offered important advice for our project thirty years later. Other partners from this early history include Etsuko and Joe Price, longtime patrons of Goff who facilitated the 1990 donation through their Shin'enKan Foundation, and the family's current generation, Sachi and Shinobu Price and Ken Perkins; and professor David G. De Long, whose important research guided the acquisition and has impacted all subsequent Goff scholarship.

We are deeply grateful to catalogue authors Lawrence Chua, David G. De Long, Penelope Dean, Scott Herring, Hadley Jerman Bruss, Kelly Keegan, Paula Lupkin, and Nolan Vallier, whose insightful essays radically expand and enrich Goff's legacy. In addition, a beautiful photography portfolio by artist Janna Ireland captures the material richness of one of the architect's last works, the Al Struckus House, built over 1977–88 in the Woodland Hills neighborhood of Los Angeles.

In our efforts to understand the lived reality of the architect's work, we relied on many people to facilitate visits to Goff-designed houses across the United States. In particular we are indebted to Sidney Robinson, Aurora, Illinois; Ann and Kevin Marshall, Woodland Hills, California; Rod Parks, Kansas City, Missouri; Laura Warriner, Oklahoma City; Daniel Naegele and Jennifer Russell, Sapulpa, Oklahoma; and Su Plunkett, Tyler, Texas, all of whom shared their passion and expertise on multiple visits. Other generous Goff homeowners, residents, and stewards include Lincoln Allen, James Robert Batterson and Todd Jordan Green, Matt Bauman and Laura Gawlinski, Jamie Nicol Bowles, Jay Brown and Julie Taylor, Susan Caldwell, Chris Davenport, Della Deme, Cassie Edmonds, Jason and Jennifer Gee, Loxi Hagthrop, the Hopewell Heritage Foundation, Dave and Jan Johnson, Linda Jones, Randy Judd, Scott Lane, Amanda Morgan, Mary and Jack Neuschwander, Lyman and Rhonda Page, Carole Pence and R. Leon Price, Jody Risley, Denise Shepard, Walter Slager, Bethany Stone, Mark and Rhonda Stovey, Pauline and Randy Taylor, Susanne Whiting and Jody Sims with Melissa Whiting, Edward and Sara Williams, and Tamar Zinguer.

Many individuals graciously contributed their expertise and memories to our research and planning over the years. In particular, we extend our gratitude to Goff's former students and colleagues Bart Prince, Herb Greene and Lila Cohen, Eugene Tssui, Douglas Harris, Robert Alan Bowlby, Bob Faust, Nelson Brackin, Tom Hart, and Michael Knorr, as well as the Friends of Kebyar. Current and former faculty and staff of the University of Oklahoma and the Fred Jones Jr. Museum of Art, including Luca Guido, Hadley Jerman Bruss, Jennifer M. McKellar, Angela Person, Stephanie Pilat, Thomas Brent Smith, Brad Stevens, and Emily Warner, offered us local connections and research support. We received invaluable advice, loans, and introductions from colleagues at other institutions: Bobbye Tigerman and Christel Guarnieri Quinn, Los Angeles County Museum of Art; Jennifer Dunlop Fletcher, San Francisco Museum of Modern Art; Maristella Casciato, Getty Research Institute; Martino Stierli and Paul Galloway, Museum of Modern Art; Monica Obniski, High Museum of Art; and Janis Staggs, Neue Galerie. In Oklahoma, Donna Keffer, Deshane Atkins-Williams, and Price Connors, formerly of the Price Tower Arts Center; Linda Pierson; and Karl Jones and Britni Harris, cofounders of the Goff Fest, imparted valuable insight. Locally we benefited from conversations with Iker Gill, Geoffrey Goldberg, Barbara Gordon, Sarah Herda, Ania Jaworska, Peter Jefferson, Thomas Kelley, Ann Lui, Tim Samuelson, Marin Sullivan, and David Van Zanten, and from the research assistance of staff at Chicago Public Library's Archives and Special Collections Division; Kalo Foundation of Park Ridge; Wichita Art Museum; Philbrook Museum of Art; Kansas City Art Institute; Wolfsonian-Florida International University; Chicago History Museum; Columbia University's Avery Architectural and Fine Arts Library; Los Angeles County Museum of Art; Deutsches Architekturmuseum; Filson Historical Society; Getty Research Institute; Cooper Hewitt, Smithsonian Design Museum; Tulsa Foundation for Architecture; Museum of Tulsa History; Oklahoma Historical Society; and the University of Oklahoma.

Bruce Goff: Material Worlds reflects the Architecture and Design department's long-standing and ongoing engagement with the architect's work. We are forever grateful for the support, advice, and efforts of our departmental colleagues, in particular, stalwart chair Irene Sunwoo, along with tremendously talented colleagues Elizabeth Mescher, Thomas Huston, Joanna Abijaoude, and Anna Burckhardt Pérez, as well as former department chair Zoë Ryan, who helped initiate this project many years ago.

Publishing, led by Katie Reilly, Lisa Meyerowitz, and Lauren Makholm, offered intellectual partnership and moral support throughout this catalogue's development. In particular, Sheila Majumdar thoughtfully refined authors' essays and edited the volume, and Elizabeth Upenieks deftly managed the catalogue's production; Kristie Kahns secured images and image rights, Isella Sandoval provided administrative support, and Reagan Stevens-Keller helped proofread captions. In Imaging, led by Bonnie Rosenberg, Nathan Keay, Robert Lifson, Joe Tallarico, Jonathan Mathias, Juan Molina Hernández, and Craig Stillwell shot beautiful new photography of exhibition works, while Elyse M. Allen with Owen Conway, Kaitlyn Fultz-Campion, and Hayley Hinsberger masterfully worked on production and post-production. The insightful Maggie Taft read early essay drafts, and designers Kimberly Varella and Gabrielle Pulgar of Content Object created a stunning publication imbued with Goff's spirit.

Campus Operations' Emily Benedict, with Samantha Grassi, Juneer Kibria, and Rachel Kaplan, and Exhibitions' Becca Schlossberg and Morgan McCommon deftly steered the complex planning of the inaugural exhibition in the museum's relocated Regenstein Hall, with an innovative exhibition design by New Affiliates, the architecture studio of Ivi Diamantopoulou and Jaffer Kolb with David Deckelbaum. Headed by Michael Neault, Experience Design was an important partner, in particular Christine Zavesky, who captured Goff's unique personality in her custom typography for the exhibition, with support from Visual Design's Layne Thue-Bludworth, Erin Fenton, and Kari McCluskey. Devin Davis, Jesus Reyes, and Chris Wood from AV Services and Gina Giambalvo, Kirill Mazor, and Alex Quintanilla produced exceptional multimedia content, including a player piano transformed for twenty-first-century audiences and an in-depth biographical video.

We extend warm gratitude for the enthusiastic collaboration of the Conservation and Science department, led by Francesca Casadio and directors Allison Langley, Sylvie Penichon, and Rachel Sabino, especially Mary Broadway, Megan Creamer, Christine Fabian, Annette Gaspers, Kristen Gillette, Beth Iska, James Iska, Kelly Keegan, Gillian Marcus, Emily Mercer, María Cristina Rivera Ramos, Andrew Talley, and Cecile Webster, with support from Ken Sutherland, Clara Granzotto, Ruthie Rolfsmeyer, Jann Trujillo, and Giovanni Verri. Erin Gordon with Michael Hall, Michael Kaysen, Ben Javellana, and Tim Campos from Collections and Loans, led by Cayetana Castillo, skillfully coordinated and received exhibition loans, with sensitive installation provided by our expert technicians. In Facilities and Logistics, Robert Ciesla, Darret Maddox, Matthew Rift, and their colleagues provided the highest caliber work, alongside exhibition casework fabricated by Navillus Woodworks. Corey Burrage and his Protection Services staff oversaw security and visitor safety with their customary vigor and grace.

Our project was deeply informed by the collections and expertise of the Research Center, led by Jill Bugajski, and the Ryerson and Burnham Libraries, headed by Violet Jaffe, and we thank Leslie M. Wilson and Rachel Joy Echivirri Rowland from Academic Engagement and Research and the entire library staff. We received major assistance on checklist development and research from Nathaniel Parks's team in Archives, in particular JT de la Torre, Jessica Smith, and Dave Hofer. Curatorial colleagues Ellenor Alcorn, Lois Taylor Biggs, Lisa Ayla Çakmak, Jay Clarke, Andrew James Hamilton, Janice Katz, Christopher Maxwell, Sarah Kelly Oehler, Elizabeth Pope, Katharine A. Raff, Kevin Salatino, Tao Wang, and

Matthew S. Witkovsky generously shared their expert opinions. In Interpretation, director Emily Fry and Marielle Epstein helped shape a discerning interpretive voice for exhibition didactics, and Sam Ramos, Nancy Chen, and Kristen French organized engaging tours and public programs. The Ryan Learning Center team, led by Robin Schnur, was instrumental in creating dynamic programing for young audiences. In Marketing, Communication, and Public Affairs, Katie Rahn with Nora Gainer, Megan Michienzi, Lauren Schultz, and Shannon Burke expertly promoted this exhibition to our diverse audiences. The stellar group in Engagement produced dynamic programs and events, led by Joe Iverson and Stephanie Henderson with Miguel Perez and Mel Harris. We are grateful for Philanthropy's assistance, especially Anna Maria Carvallo VanMeter, Erika Lowe Mullins, Jennifer Oatess, and Teresa Sutter. Special appreciation goes to General Counsel's indefatigable Troy Klyber. Lastly, we thank Heather Reinholtz and Pete Smiler and the teams in the Museum Shop and Visitor Engagement for their vision and collaboration.

Bruce Goff: Material Worlds benefited from the extraordinary support of James Rondeau, President and Eloise W. Martin Director of the Art Institute. Throughout exhibition planning, we received sage counsel from Sarah Guernsey, Deputy Director and Senior Vice President for Curatorial Affairs; Sarah Kelly Oehler, Vice President of Curatorial Strategy and Field-McCormick Chair and Curator, Arts of the Americas; and Ann Goldstein, Deputy Director and Senior Curator at Large; along with welcome assistance from the staff of the Office of the President and Director, including Claire Burdulis, Maureen Ryan, and Kate Tierney Powell. The support of other institutional leaders, including David Nacol, Senior Vice President, Philanthropy; Amy Allen, Vice President, Engagement; and Aaron Andersen, Associate Vice President, Financial Planning and Analysis, has been equally crucial to the project's success.

Finally, we extend a note of thanks to our families and friends, whose support allowed us to inhabit Goff's dazzling world for the past few years.

ALISON FISHER
Harold and Margot Schiff Curator of Architecture and Design
The Art Institute of Chicago

CRAIG LEE
Assistant Curator of Architecture and Design
The Art Institute of Chicago

Note to the Reader

This project mixes two broad genres of objects: drawings and paintings made by Bruce Goff and materials from Goff's personal collection, including original artworks (and reproductions) by other artists, as well as non-art materials like natural specimens, building materials, and mass-produced trinkets that are collectively described in archival terminology as *realia*. These realia objects, with the exception of those in the Object Atlas (pp. 31–49), have simplified captions with a descriptive title, date (when known), and collection but no dimensions or media descriptions.

Of the objects featured in this publication and exhibition, more than 80 percent are held in the collection of the Art Institute of Chicago. Given our dual focus, the works illustrated are primarily drawn from the museum's Architecture and Design department and the Ryerson and Burnham Art and Architecture Archives, with smaller suites of work from the departments of Arts of Asia and Prints and Drawings, and from private and institutional lenders. The Bruce A. Goff Archive, gift of Shin'enKan, Inc., Ryerson and Burnham Art and Architecture Archives, The Art Institute of Chicago collection line has been shortened to *Bruce A. Goff Archive* in captions.

The titles of Goff's architectural drawings are based on an institutional style that includes several pieces of information in a fixed order: project name, often the name of the client(s); location by city and state for projects with a specific site; and architectural drawing type. Unbuilt projects are identified in the title. The associated date refers to the drawing itself. Date ranges for built projects discussed in the text span the initial commission through completed construction.

More recently, we adapted these titles to better reflect the clients who commissioned Goff's many custom houses. Historically, it was conventional to include the name of only the male client in a heterosexual couple, omitting the names of many female clients who played equal—or even more active—roles in shaping these commissions. We have restored these names, listing couples in alphabetical order. As a result, the drawing titles and project names in this book might be slightly different from those used in other publications on Goff, including the Art Institute's 1995 catalogue.

Unless otherwise noted, measurements for architectural drawings and other works on paper pertain to the overall sheet, not the image. Many drawing images have been cropped for this publication. For nonlinear objects, measurements are clarified with the following abbreviations: diam. = diameter; and h. = height.

Bruce Goff called his paintings "compositions," but very few were given formal titles. Therefore, we have used *Untitled (Composition)* as the title for these works. Many are also undated. These compositions are either labeled "n.d." (no date) or given an approximate date based on scholarly assumptions when adequate documentary or contextual evidence exists. These approximate dates are labeled with the convention "c. 1925," which indicates that the work was likely made sometime between 1920 and 1930.

Bruce Goff: Beyond Architecture

David G. De Long

The striking originality of Bruce Goff's work attracted widespread and varied attention.[1] Reyner Banham, a leading English historian of modern architecture, wrote that Goff had "existed too long on the margins of fame, designing houses of unclassifiable originality in the Middle West. . . . For my money, the hundred percent pure, good-to-the-last-drop, rolled from better leaf, American architect is Bruce Goff."[2] Adding to this praise, *New York Times* architecture critic Ada Louise Huxtable wrote, "Bruce Goff is a phenomenon, part of an indigenous American tradition of the unspoiled, romantic, land-loving loner."[3] Others were less generous. One critic, for example, characterized him as the "Michelangelo of Kitsch," and noted Philadelphia architect Louis I. Kahn, when shown pictures of Goff's work, dismissed it as "an architecture of Coke bottles and old locomotive parts."[4]

Kahn evidently viewed such found materials as unnecessary distractions that compromised architectural integrity. But for Goff, using things like coiled rope for the ceilings of the Ruth and Sam Ford House, Aurora, Illinois (1947–50), or affixing goose feathers to the upper ceiling planes of the Joe Price Studio, Bartlesville, Oklahoma (1956–58), intensified each home's personal expression and reflected a diversity he sought, a diversity unbound by architecture conventions. In contrast to his exuberant work, Goff himself was a gentle, soft-spoken individual, a surprise for those expecting a stronger, more domineering personality. Goff's commissions were primarily for houses located in Midwestern sites of no particular distinction, and his designs provided those missing distinctions while expressing the individual nature of his clients.[5] The many clients I interviewed supported his work and thought their houses uniquely expressed their needs—a kind of architectural portrait.

I got to know Goff while completing research for my doctoral dissertation during the summer of 1974, when I stayed in Tyler, Texas, as his guest along with his mother.[6] By then he was living in a comfortable seven-room house provided by Bruce Plunkett, an important client whose family previously owned it. His day began early, ministering to his beloved cat, Chiaroscuro. His mother next prepared the ample breakfast that followed, providing a leisurely time for relaxed conversation. Goff then retreated to the small room at the front of the house that he used as an office (fig. 2).

The room was lined with shelves showcasing his extensive collection of phonograph records rather than evidence of the work that architects ordinarily display. At the center, a glass-topped table served as his desk, where he tended to correspondence and sometimes sketched ideas for his current commissions. Meanwhile

FIG. 2 Bruce Goff in his home office, Tyler, Texas, 1973. Photograph by Takenobu Mohri. Bruce A. Goff Archive.

1. In general, for documentation of my comments in this introduction, see David G. De Long, *Bruce Goff: Toward Absolute Architecture* (Architectural History Foundation; MIT Press, 1988), esp. 299–309.
2. Reyner Banham, *Guide to Modern Architecture* (Architectural Press, 1962), 64–65.
3. Ada Louise Huxtable, "Peacock Feathers and Pink Plastic: A New Yorker Sees Bruce Goff," *New York Times*, Feb. 8, 1970, D25.
4. Charles Jencks, "Bruce Goff: The Michelangelo of Kitsch," ed. John Sergeant and Stephen Mooring, special issue, *Architectural Design* 48, no. 10 (1978): 10–14. Louis I. Kahn made these remarks in the fall of 1962 in a master's class at the University of Pennsylvania that I attended as a student.
5. Goff himself lived simply in rented accommodations that were distinguished by his library and collection of phonograph records, rather than by any transforming interventions.
6. See David G. De Long, *The Architecture of Bruce Goff: Buildings and Projects, 1916–1974* (Garland, 1977).

FIG. 3 Dorothy and William Dace House, Beaver, Oklahoma, c. 1984. Photograph by Robert Alan Bowlby. Bruce A. Goff Archive.

I was in the former family room set up as a drafting studio, studying and organizing his more than seven thousand drawings. As I compiled a documented list of his projects, at least once a day I would review my progress with Goff. He generously took time to help me refine the list and answered questions about specific commissions.

Lunch was simple—usually sandwiches that I made—then back to work for the remainder of the afternoon. Goff stopped work promptly at 4:30 p.m. to watch *Star Trek*, one of his favorite television programs, and later *The Twilight Zone*, another favorite. Goff's enjoyment of these programs and others reflected an engagement with popular culture that was never condescending, but sincere.

Goff surrounded himself with objects he found attractive. On his desk this included a vase of peacock feathers, a Wiener Werkstätte dish, and various smaller items, such as Christmas ornaments. The source of inspiration for some things, like the peacock feathers and the crystals and shells in the drafting studio, was clearly traceable: These recalled his great-grandmother's collection of crystals, shells, and feathers that Goff remembered being drawn to as a boy. But most pieces reflected an eclecticism based more on personal taste than on aesthetic merit or monetary value.

Surrounding the house, an expansive yard went largely unused. On the few occasions Goff went outside—usually for the short walk to the garage—he favored the paved sidewalk even though it took much longer than walking across the grass, which he studiously avoided. He seemed to get no pleasure from being outside, an attitude that put him at odds with Frank Lloyd Wright's concept of organic architecture. Goff found that concept too limiting, and he sometimes challenged certain of its aspects, as in the Dorothy and William Dace House (fig. 3). Instead of integrating the house in its natural setting, he sought to contrast it with the landscape and designed an interior world largely closed to the outside world, an approach he took in many other designs.

Goff left his estate to Shin'enKan, the foundation established and led by Joe Price, his most important patron. After Goff's death, Price asked me to sort through his belongings and recommend their placement. His papers and drawings went with me temporarily to Columbia University, where I was teaching at the time. Student assistants and I organized these extensive papers and correspondence files, and I catalogued his drawings, conserving those in need of special treatment and preparing things for archival deposit. The collection was later donated to the Art Institute of Chicago, along with his Japanese prints and many objects from his house—even his clothes, receipts, material samples, and all those objects he collected—where they remain, constituting a rich and most unusual archive.

Joe Price was Goff's most important patron, providing an ongoing series of commissions that began in 1953 with the design of his own Bartlesville house and culminated in 1978 with the Pavilion for Japanese Art. Although Goff died before the pavilion was completed, his design was faithfully realized at the Los Angeles County Museum of Art by Albuquerque architect Bart Prince, Goff's trusted colleague. Prince and I were with Goff in Tyler, Texas, during the last days of his life. He remained lucid to the very end, still speaking more of the work of others than of his own. I have never known anyone more even tempered, nor more generous with his time. He seemed always focused on those around him rather than himself, giving friends, colleagues, and clients alike a feeling of unique importance.

FIG. 4 Bruce Goff at the drafting table in his office at the University of Oklahoma, Norman, c. 1954. Photograph by Philip B. Welch. Bruce A. Goff Archive.

Introduction

Alison Fisher and Craig Lee

"I've been controversial ever since I started. I can't help it. I'm neither ashamed nor proud of it. That's just what happened."[1]

While much of the architectural world focused on creating fine-tuned, minimalist structures, Bruce Goff openly reveled in color, decoration, and materials. Where celebrated modernist Ludwig Mies van der Rohe successfully pared the architectural palette down to glass, steel, and brick, Goff went maximal with mosaics, shag carpeting, prismatic windows, and other materials that defied convention. Some critics derided his singular approach with loaded words like extravagant, whimsical, bohemian, and kitsch, but Goff proved again and again that he could build nearly everything he dreamed up. Even more unusual, he charted this independent path from a place of relative obscurity, working in towns and cities in Oklahoma and Texas, far from the established centers of art and culture on the US coasts. Goff's remarkable life story also factors into his exceptionalism; as a child prodigy, he built his first projects at fifteen years old, and as an adult autodidact he would lead a remarkably successful architecture school.[2]

Yet Goff also fits the mold of an established mid-century architect, having received national and international recognition early in life for the 1926 Boston Avenue Methodist Episcopal Church South (fig. 5), his luxurious Art Deco design created while working with the Tulsa firm Rush, Endacott and Rush.[3] Architect Richard Neutra included a photograph of Goff's bold, geometric 1927 Page Furniture Depository and Warehouse (fig. 6) in his German-language publication *Amerika* as part of his survey of new buildings in the United States in 1930, a major moment in the development of International Style modern architecture.[4] After a productive creative period in Chicago during the Great Depression and a few years in the US Navy in the 1940s, his reputation was solidified by an appointment to serve as professor, then chair, of the School of Architecture at the University of Oklahoma. During this period, Goff cemented his standing with a trifecta of major commissions: the Hugh Ellis and Lois Ledbetter House (1947–48), the Ruth and Sam Ford House (1947–50), and the Eugene and Nancy Bavinger House (1950–55). Each project featured in stand-alone articles in *Life*, introducing his work to large audiences as part of the heady zeitgeist of postwar domestic architecture.[5]

Goff's work had a second resurgence of popular coverage in the swinging 1970s, with the splashy publication

FIG. 5 Bruce Goff (American, 1904–1982); Rush, Endacott and Rush, Architects (American, 1905–1929). *Boston Avenue Methodist Episcopal Church South, Tulsa, Oklahoma, Perspective Study*, 1926. Graphite on cyanotype; 19 × 17.5 cm (7½ × 6 15⁄16 in.). The Art Institute of Chicago, gift of Shin'enKan, Inc., 1990.891.8.

of Shin'enKan, Joe and Etsuko Price's spectacular home in Bartlesville, Oklahoma, in the pages of *Vogue* in 1972 and ample coverage of the Pavilion for Japanese Art at the Los Angeles County Museum of Art, a major public project commissioned in 1978 and completed after Goff's death in 1982.[6] Far from being sidelined by his outsider status, Goff remained in active dialogue with culture in the United States—its economies, images, and materials—as, in the words of Frank Lloyd Wright, "one of the most talented members of the group of young architects devoted to an indigenous architecture for America."[7]

MATERIAL WORLDS

Although still not a household name, Goff commands great devotion from his former students and followers, and his work has been creeping into both popular culture and scholarship in recent years.[8] Building on the Art Institute of Chicago's 1995 monograph, this exhibition and publication seek to renew our understanding of Goff's architecture by capitalizing on his engagement with themes of contemporary significance, including questions of creativity and queerness, the slippery

1. Bruce Goff, interviews with Robert Morris, Feb. 1979 and Apr. 1980, in "Autobiography in the Continuous Present: An Interview with Bruce Goff," *Cite* 3 (Spring 1983): 7; republished in "The Hidden Sides of Architect Rebel Bruce Goff—A Rare Look at a Generous Genius," *PaperCity*, Jan. 26, 2019.
2. After visiting the University of Oklahoma campus in 1953, German émigré architect Erich Mendelsohn wrote to his wife, "Bruce's School is in excellent shape and [is] . . . full of extraordinary young men and women. Though very much tucked away from the main streams of the U.S., you feel to be inmidst [*sic*] of a vibrating power field of history making." Erich Mendelsohn to Luise Mendelsohn, Mar. 5, 1953, Correspondence of Erich and Luise Mendelsohn 1910–1953, Erich Mendelsohn Archive, Kunstbibliothek, Staatliche Museen zu Berlin, ema.smb.museum/1409. For more on Goff's biography, see David G. De Long's authoritative book *Bruce Goff: Toward Absolute Architecture* (Architectural History Foundation; MIT Press, 1988) and "Chronology" in *The Architecture of Bruce Goff, 1904–1982: Design for the Continuous Present*, ed., Pauline Saliga and Mary Woolever (Prestel; Art Institute of Chicago, 1995), 109–11.
3. See, for example, Heinrich Klumb, "Eine Kirche in Tulsa, Oklahoma, U.S.A.," *Deutsche Bauzeitung*, Feb. 11, 1931, 85–88.
4. Richard J. Neutra, *Amerika: Die Stilbildung des neuen Bauens in den Vereinigten Staaten* (A. Schroll, 1930), 93. The building was also published in "The Page Furniture Depository and Warehouse," *Art in Architecture*, June 1928, 10–14.
5. "Consternation and Bewilderment in Oklahoma," *Life*, June 28, 1974, 71–74; "The Round House: Steel, Glass, Marbles, Copper, Rope and Coal Make a $64,000 Quonset-Hut Mansion," *Life*, Mar. 19, 1951, 70–75; and "Space and Saucer House: Oklahoma Family Lives in Suspension in a Unique New Structure," *Life*, Sept. 19, 1955, 155–56.

relationship between modernism and non-European art, and his deep engagement with material culture.

To realize our goals we turned to an embodied life story inspired in part by the extraordinary cache of Goff's realia, or everyday objects, in the Ryerson and Burnham Art and Architecture Archives in addition to his correspondence, clippings, and project files.[9] Where one might expect to find just a few personal items, Goff's archive of materials is unusually comprehensive, including patterned polyester shirts and bolo ties, geometric desk toys, collections of shells and crystals, and a steamer trunk safeguarding letters from friends and lovers.

Thus, both the publication and exhibition begin with a selection of Goff's belongings that serves as a kind of "object atlas," or an illustrated introduction to essential themes and drivers in his life and work, as well as major categories in his broad collection of realia. This presentation was inspired by the exuberant and artful installation of "stuff" in Goff's homes and office spaces, as well as his architectural commissions. As many friends and colleagues recalled, Goff acknowledged the unusually dense materiality of his immediate environment and, by extension, his worldview. When a journalist in 1979 paid a visit to Goff's home in Tyler, Texas, for example, she was so taken with his displayed collections that they serve as the anchor for the whole article, which describes Goff's groups of work by Asian and Native American artists, sofas with black-and-white striped

FIG. 6 Page Furniture Depository and Warehouse, Tulsa, Oklahoma, 1927. Photograph by Miller. Bruce A. Goff Archive.

6. Valentine Lawford, "Masterwork for Mr. and Mrs. Joe Price," *Vogue*, Feb. 1, 1972, 182–90. For the Japanese Pavilion, see Sam Hall Kaplan, "New Japanese Pavilion Is a Work of Art Itself," *Los Angeles Times*, Sept. 25, 1988, among others.

7. Frank Lloyd Wright, letter of support, Nov. 12, 1946, series I, box 25, folder 7, Bruce A. Goff Archive, Ryerson and Burnham Art and Architecture Archives, The Art Institute of Chicago (hereafter BGA, AIC). There is obvious irony in Wright's discussion of Goff as an indigenous architect, especially given the large population of Native Americans in Oklahoma.

8. Goff's legacy has been promoted by the nonprofit group Friends of Kebyar since 1983, with new research appearing in their eponymous journal. For recent press coverage, see the selected bibliography in this volume. For recent scholarly work, see Luca Guido et al., eds., *Renegades: Bruce Goff and the American School of Architecture* (University of Oklahoma Press, 2020); and the efforts to expand the American School of Architecture Archive at the University of Oklahoma.

9. This collection was donated by the Shin'enKan Foundation, an organization led by Joe Price, the executor of Goff's estate, and was organized by professor David G. De Long. For more, see Saliga and Woolever, *The Architecture of Bruce Goff.*

upholstery, a mobile of disco ball ornaments kept in motion by a hidden fan, and a monumental landscape painting by Austrian artist Gustav Klimt.[10] When asked to categorize this array, Goff reflexively answered that he was a bit of a pack rat before pausing to reflect on what he termed his "aware-house," an interior whose diverse and stimulating contents served as an essential spark for his creative practice.[11]

On the one hand, this proliferation offers a new way to understand the unconventional materiality of many of Goff's architectural projects. Yet his curiosity and openness were not confined to building materials. A closer look at this constellation of realia reveals Goff's particularly modern exploration of the world, largely by correspondence and postal mail, as seen in his large catalogue of magazine subscriptions, gallery brochures, and a library covering subjects ranging from music to anthropology and astronomy. Contributor Paula Lupkin's essay extends this phenomenon to Goff and the television, a new device of audiovisual media that stood at the center of his work for Joe Price and, more broadly, revolutionized the design and functions of the modern home.

These possessions pushed us to seriously consider Goff's widely varied sources of inspiration.[12] The plastic puzzles, sparkly vinyl, and mirrored ornaments, for example, suggest the ways that humble trinkets purchased at dollar stores and secondhand shops transported him to new worlds of perception. The natural world also fed directly into Goff's unique architectural environments, geometries, and materials, reflected in his large collections of minerals, shells, and brilliantly colored butterflies. Exhibition co-curator Alison Fisher explores this duality in his work, the blending of artificial and natural. Goff's preoccupation with star charts and sci-fi magazines feeds into Penelope Dean's essay, which interrogates the cracks and fissures in Goff's engagement with twentieth-century concepts of scientific progress and consumerism.

This project publishes new research on underexplored areas of his life and work, such as a serious practice of abstract painting resulting in more than five hundred works, as explored by exhibition co-curator Craig Lee and conservator Kelly Keegan, and his parallel engagement with modern classical music, explored in new depth by Nolan Vallier. Goff's work with painting and music fed into a broader network of creative and romantic relationships, traced by Scott Herring, which have been largely sidelined in favor of a more sensationalist narrative about his departure from the University of Oklahoma in 1955.

Several contributors have responded directly to his more formal areas of collecting. Lawrence Chua discusses Goff's many Japanese prints and sculptures and music from Southeast Asia, and Hadley Jerman Bruss covers Goff's engagement with the culture and art of Native American tribal groups of Oklahoma and the resulting complex history of collecting and architectural projects. Lastly, Los Angeles–based artist Janna Ireland's photographic portfolio of the Al Struckus House in Woodland Hills, California, highlights the material mix and details inherent to this late masterpiece.

In short, these materials enabled a deeper exploration of Goff's work than his architectural projects alone could. Just as Goff created new worlds for his clients, his work was deeply rooted in his own rich, materialist worldview, forged across the unlikely threshold of modern avant-garde practices in Asia, Europe, and the windswept plains of Oklahoma.

FIG. 7 Le Corbusier and Pierre Jeanneret's buildings at the Weißenhofsiedlung, Stuttgart, Germany, c. 1928. Photographer unknown. Mercedes-Benz, Archive number 6075.

10. Betty Leigh, "Interview: I Do What Comes Naturally," *Inland Architect* 23, no. 8 (Dec. 1979): 18.
11. Leigh, "I Do What Comes Naturally," 18.
12. The other great cache related to Goff's personal collections, including his nearly eight thousand record albums, is at Price Tower, Bartlesville, Oklahoma.
13. This list comes from the individuals who wrote letters supporting Goff's Crystal Chapel project of 1949, see series I, box 4, folder 38, BGA, AIC.
14. Bruce Goff, "As an Architect," in *Architecture by Bruce Goff* (Yellowstone County Fine Arts Center, 1978), xxx.
15. Adolf Loos, "Ornament and Crime," in *Ornament and Crime: Selected Essays*, trans. Michael Mitchell (Ariadne Press, 1998), 67–77. Many scholars have discussed the racism and sexism of Loos's theories of ornament. See, for example, Irene Cheng, Charles L. Davis II, and Mabel O. Wilson, eds., *Race and Modern Architecture: A Critical History from the Enlightenment to the Present* (University of Pittsburgh Press, 2020).
16. Franz Schulze and Edward Windhorst, *Mies van der Rohe: A Critical Biography* (University of Chicago Press, 2012), 205. Louis H. Sullivan, "The Tall Office Building Artistically Considered," *Lippincott's Magazine*, Mar. 1896, 408. The modern movement was predisposed to maxims and manifestos; see many in Ulrich Conrads, ed., *Programs and Manifestos on 20th-Century Architecture* (MIT Press, 1971).
17. Frank Lloyd Wright, "In the Cause of Architecture," *Architectural Record* 23, no. 3 (Mar. 1908): 156.

WHAT KIND OF MODERNISM?

This material complexity has a direct bearing on Goff's status in the modern movement. He clearly considered himself a modern architect; early in his career he established contacts with the most radical architects of his time, including Louis Sullivan and Frank Lloyd Wright, and later counted Walter Gropius, Philip Johnson, Richard Neutra, Erich Mendelsohn, and Eero Saarinen among his supporters—a veritable who's who of midcentury modern architects in the United States.[13] Yet he stood defiantly apart from the architectural elite, both geographically as well as through his professional claims (perhaps disingenuous) to never participate in competitions or seek out publicity.[14] More revolutionary, however, was his early denunciation of mainstream modern architecture's sterility, especially the form from Europe known as the International Style.

It is not an exaggeration to assert that modern architecture's primary preoccupation in the twentieth century was eliminating applied ornamentation. One standard bearer of this message, Austrian architect Adolf Loos, wrote the famously titled essay "Ornament and Crime" in 1910 arguing that the current preference for ornamented objects was out of step with modern attitudes and technologies and, even worse, veered into cultural degeneracy.[15] Loos's essay provided one of the many catchphrases that emerged from this modern rejection of the decorative, including "less is more," spoken by famous minimalist Ludwig Mies van der Rohe, and "form follows function," a correct yet decontextualized claim from Sullivan, a famed ornamentalist.[16] In 1908 Wright added to this pile-on, criticizing some architects' "excessive love of detail" as hopelessly vulgar, a quality that made houses appear as "mere notion stores, bazaars or junk-shops."[17]

In the 1920s this stripped-down aesthetic spread widely as modern architecture was promoted as a tool for municipal planning in campaigns by groups such as CIAM and in projects like the Deutsche Werkbund's Weißenhofsiedlung (fig. 7).[18] In Tulsa, Goff followed these developments closely, reading about Mendelsohn's work in *Dial* in 1921 and ordering Le Corbusier's book *Towards a New Architecture* (1927) and a set of books about Bauhaus work and teachings.

The political and programmatic direction of modern architecture shifted after it was introduced to the United States in the 1930s. Curators at the Museum of Modern Art in New York played a decisive role in this development, organizing a 1932 exhibition on modern architecture that celebrated the refined aesthetic principles of European designers Le Corbusier, Walter Gropius, and Mies van der Rohe.[19] With the arrival of a critical mass of émigré architects leading up to World War II, the International Style quickly became depoliticized, trumpeted by stylish architects and adopted by governments and major corporations from the 1950s onward.[20]

FIG. 8 Adolf Loos's bedroom for Lina Loos, Vienna, c. 1903. Photographer unknown. Albertina Museum, Vienna.

Of course any straightforward historical narrative leading to material purity in modern architecture is to some degree a fabrication. Some of the loudest early evangelists railing against architectural adornment, like Loos and German architect Peter Behrens, created buildings with colorful, expressionist, and sumptuous interiors (fig. 8).[21] And there were always outliers: Scandinavian modernism was warmer and more accommodating of local influences, Wright's modernism embraced curves and organic materials, and the movement encompassed many idiosyncratic individuals, from Spanish architect Antoni Gaudí to German architect Hans Scharoun and Austrian architect Josef Hoffmann. Tellingly, it was in this diverse group that the self-taught, radically independent young Goff would find his personal heroes as he forged his own path.

So while he integrated some qualities of architectural modernism, including new materials, flat roofs, and bold

18. CIAM is the International Congresses of Modern Architects. See Eric Mumford, *The CIAM Discourse on Urbanism, 1928–1960* (MIT Press, 2002); and Richard Pommer and Christian F. Otto, *Weissenhof 1927 and the Modern Movement in Architecture* (University of Chicago Press, 1991).

19. *Modern Architecture: International Exhibition* (Museum of Modern Art, 1932). In the 1950s Goff was in touch with architecture curator Arthur Drexler, who included the Bavinger house in the 1965 exhibition and publication *Modern Architecture, U.S.A.* at the Museum of Modern Art.

20. For more on the corporate absorption of modernist ideals, see Grace Ong Yan, *Building Brands: Corporations and Modern Architecture* (Lund Humphries, 2020).

21. The many inconsistencies and neuroses underpinning modern architectural purity formed a major topic in 1990s and early 2000s scholarship. See Hal Foster, *Design and Crime and Other Diatribes* (Verso Books, 2002); and Mark Wigley, *White Walls, Designer Dresses: The Fashioning of Modern Architecture* (MIT Press, 1995).

geometries, Goff also championed difference, freedom, and a staunch individualism. Roundly rejecting disciplinary conformity, he stated in a 1966 piece in *Architectural Forum*: "Mies says that he has no use for an architect who thinks he has to invent a new style of *architecture* [italics in original] every Monday morning; I think you have to invent one for each building, whether it is Monday morning or not."[22]

A NEW ORGANIC

Goff's work is frequently associated with organic architecture, a vast and often imprecise category describing projects by many different designers working with natural forms and materials.[23] Wright first defined the term and many of its now-accepted qualities in a 1908 article; these include a completely integrated character ("true forms"), a design in harmony with the landscape ("a building should appear to grow easily from its site"), and a kind of honesty in materials ("natural characteristics").[24] Because of Goff's use of natural materials and his association with Wright, he is often included in the next generation of organic architects, alongside Alden B. Dow, E. Fay Jones, and William Wesley Peters. However, scholars still struggle to incorporate Goff into this lineage, describing him as the creator of "futuristic organic architecture."[25] He himself expressed a similar unease: "I'm what you might call Prairie School based in some senses, and in other senses I'm a 'black sheep.'"[26]

FIG. 9 Goff and Herb Greene (American, born 1929). *Crystal Chapel, Norman, Oklahoma, Interior Perspective* [unbuilt], 1949. Colored pencil and graphite, with opaque watercolor, on tracing paper; 85.1 × 59.7 cm (33½ × 23½ in.). The Art Institute of Chicago, gift of Shin'enKan, Inc., 1990.854.1.

Despite his deft use of natural building materials, Goff relished the artificial. One of his most elaborate unbuilt public buildings was the Crystal Chapel (fig. 9) designed in 1949 for the University of Oklahoma. This large crystalline structure featured a soaring sanctuary, an elaborate bell tower, and reflecting pools inside and out. However remarkable the complex was, with its compound triangular geometries, perhaps the most striking aspect was its proposed material: two layers of glass sandwiching bright-pink fiberglass insulation, something typically hidden in the walls and roofs of suburban tract houses. Beyond its thermal properties, Goff chose this material for its quality of light diffusion and its remarkable color, which determined the scheme down to the supporting piers of pink granite. This project was certainly well integrated, but natural it was not.

Landscape is another point of difficulty for Goff's association with the organic. Although he admired the qualities and uniqueness of natural settings, his buildings were not in seamless harmony with their surroundings, but often appeared totemic, a kind of distillation or exaggeration of nature that took on a life of its own. Several projects, including the Bavinger house and the unbuilt Bob and Doreen Barns House (fig. 144), employed narrow, outdoor footbridges draped with netting that resemble spiderwebs. Similarly, for a built work in Mountain Lake, Minnesota, Goff designed a large house for turkey farmers Glen and Luetta Harder on a vast plain of native grass bordering cornfields (fig. 10). The house was anchored by three great cairn-like chimneys that almost appear to be blown by wind rushing over the landscape. The boulders and stones for the chimneys were sourced from the site, but the house does not so much mimic the natural expanse as hover over it, an effect heightened by a dramatic roof clad in bright red-orange carpeting, with deep-scalloped eaves that recall a flying carpet. With matching interior floor coverings, this structure is both of the land and its own

22. "Architects on Architecture," *Architectural Forum* 75, no. 4 (Nov. 1966): 67. Similarly, Goff often spoke about his desire to remain an "amateur" in his field, approaching each project anew. This idea echoes his long-standing interest in the "continuous present," a concept borrowed from the writings of Gertrude Stein. See David G. De Long, "Bruce Goff Reconsidered," in Saliga and Woolever, *The Architecture of Bruce Goff*, 29–30.

23. See foundational scholarship by historian Bruno Zevi, *Towards an Organic Architecture* (Faber and Faber, 1950), originally published in 1945 in Italian; work by Bruce Brooks Pfeiffer, including "Organic Architecture," *AV Monographs*, no. 54 (1995): 20–23; and Sidney K. Robinson and Elizabeth A. Scheurer's exhibition catalogue, *The Continuous Present of Organic Architecture* (Contemporary Arts Center, 1991).

24. Wright, "In the Cause of Architecture," 157–58. See also Frank Lloyd Wright, *An Organic Architecture: The Architecture of Democracy* (Lund Humphries, 1939). This term might also describe the work of John Lautner and Paolo Soleri, who, like Goff, were among Wright's more independent students.

25. David Pearson, *New Organic Architecture: The Breaking Wave* (University of California Press, 2001), 39.

26. Bruce Goff, speech, Milwaukee, Oct. 29, 1977, typescript, series V, box 2, folder 1, BGA, AIC.

FIG. 10 Glen and Luetta Harder House, Mountain Lake, Minnesota, 1970. Photograph by Julius Shulman. Getty Research Institute, Los Angeles, 2004.R.10.

coherent world, one that proposes a very different relationship to nature than Wright's early engagement with the Illinois prairie.

LOCATIONAL AESTHETICS

Goff's work, particularly in the late 1940s and 1950s, shows the development of another kind of site specificity based on man-made rather than natural landscapes. The Hopewell Baptist Church, for example, was a low-budget project he designed in 1948 for a rural community in Edmond, Oklahoma. The congregation contained many families of oil-field workers—drillers, pipe welders, and riggers—who came to the project with limited means but the skills and motivation to assist in its construction.[27] Goff's design was both simple and staggering: a ninety-foot-tall conical sanctuary with an exposed metal structure that was lit by a single monumental, star-shaped skylight and a full-height hanging sculpture-cum-light-fixture (fig. 11) made from dime-store aluminum cake pans.[28] Described by architect Paul Nicolaides as a cross between "a tee-pee and an oil derrick," the church incorporated a large quantity of oil pipe donated by a local oil company, which Goff deployed to create exterior trusses and interior framing that was assembled with techniques the congregants used in their day jobs.[29] The result was a widely acclaimed work of modern ecclesiastical architecture seamlessly embedded in the local culture, materials, and landscape.[30]

Goff employed this strategy in more limited ways for many projects of this period, marrying more-

27. Paul Nicholas Nicolaides, "Bruce Goff and His Architecture" (master's thesis, Kansas State University, 1960), 100, series VI, box 2, folder 1, BGA, AIC.
28. De Long, *Bruce Goff*, 99.
29. Ibid. See also Hadley Jerman Bruss's essay in this volume. An article on the website Abandoned Oklahoma notes that church construction was led by chairman of the board of deacons J. R. "Ike" Thomas, who was also the foreman for a local oil company. Michael Schwartz, "Bruce Goff's Disappearing Architectural Gem," Abandoned Oklahoma, Sept. 2, 2010, abandonedok.com/hopewell-baptist-church/.
30. "Drill Pipe, Faith and Hard Work," *Architectural Forum* 101, no. 6 (Dec. 1954): 122–23.

FIG. 11 Hopewell Baptist Church, Edmond, Oklahoma, interior, 1953. Photograph by Philip B. Welch. Bruce A. Goff Archive.

conventionally-built structures with striking elements repurposed from farming and other industries. The carport and garden of the Hugh Ellis and Lois Ledbetter House of 1947–48 (fig. 12) are sheltered by large disks that were originally grain silo covers, cantilevered from the flagstone and glass house and painted bright red-orange. In the mid-1950s complete grain bins provided architectural volumes for several projects, including a brightly colored gas station in Pawhuska, Oklahoma; a number of unrealized houses; and a daring design for an art school in Amarillo, Texas, with shortened bins elevated on radial pipe pilotis.[31] Together these architectural readymades represented an alternative form of site specificity that paid attention to local materials and expertise, as well as their contested histories.

Goff's attention to place extended beyond material considerations to a deep engagement with the national image and aspirations for the American West. This ideal is perhaps most visible in his unrealized designs for roadside architecture, the quirky and often nostalgic buildings—coffee shops, diners, gas stations, and motels—built in the 1940s and 1950s to support growing middle-class tourism by car in the United States.[32] Variously called roadside vernacular, Googie, and Doo Wop architecture, this typically anonymous style did attract a few notable architects, such as Morris Lapidus, John Lautner, and Helen Liu Fong.[33] Perhaps most importantly, roadside architecture was also part of Goff's lived experience; Route 66, the historic highway linking Chicago and Los Angeles, crossed nearly all of Oklahoma and many of the places in which he built.

Through his canny engagement with different genres of roadside architecture, Goff negotiated a particular kind of modern Western identity. For example, Black Bear Motor Lodge (fig. 13) in Jackson Hole, Wyoming, suggests his familiarity with a style now called "NPS Rustic," which describes the grand timber and stone architecture developed at many western national parks.[34] And two spectacular large-scale projects, a 1955 competition entry for the Cowboy Hall of Fame in Oklahoma City (fig. 203) and his 1961 Viva Casino and Hotel (fig. 14) in Las Vegas, show Goff engaging at a high level with the popular culture of his time. For these, he designed buildings with exterior forms so vivid—the first resembling six monumental horseshoes, and the second, a circus tent with Miami-style neon tubing—that he effectively "out camped" both the rodeo and the Las Vegas Strip.[35]

Located at the beating heart of fantasies about the American West, these works pushed Goff's creativity and playful irreverence to the extreme. A decade before the British architect Reyner Banham's pop-critical fascination with Los Angeles and Philadelphia-based Denise Scott Brown and Robert Venturi's taxonomy of the Strip brought greater professional and critical attention to this roadside, commercial vernacular, Goff had already embraced the winking charms and superficial reality of the new West—as a native, not a tourist.[36]

BUILDING RELATIONSHIPS

The project also seeks to correct (or soften) a common perception that Goff was a loner, a solitary figure who deliberately held himself apart from his local communities throughout his life: "A close examination of Goff's habits shows that he was essentially rootless. He moved from place to place in response to possibilities of work, and he treated each place in the manner of an impermanent camp, never establishing strong ties."[37] It is true that Goff moved many times in search of better opportunities,

31. These domestic projects include the C. Watkins House, Sapulpa, Oklahoma (1956), Raymond Darling House, El Dorado, Kansas (1958), and the A. E. Stull House, Dewey, Oklahoma (1958), as well as the Dord Fitz Studios. See De Long, *Bruce Goff*, 153–54.
32. Gabrielle Esperdy, *American Autopia: An Intellectual History of the American Roadside at Midcentury* (University of Virginia Press, 2019).
33. For more, see Jim Heimann and Rip Georges, *California Crazy: Roadside Vernacular Architecture* (Chronicle Books, 1980); and Alan Hess, *Googie: Fifties Coffee Shop Architecture* (Chronicle Books, 1986).
34. For background on national park rustic, see Linda Flint McClelland, *Building the National Parks: Historic Landscape Design and Construction* (Johns Hopkins University Press, 1998).
35. Ada Louise Huxtable used the term "space camp" to describe some of Goff's projects from this era. See Huxtable, "Peacock Feathers and Pink Plastic: A New Yorker Sees Bruce Goff," *New York Times*, Feb. 8, 1970, D25.
36. Banham visited Los Angeles in 1968 and Scott Brown brought Venturi on a trip out West in 1966 that informed their seminal publications on Las Vegas. See Reyner Banham, *Los Angeles: The Architecture of Four Ecologies* (Harper and Row, 1971); and Robert Venturi, Denise Scott Brown, and Steven Izenour, *Learning from Las Vegas: The Forgotten Symbolism of Architectural Form* (MIT Press, 1972).
37. De Long, "Bruce Goff Reconsidered," 17.

FIG. 12 Hugh Ellis and Lois Ledbetter House, Norman, Oklahoma, 1948. Photograph by Michael Rougier. Bruce A. Goff Archive.

FIG. 13 Goff. *Black Bear Motor Lodge for Creager Enterprises, Jackson Hole, Wyoming, Perspective* [unbuilt], 1961. Graphite on tracing paper; 70.5 × 91.5 cm (27¾ × 36 in.). The Art Institute of Chicago, gift of Shin'enKan, Inc., 1990.890.1.

FIG. 14 Goff. *Viva Casino and Hotel, Las Vegas, Nevada, Perspective* [unbuilt], 1961. Graphite on tracing paper; 77.6 × 78 cm (30 9/16 × 30 3/4 in.). The Art Institute of Chicago, gift of Shin'enKan, Inc., 1990.807.1.

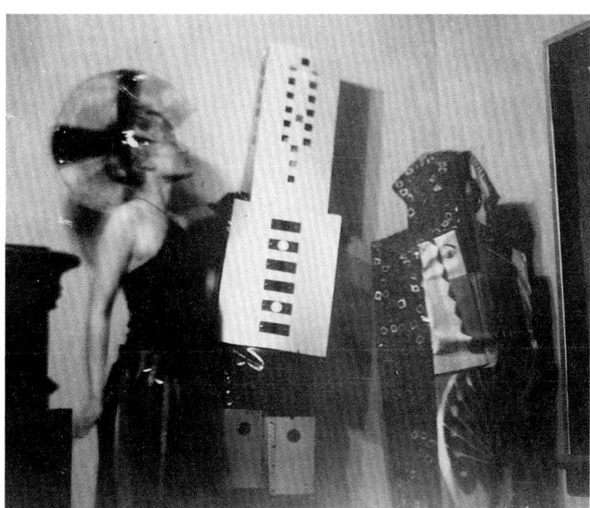

FIG. 15 From left to right: Evelyn Hall, Bruce Goff, and Olinka Hrdy dressed as modern dance, architecture, and painting, respectively, at a costume party in Tulsa, Oklahoma, 1929. Photographer unknown. Bruce A. Goff Archive.

yet each time he developed networks of robust, often lifelong relationships, all while maintaining earlier connections. And although Goff often railed against groupthink and even teamwork in architectural practice, his friendships and creative collaborations were at the core of his development as an architect and were key to his longevity in the field.[38]

After his teenage apprenticeship in the large architectural firm Rush, Endacott and Rush, he found new inspiration in a creative circle in Tulsa that rivaled the avant-garde spaces one usually associates with Paris or New York in the 1920s. The group included painter Olinka Hrdy, poet and later romantic partner Richard San Jule, composer Ernest Brooks, art teacher Adah Robinson, and dancer Evelyn Hall, Goff's wife from 1928 to 1932. With Hall, Goff held a kind of salon in an apartment decorated with stark black-and-white decor, where he introduced others to modern art and music, collaborated on the short-lived magazine *Tulsart*, threw masquerade parties (fig. 15), and created improvisational musical compositions.[39]

Goff met Chicago sculptor Alfonso Ianelli around this time, which led to Goff's second creative community in Chicago, where he moved with San Jule in 1934, following the stock market crash and the subsequent dissolution of his Tulsa architecture firm, Rush, Endacott and Goff. First joining Iannelli's studio, Goff eventually forged his own path, working for the Libbey-Owens-Ford glass company, painting, performing music, and, on Iannelli's recommendation, teaching at the Chicago Academy of Fine Arts, owned by painter Ruth Ford. This experience proved very fruitful, giving him his first opportunity to teach and leading to two of the most important commissions of his early solo practice: the Irma Bartman House in Louisville, Kentucky, for the mother of one of his Chicago students, and the Ruth and Sam Ford House in Aurora, Illinois.

The Ford house was a watershed in Goff's practice, a single-family home whose distinctive pumpkin- or dome-like shape was the result of a unique, prefabricated framing system—metal ribs from a temporary shelter developed for military use during World War II, the Quonset hut. Goff first repurposed the Quonset hut, using its more conventional half cylinder shape, in his design for Camp Parks Chapel, a church on a US Navy base near San Francisco built during his time in the Seabees during the war.[40] For the Ford house, however, Goff organized these metal ribs—painted a bright red-orange—around a central copper mast to create a dramatic double-height volume with a skylight that accommodated Ruth's cantilevered painting studio and kitchen below (fig. 16). This project also incorporated indoor-outdoor fireplaces and terraces, round bathing tubs lit by acrylic plastic domes salvaged from military aircraft, soffits covered with surplus rope, and Goff's first use of what would become a signature masonry treatment: deep-black coal blocks and blue-green unprocessed glass chunks, or cullet. The final result was so unusual that the Fords felt the need to preemptively fend off criticism during its construction with a bold, hand-painted sign that declared to the suburban passersby: "We don't like your house either" (fig. 118).[41]

Goff designed houses for clients of all kinds, from bankers and dentists to shoe store owners and turkey farmers, yet he seemed to forge especially close and creatively productive relationships with his many clients in the visual arts or music. This began in 1928 with a remarkable Tulsa home and music school for Patti Adams Shriner, continued in the 1940s with houses for Ford and recording engineer Myron Bachman in the Chicago area, and came to a new height with houses for several artists on faculty at the University of Oklahoma, including ceramist Roger Corsaw and Eugene and Nancy Bavinger, a painter and sculptor, respectively. In these projects Goff realized a community of the arts, albeit temporarily, with architectural designs actively supporting his clients' artistic talent and ambitions to live differently.[42]

Relationships also kept him afloat during one of the most difficult moments of his life, after a homophobic sting operation in Norman on November 26, 1955,

38. For more on his criticisms, see Bruce Goff, "A Young Architect's Protest for Architecture," *Perspecta* 13/14 (1971): 331; and Arn Henderson, *Bruce Goff: Architecture of Discipline in Freedom* (University of Oklahoma Press, 2017), 89–127.
39. De Long, *Bruce Goff*, 30 and 46. See also the documentation of parties and musical compositions by Goff, Brooks, and Hrdy, series IX, BGA, AIC.
40. De Long, *Bruce Goff*, 72–75.
41. "The Round House," 70.
42. See Velma Riggs, "A Five-Bowl Efficiency Makes Life Interesting," *Daily Oklahoman*, Feb. 23, 1958, F1 and F5.

resulted in his arrest and charges on moral grounds for contributing to the delinquency of a teenage boy.[43] Despite vocal and steadfast support for Goff among the administration and students—who solicited letters from prominent American architects—he seemed to understand that local police and community members were intent on disrupting his life and work at OU, with the full backing of the McCarthyite federal government.[44] At great personal and professional cost, he resigned as chairman of the School of Architecture in December 1955, officially citing "bad health."[45] A friendship made with Joe Price, an engineering student he met in 1947, would prove a lifeline during this difficult transition.[46]

Goff relocated to Bartlesville in 1955 and established a live-work space in the newly completed Price Tower (see back endpaper), a mixed-use corporate headquarters that Frank Lloyd Wright designed for Joe Price's father's company in 1952. There he regained his bearings and rebuilt his career with the support of this powerful local family. This move began a nearly thirty-year professional relationship with Price, during which time Goff gradually created his magnum opus, Shin'enKan, a spectacular house and gallery built in three phases for the Price family. In many ways, this project was a monument to Goff and Price's shared passions for progressive living, beauty, architectural innovation, and Japanese art.

CONCLUSION

Goff has often been considered an outsider in terms of both personality and position in the discipline, intent on pushing the limits of material and geometry. Yet he was also an insider, an architect with a productive practice who lectured widely and received widespread national and international attention throughout a long career. He was known for his remarkable relationships with clients, for listening carefully to their needs, both prosaic and aspirational, and revisiting designs multiple times in response. Unlike many famous architects of his time, Goff was also willing to design for every price point, finding moments for experimentation and discovery within even the most modest commissions.

As this volume attests, Goff was also an insider by virtue of his deep connections with the zeitgeist of his time, reflecting the massive changes in US consumer culture, household technologies, and artistic currents from the 1920s to the 1980s. This timeliness set him apart from his modernist peers with nostalgic tendencies and can be charted in his collections, where we see his ready adoption of new technologies (hi-fi speakers), new materials (lenticular plastic) and new ways of seeing the world (*Omni* magazine; fig. 273).

Although he formed dear and lasting relationships, Goff was never able to achieve his dream of building his own permanent artistic community. However, he was far from being a rootless wanderer in America; Goff was anchored by his connection to place—an amalgamation of landscapes, popular culture, and friendships. The architect dreamed of buildings that pushed the boundaries of feasibility and taste, and when budgets, zoning, and clients aligned, the results were so extraordinary that they challenged many to rethink their conceptions about the very nature and function of architecture itself. He was a wild and often disobedient architect, but he did not build fantasies. For Goff every building and every client was real.

43. "Goff Resigns as Architect Head," *Oklahoma Daily*, Nov. 30, 1955; Pierre-Rene Noth, "Cross Says Goff Wasn't 'Pressured,'" *Oklahoma Daily*, Dec. 6, 1955; "Architect Fined in Morals Case," *Daily Oklahoman*, Sept. 12, 1956; and De Long, *Bruce Goff*, 136.

44. For a thoughtful analysis of this event in the context of the US Lavender Scare, see Carol Mason's chapter "Bruce Goff: How to Stop Enjoying and Learn to Fear Queer Art," in *Oklahomo: Lessons in Unqueering America* (State University of New York Press, 2015), 111–37. Mason also mentions the persecution of queer artist and Oklahoma native Dord Fitz, who was ousted from the University of Kentucky for homosexual relationships and went on to commission the design for an unbuilt art school from Goff in 1957. See Mason, *Oklahomo*, 125–26.

45. Bruce Goff to George Lynn Cross, President of University of Oklahoma, Nov. 28, 1955, series XI, box 1, folder 2, BGA, AIC.

46. Joe D. Price, "Introduction: Adventures in Architecture," in *Bruce Goff: A Creative Mind*, ed. Scott W. Perkins (Fred Jones Jr. Museum of Art, University of Oklahoma; Price Tower Arts Center, 2010), 15.

FIG. 16 Ruth and Sam Ford House, Aurora, Illinois, 1951. Photograph by Eliot Elisofon. Published in *Life*, Mar. 1951.

OBJECT ATLAS

FIG. 17 Glass cullet. Unprocessed glass; 10.2 × 21 × 10.2 cm (4 × 8¼ × 4 in.). Private collection.

GLASS CULLET

Few things are more associated with Bruce Goff than glass cullet, the blue-green chunks of unprocessed glass left over from soda bottle manufacturing. So essential was this material in his designs that it was chosen to adorn Goff's headstone in Chicago's Graceland Cemetery, a legendary resting place for the titans of modern architecture—among them Marion Mahony Griffin, Ludwig Mies van der Rohe, and Louis Sullivan. Goff's grave marker was designed in 2000 by former student Grant Gustafson, using a particularly Goffian complex geometry: the rounded-edged, or Reuleaux, triangle. Cast in green-tinged bronze, the headstone supports a slim piece of translucent cullet mounted like a solitaire diamond.

The fragment was salvaged from Goff's chef d'oeuvre, the monumental house for Etsuko and Joe Price in Bartlesville, Oklahoma, also known as Shin'enKan (completed in 1976), which was destroyed by a fire in 1996. Much of the resulting debris was scattered, and today it seems like almost everyone in the area has a piece or two of salvaged aqua cullet in their backyard. Hard, heavy, and often sharp, these chunks of glass may seem like funny things to galvanize a community, but in Bartlesville they do, where they are displayed in gardens and were used to build the Goff-designed social hall of the Redeemer Lutheran Church (1959–61).

With the exception of Shin'enKan's monumental walled gardens, the church has the largest concentration of glass cullet in Goff's oeuvre. Although the structure is a modest cube, Goff used the commission to experiment with as many cullet applications as possible, beginning with discrete chunks sticking out of mortar between the flat stones of the facade. But Goff also used cullet *as* masonry for the jewel-like entry vestibule, creating a total enclosure of turquoise glass that evokes the feeling of being under water or a thick layer of ice. This application resembles building with glass block, a popular material during the 1920s and 1930s that was used alongside tinted structural glass by Vitrolite, Goff's one-time employer. Finally, Goff encrusted the building's corners so completely with cullet that they take on a sculptural quality, like horns or cyan flames rising from the structure.

Although drawings suggest that Goff contemplated swapping purple for teal cullet in at least one project, his built work remained true to this original color, whether due to aesthetic choice or supply issues. As a result, Goff's glass cullet has become an improbable material signature, as unique and recognizable as Paul Rudolph's concrete or Frank Gehry's undulating stainless steel. –AF

TEMARI BALL

Suspension was a powerful device Goff used to call attention to objects or utilitarian spaces. In his architectural projects this could look like the living and sleeping pods hanging in the Eugene and Nancy Bavinger House in Norman, Oklahoma (1950–55) or the steel cables holding up the roof, which enabled its open, column-free interior. Beyond making structural interventions, however, Goff altered spaces simply by hanging objects from the ceiling. Whether he installed small ornaments or entire rooms, they all had the effect of animating environments with unexpected drama—defying gravity with string and wire.

Goff festooned his personal spaces with all manner of items as well. His office at the University of Oklahoma was perhaps the most notorious, a riot of objects loosely, yet carefully, arranged. Covering the ceiling, a maze of string held a layer of tumbleweed aloft, while groupings of paper lanterns, disco ball ornaments, and beaded garlands dangled midair. By reimagining these modest materials in an original ensemble, Goff created an interior world that encapsulated his personal taste and approaches to design and teaching.

Among the most eye-catching of these hanging objects is this temari ball, a large Japanese decorative craft ornament constructed from fabric strips and brightly colored embroidery thread. A rigorous geometric pattern covers the surface, demonstrating how a simple line, when repeated and varied, could result in a striking design. Goff followed this principle in his own work, installing parabolic curves of string that decorated interiors or divided spaces, such as in his Chicago home and studio or in the Star Bar Lounge at Camp Parks in Dublin, California, respectively.

Goff would hang anything of interest, but he had an affinity for the various East Asian objects in his collection, including paper fans, painted scrolls, wind chimes, a gong, and numerous *kusudama*, or origami flowers. He was also an avid collector of Japanese prints and other ephemera. Although he did not visit Japan until he was sixty-five, throughout his life he received gifts from friends, colleagues, and clients, such as Etsuko and Joe Price, who traveled to Japan, and he frequently wrote to dealers and merchants to further add to his collections. As with so many of his long-standing interests, Goff surrounded himself with Japanese art and objects, creating displays that served as sources of inspiration and allowed him to study and appreciate this faraway culture. —CL

FIG. 18 Temari ball. Synthetic, cotton, and metallic foil thread and cord with metal pins; diam.: 33.1 cm (13 in.); overall h.: 111.8 cm (44 in.). Bruce A. Goff Archive.

FIG. 19 Black-and-white shell. Seashell; 14 × 12.7 × 8.9 cm (5½ × 5 × 3½ in.). Bruce A. Goff Archive.

BLACK-AND-WHITE SHELL

Goff had a long-standing obsession with black and white, a color combination that was most famously exhibited by his beloved tuxedo cat, Chiaroscuro. In his life and work these colors emerge everywhere: marking objects in his domestic space—natural and man-made—as well as appearing in materials for architectural projects.

The earliest known use of this high-contrast color scheme was found in his apartment in Tulsa, Oklahoma, likely the first living space he was able to personalize as a young adult, after marrying Evelyn Hall in 1928. (They divorced in 1932.) Mutual friend Olinka Hrdy described the interior: walls covered with black oilcloth, black-painted floors, and bright-white ceilings. This visual drama is matched only by photographs taken in the mid-1960s of his house in Kansas City, Missouri, which he decorated with black-and-white tapestries, with bull's-eye striped mobiles and black-and-white paper lanterns that hung above a red lava lamp and white bead curtain.

In his personal collections, too, Goff gravitated toward black-and-white objects, including the striped Hexaplex Radix Murex shell. Commonly found in the Pacific Ocean off the coast of Mexico and South America, this shell was part of Goff's large collection of natural specimens, including crystals, peacock feathers, mounted butterflies, and driftwood. As a young child, Goff recalled being inspired by a similar collection assembled by his great-grandmother Harriet Zelida York Messick, who also encouraged his interest in drawing. In addition to this naturalist array, Goff collected black-and-white furnishings and decorative art objects, including Navajo rugs, a Greek Kamares ware–style pitcher, and a totemic Native American sculpture from the Pacific Northwest.

Goff found a more adaptable form of his preferred color palette with the advent of plush polyester fabrics in the late 1960s. For the remainder of his life, photographs of his home always show a specific type of zebra-print fabric with a dramatically striped plush pattern, often deployed as a couch cover or throw. This material also featured in his architectural commissions, in particular, the basement of the Betty and James Nicol House in Kansas City, Missouri (1965–67). Departing from the green palette upstairs, the basement was decorated in black and white, including striped linoleum-tile flooring, built-in couches with alternating black and white vinyl cushion covers, and daybeds upholstered with Goff's signature zebra-print fabric.

For Goff, these choices did not seem to be limited to material performance or even simple aesthetic preferences, but were tied to a deeper appreciation of values assigned to black and white—something that is captured with the drama of ink drawings by architect Erich Mendelsohn or the shadows and light in a silver gelatin print, the almost disorienting quality of Goff's Op Art–inspired patterned shirts, or the harmony of piano keys. –AF

T SQUARE WITH MIRROR MOSAIC PIECES

Sparkle, shine, and brilliance consumed Goff's visual attention, whether in small objects or expansive environments. No plain surface was safe from his impulse to embellish and decorate, forming jaunty optical interplays of light and color. He added metallic hues to his painted compositions, dressed in colored lamé shirts, and surrounded himself at home with organic iridescence, such as a vase of peacock feathers on his desk and several box-mounted and framed butterfly specimens.

Goff also brought glamour to the mundane, everyday items he used in his profession, for a time writing to clients and colleagues on paper pressed with glitter. He also modified his tools, wrapping a few of his architectural drafting tubes in green-mirrored tiles and metallic, textured foil and adhering translucent multicolored-glass "gems" onto their cap ends. He bedazzled the head of this T square with silver, turquoise, and orange triangular mirrored tiles, enlivening a standard drawing implement so that when he marked out straight lines with this guide, the task would be imbued with a sense of delight.

This instinct to beautify through radiance carried over into his architectural projects. In one of his earliest projects, he added an abstract, multicolored composition of ceramic tiles to two side altars at Church of Christ the King in Tulsa, Oklahoma (1928). He later applied translucent plastic shapes to the doors and windows, replicating stained glass, like in his addition to the Etsuko and Joe Price House (1974–76), and created decorative mosaic designs using flexible sheets of mirrored and ceramic tile, like in the main entryway of the Redeemer Lutheran Church in Bartlesville, Oklahoma (1959–61). These efforts constitute his homespun equivalent of mosaics, usually made with tesserae of marble, glass, pearl, or semi-precious stones. The epitome of this type of work for Goff was Gustav Klimt's 1911 dining-room mosaics at the Stoclet Palace in Brussels, Belgium, which he visited in 1969 and memorialized in a photograph of him posing beneath a panel. Compared with this Gesamtkunstwerk of the Wiener Werkstätte, Goff's total work of art was just as encompassing, even if he fashioned it from the more prosaic and less precious materials available to him.

Perhaps the most dazzling example of his decorative penchant is the Durst Gee House in Houston (1976). Goff designed an addition for the new owners, Julia and Raymond Gee, revising his designs for original client Robert Durst (1958 and 1970) by trimming windows, embellishing beams, and decorating a door in a geometric riot of multicolored mirrored tile—in short, immersing the home in shimmering reflections. This drive to apply sparkle carried over into all aspects of his being—reflected in the large stock of materials he amassed over his lifetime, including mirrored tile, colored Plexiglas, glass "gems," plastic beads, and trimmings such as sequins and glitter, all shimmering remnants of his kaleidoscopic mind. –CL

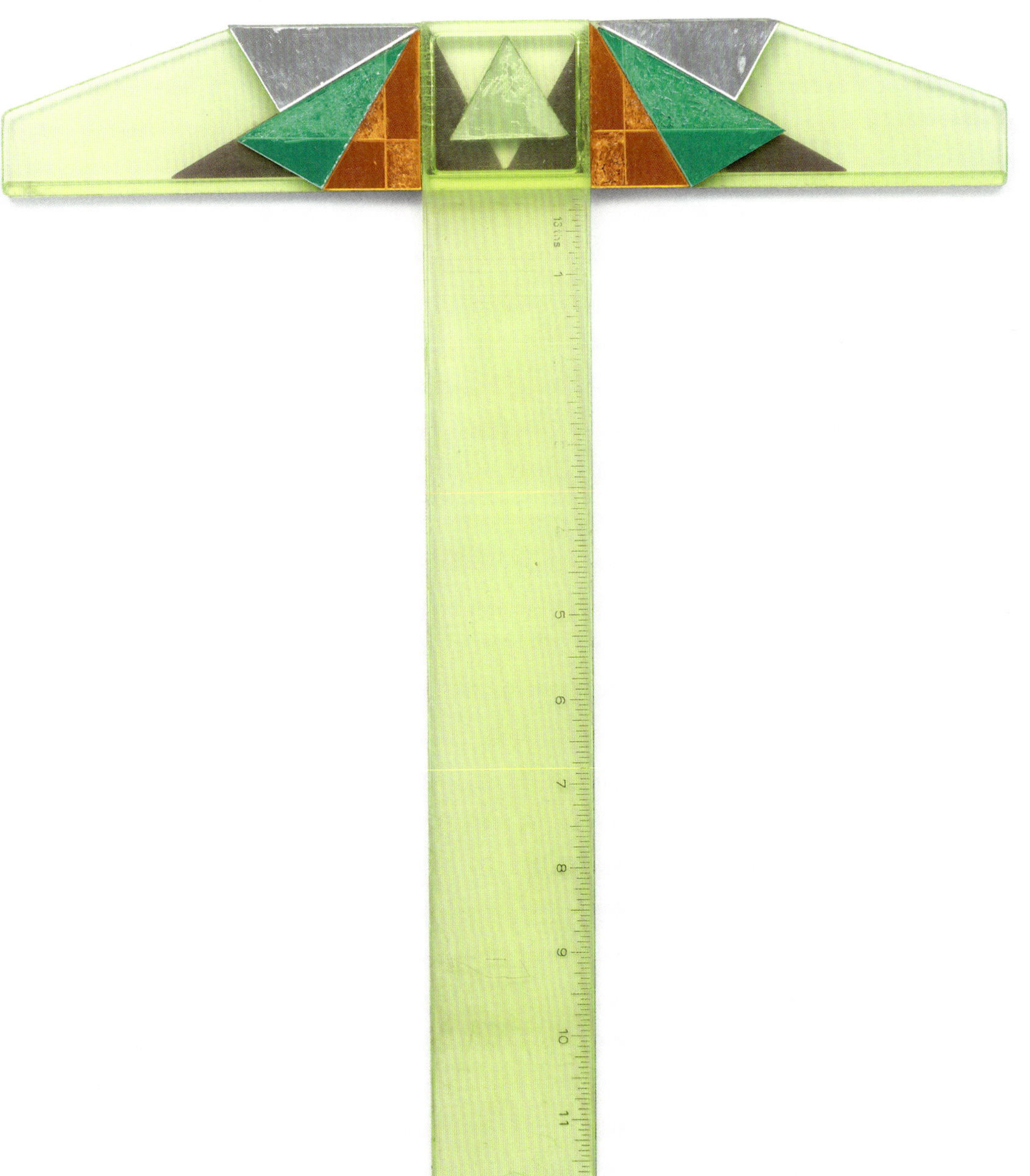

FIG. 20 T square with mirror mosaic pieces. Plastic and mirrored plastic; 35.3 × 30.2 × 1.3 cm (13⅞ × 11⅞ × ½ in.). Private collection.

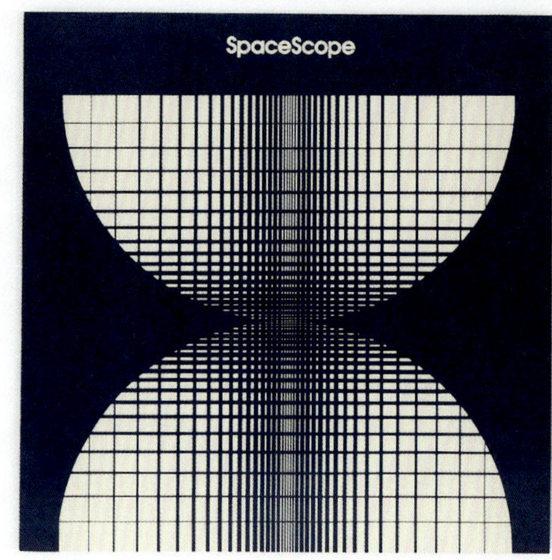

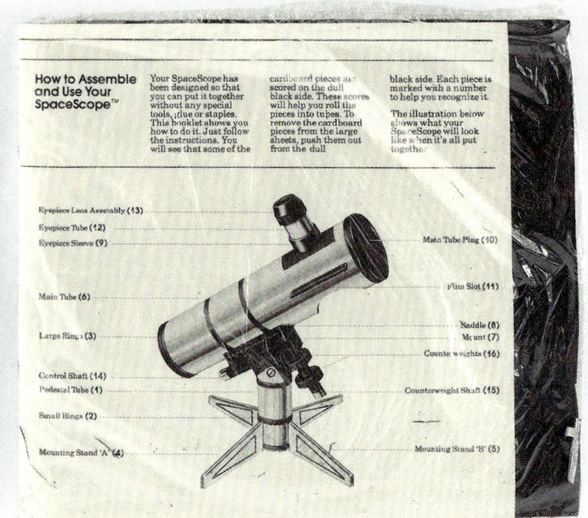

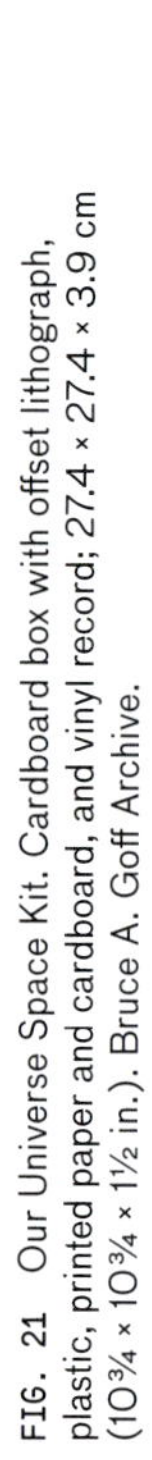
FIG. 21 Our Universe Space Kit. Cardboard box with offset lithograph, plastic, printed paper and cardboard, and vinyl record; 27.4 × 27.4 × 3.9 cm (10¾ × 10¾ × 1½ in.). Bruce A. Goff Archive.

In some ways, Goff's diverse collections echo common childhood obsessions with small objects: plastic toys, crystals, and shells. In other areas, Goff was extraordinarily precocious, for example, acquiring a rare portfolio of prints by Austrian artist Gustav Klimt from a New York bookseller at the tender age of fifteen—on a payment plan. What remained consistent throughout his life was an insatiable quest to discover cultural ideas, visual references, and artistic traditions that existed outside of his often isolated communities in Oklahoma and Texas.

Given that Goff's travel was largely regional until his sixties (he hated to fly), this self-education through objects was conducted primarily through his large network of subscriptions, catalogues, and mail-order forms. This was the origin of Goff's large music and book library, which included more than seven thousand records and books ranging from biographies of composers and art books to tomes on travel and the ethology and landscapes of faraway places. Therefore it was by correspondence that Goff became influenced by such diverse traditions as Balinese Gamelan music and the fantastic illustrations of turn-of-the-century English artist Arthur Rackham.

But for all of this acquisition of information, what was Goff's engagement with the present? Although Goff became a devotee of television programs—*The Love Boat* and *Star Trek* were his favorite shows—his friends and colleagues noted that this interest developed in the 1970s, relatively late in life. And despite his speed in adopting new influences in his architectural practice, he was fairly uninterested in current events, rarely watching the news or reading newspapers.

Again and again in his library and biography, objects stand in for and supersede events. For example, while such seismic occurrences as the 1969 Apollo 11 moon landing elicited just a shrug from Goff, he treasured his collection of sci-fi magazines and collectables, such as this Our Universe Space Kit. Created by National Geographic in 1980, this boxed set was designed to expose children to diverse extraterrestrial ideas, including a record of "space sounds," stories on the link between constellations and Greek and Roman myths, and a customizable star chart.

A symbol of his indefatigable and lifelong sense of curiosity and wonder, this kit is also evidence of Goff's distance from visceral experience. He was content to experience the world at a remove, listening to the sounds of space from his armchair, thumbing through magazines with pictures of distant peoples and lands, and becoming an expert on classical music through records rather than live performances. In the end, perhaps there is nothing more contemporary about Goff than his comfort with mediated experience, portending our future of virtual communication and creative expression. –AF

BOLO TIE

Goff's personal fashion sense was much remarked upon by friends and critics alike. In many cases, his unique and colorful attire—wildly patterned shirts, velvet pants, purple suede shoes—was seen to clash with his soft-spoken and unassuming demeanor. "He wore garish clothing as if to shock people," remarked one colleague in a feature published in *The Christian Science Monitor* (Sept. 3, 1982), sartorial choices that were associated with his identity as either an avant-garde artist or a gay man, or both. Others commented that the color and material of his clothes might have been unusual but that his manner of dress was neat and fastidious in keeping with his personality.

In the 1950s and 1960s, Goff wore turtleneck sweaters and collarless jackets that raised some eyebrows in Norman and Bartlesville, Oklahoma. By the 1970s he had moved on to imported silk and polyester shirts with daring geometric patterns, metallic threads, and exaggerated collars. Most consistent was his interest in creating extreme color contrasts, such as a white coat and crimson shirt with dark slacks, or monochromatic effects, like a dark-green satin shirt and matching velvet pants—not unlike the color schemes of the buildings he designed. Neither the style of a sixties beatnik nor of a disco kid, Goff's fashion evolved with the times, more like the students and apprentices he mentored than the middle-aged man he was.

One item in Goff's wardrobe invited an extra level of attention: the bolo tie. This is distinguished from the conventional tie, a symbol of conformity and professionalism that Goff almost never wore—in contrast to modern architect Ludwig Mies van der Rohe, who was always photographed wearing a white shirt, dark suit, and tie. This uniform was also adopted by many American architects of Goff's generation, including Philip Johnson, Eero Saarinen, and Marcel Breuer, mimicking the anonymous cadre of white-collar workers that quickly expanded in US cities after World War II.

The bolo tie, associated with the American Southwest and rock and roll, represents the opposite of the corporate and universal. This modern accessory had an independent edge that grew out of a number of western traditions in the 1940s, including the silver scarf slides made in Native American communities in Oklahoma and Kansas and cowboy neckwear, before gaining wide exposure in TV shows of the 1950s. Goff owned many bolo ties, amply documented in his portraits over the years. This example is unsigned but features the inlaid style of Zuni tribal silversmiths from New Mexico, with a circular Sunface motif and traditional materials of mother-of-pearl (white), jet (black), coral, and turquoise.

When worn with one of his signature patterned shirts, Goff's bolo ties expressed the kind of freedom that he adopted for life, work, and attire. Either admired for its beauty or derided as unusual, Goff's clothing was part of a persona that was at once folksy and unassuming, eclectic and flamboyant. —AF

FIG. 22 Bolo tie. Leather, silver, mother-of-pearl, coral, jet, and turquoise; pendant diam.: 2.6 cm (1 in.); overall h.: 45.8 cm (18 in.). Bruce A. Goff Archive.

FIG. 23 Shag carpet examples. Nylon, metal, and paper; 40.7 × 66.1 × 11.5 cm (16 × 26 × 4½ in.). Private collection.

SHAG CARPET SAMPLES

Recognized for structures with daring, over-the-top geometries, Goff is equally an architect of cladding. Beginning in the 1940s and continuing through his final projects, Goff transformed the practice of architecture with surface materials that subvert convention and, in doing so, suggest new and unusual connections between outside and inside, up and down.

An early example of this phenomenon can be found in a house he designed for artist Ruth Ford and her husband, Sam, in Aurora, Illinois, completed in 1950. Here Goff used an unusual material—army surplus jute rope—to define a series of rounded exterior soffits (the underside of a roof edge) on the carport and the small roofs over two bedroom wings. Laid out in straight lines and nailed to the curved plywood underlayer, these rope-clad soffits continue inside under plate glass windows, creating an unexpectedly dense, ribbed materiality in the entryway and bedrooms that frames views out into the landscape.

Goff's attention to surfaces echoes an important theory of cladding in Gottfried Semper's 1851 text *The Four Elements of Architecture*. Semper argued that the earliest human enclosures were textiles, such as rugs and mats, draped over simple frames, which clothe the structure just like garments on the human body. Similarly, Goff's claddings often serve to obscure the building's structure and create unexpected visual effects or links between unrelated parts.

As Goff's career evolved, so did the range of available cladding materials. The advent of plastics in the 1950s and 1960s led to a huge expansion of commercial products for the home: laminate countertops, vinyl flooring tiles, and brightly colored acrylic carpeting. This sample of shag carpet squares illustrates a particular focus on covered surfaces in his later work. Goff selected lime-green shag to unite multiple levels of seating and flooring in the conversation pit of his Betty and James Nicol House (1964), and he affixed pink carpet to the back of a bathroom door in the Grace Lee and John Frank House (1955–56), providing a sense of enclosure and sound dampening and creating a harmonious color environment with the room's matching tile floor and soft-gray fixtures.

Perhaps his most notable application of shag carpeting appears in the Al Struckus House in Los Angeles, begun in 1979. Inside the barrel-shaped house, Goff used rose-colored carpeting to define the house's monumental, exposed staircase. Rising more than three stories in height, pink shag covered the staircase's curvilinear walls and stair treads, creating a lush backdrop for floor-to-ceiling bookshelves and integrating deep window wells framing the building's distinctive bubble windows. Cladding, which Goff used to soften and animate, enclose and protect, formed an indispensable part of the architect's integrative language, uniting exterior, interior, walls, floors, and ceilings, as well as parts without names. –AF

RECORD ALBUM

Goff took music appreciation seriously. When playing an album, he sat down to listen and only listen, learning to discern the nuances between different recordings of the same piece. (His many duplicate albums—some worn down—attest to their frequent use.) In many homes he included spaces dedicated solely to this activity, installing high-fidelity speakers and decorations to facilitate listening. Yet he also turned this solitary pursuit into a social activity, insisting that others partake in listening sessions. These gatherings with friends at his Tulsa home in the 1920s and later with apprentices in his small office in Tyler, Texas, would remain a fixture of his life. At the University of Oklahoma, music was a key, if informal, part of his architectural curriculum. As students worked at their desks into the evening, Goff invited them to the lecture hall and played a selection of records. Music was meant to be shared, to bring people together.

The seeds of this intense interest were planted early in high school, when Goff first heard work by French composers Claude Debussy and Maurice Ravel. Since that formative moment, he subsequently surrounded himself with music: He composed it, performed it, and, more than anything, collected it. Through placing catalogue orders and visiting record shops, he amassed nearly eight thousand record albums, more than twice the number of books in his library and by far his largest collection. Dedicated shelving lined his walls, so hazardously full that in one instance it fell and narrowly avoided crushing him. Although he primarily focused on classical music—Debussy, his favorite composer, for example, comprised 20 percent of his collection—he had varied tastes and was receptive to new approaches. He acquired traditional and folk records from African and Asian cultures, avant-garde work by American composer John Cage, and 1970s Japanese electronic music. For a self-taught and curious mind, record albums provided nearly unlimited possibilities.

Music also played a large role in fostering Goff's community. It formed a common bond between him and his partner Richard San Jule. It connected him with architectural clients and enhanced his instruction of university students. And it led to friendships with musicians, including American jazz pioneer Duke Ellington and French-born composer Edgard Varèse. Architecture was his profession, and painting was a lifelong, self-described "relaxing" activity, but among the arts, music was Goff's passion. –CL

FIG. 24 Record album. Vinyl record and cover with offset lithograph; 30.5 × 30.5 cm (12 × 21 in.). Private collection.

FIG. 25 Keys and key case. Metal, leather, paper, and ink; keyholder, open: 8.9 × 15.3 × 1.3 cm (3½ × 6 × ½ in.). Bruce A. Goff Archive.

KEYS AND KEY CASE

The self-designed house is a tantalizing prospect for an architect because it can offer the clearest demonstration of their architectural vision. Many of Goff's students and apprentices, such as Herb Greene and Bart Prince, designed their own homes as testaments to their work and specific approaches. Yet for all the remarkably individualized houses Goff built throughout his career, he never lived in one of his own design. He was a peripatetic architect and moved where opportunity and circumstance took him: from Tulsa, Oklahoma, to Chicago (with a short time in Toledo, Ohio); then Berkeley, California, after being stationed in Alaska's Aleutian Islands and at Camp Parks, California; to Norman and Bartlesville, Oklahoma; then Kansas City, Missouri; and finally Tyler, Texas. In each successive place—whether a modest apartment, a live-work unit in Frank Lloyd Wright's Price Tower, or a single-family house—he used interior design and his vast collections to create a home, by designing built-in furniture, adding decorative wall treatments, and surrounding himself with inspiring objects.

That is not to say that Goff did not envision a house of his own. A project called Kebyar was perhaps his most audacious plan, capturing his ideal for what constitutes home. Theatrics of the proposed structure aside—it would have been suspended across a waterfall on a site that he bought in 1941 outside Louisville, Kentucky—it was a place where he and his partner Richard San Jule could live in creative community with others. After San Jule died unexpectedly in 1946, however, their shared ambition was never realized. For Goff, such a home remained a dream.

In lieu of a permanent home, Goff amassed numerous keys, like this set, that unlocked the many places where he lived, worked, and stored his things over the years. Near the end of his life, he revisited the idea of designing a house for himself. Joe Price, a friend and patron, offered him a barn on his property in Bartlesville, and Goff drew designs that opened up the gable ends with large hexagonal and triangular windows. In Tyler, Goff spoke of designing himself a house that would float on Lake Palestine, part of the lakeside community he was working on with developer Bruce Plunkett. Any idea for a house of his own, however, remained merely that. In the end, Goff's most elusive client was himself. —CL

FIG. 26 Bruce Goff, Chicago, c. 1936. Photographer unknown. Bruce A. Goff Archive.

The Queer Modernism of Bruce Goff and Richard San Jule

Scott Herring

In the summer of 1940 while visiting family in the San Francisco Bay Area, Richard (Rik) San Jule wrote to his lover Bruce Goff about how much he wished to be homeward bound. He sorely missed Goff and looked forward to reuniting, with "October as a deadline to be back in Chicago." His letter updated Goff about the health of San Jule's parents and commented on the city's beauty. More than once it emphasized how much the two meant to each other—personally and creatively. "How can I tell how much I miss the living warmth and richness of your friendship; and not just the music and architecture," San Jule wrote. He ended with a nod to their queer affection that took precedence over that of his biological kin: "Please take care of yourself. They say blood is thicker than water. How much nearer you are to me than any of my own relatives, than anyone else."[1]

Such intimacies between Goff and San Jule have gone largely unremarked in the scholarly record. Cultural critic Carol Mason correctly observed in 2015, "Most Goff aficionados and art historians have veered away from acknowledging the queer aspect of Goff's 'continuous present' and in general downplay his homosexuality."[2] While unfortunate, this long-standing oversight nevertheless presents a valuable opportunity to refine Mason's important insights into Goff's creative practices. Focusing on Goff's time at the University of Oklahoma School of Architecture from 1947 to his resignation in 1955, Mason insisted on "the queerness of his designs and his life."[3] To do so she interpreted the shirts Goff wore during and after his tenure as instances of "rustic glam" that signified his non-normative desires: "Goff often used metallic hues in his paintings [and] had a wardrobe containing a gold lamé shirt and bolo ties."[4] The Bruce A. Goff Archive at the Art Institute of Chicago houses many of these shirts (fig. 27), and this realia stands in sharp relief, Mason contended, to the staid US heteronorms of the Cold War era.

This essay looks at the years before, returning queerness to Goff's lengthy career—but not only to University of Oklahoma's hallways, where his attire announced "a contemporary gay aesthetic," or to the decades thereafter.[5] I am instead most keen to understand how his sexual orientation infused his creative years in Chicago, from 1934 to 1942, when he coupled with San Jule and self-identified as an upstart modernist experimenting with interior decoration, poetry, and prose. According to architect and scholar David G. De Long, these years facilitated an aesthetic breakthrough that would help Goff launch his illustrious career.[6] Goff's intimacies with his partner were part of this development.

FIG. 27 Polyester shirt, n.d. Bruce A. Goff Archive.

Documents in the Art Institute of Chicago's Ryerson and Burnham Art and Architecture Archives confirm as much. In addition to numerous architectural designs, the Bruce Goff archive contains published and unpublished essays, photographs of Goff and San Jule's Chicago apartment and their intended home site in Kentucky, poems, and what De Long refers to as "a large cache of intimate love letters" that illuminates the foundational influence of their relationship on what would become Goff's astounding architectural record—especially given that "for an architect such as Bruce Goff, the term 'architectural record' resists concise definition."[7] As I noted at this essay's start, this correspondence illuminates how important the two were to each other when they lived together or when they were apart from each other on their respective travels. "And remember,"

1. Richard San Jule to Bruce Goff, postmarked 1940, series I, box 20, folder 11, Bruce A. Goff Archive, Ryerson and Burnham Art and Architecture Archives, The Art Institute of Chicago (hereafter BGA, AIC). For more on queer (male) intimacies and letter writing, see Nicholas L. Syrett, "Mobility, Circulation, and Correspondence: Queer White Men in the Midcentury Midwest," *GLQ: A Journal of Lesbian and Gay Studies* 20, nos. 1–2 (2014): 75–94.
2. Carol Mason, *Oklahomo: Lessons in Unqueering America* (State University of New York Press, 2015), 115.
3. Ibid., 120.
4. Ibid., 119.
5. Ibid.
6. David G. De Long, *Bruce Goff: Toward Absolute Architecture* (Architectural History Foundation; MIT Press, 1988), 53.
7. David G. De Long, "The Historian's View," *American Archivist* 59, no. 2 (1996): 158 and 161.
8. Richard San Jule to Bruce Goff, postmarked Aug. 2, 1940, series I, box 20, folder 11, BGA, AIC.
9. For more on queer US modernity, see Siobhan B. Somerville, *Queering the Color Line: Race and the Invention of Homosexuality in American Culture* (Duke University Press, 2000); Scott Herring, *Queering the Underworld: Slumming, Literature, and the Undoing of Lesbian and Gay History* (University of Chicago Press, 2007); and Jonathan Flatley, *Like Andy Warhol* (University of Chicago Press, 2017).
10. Mason, *Oklahomo*, 119.
11. De Long, *Bruce Goff*, 51.

San Jule wrote to Goff in another letter from the summer of 1940, "more than anything, there is no one and nothing which means as much to me as you do and what you stand for. Remember I really won't be happy or truly alive to the imaginative beauty of things until I'm back with you again."[8]

Reviewing how these letters captured their shared commitments to beauty in modern art, in queer male life, in their living space, and in each other, I find these materials beholden to an American strain of queer modernity, in particular, and to international modernism generally, both of which paved the way for Goff's "contemporary gay aesthetic."[9] At the same time, the archive also contains San Jule's own modernist writings folded into Goff's collections. These extensive yet understudied resources illuminate how the two men—through art, poetics, and everyday intimacies—collaborated on a queer male modernism that anticipated Goff's midcentury "rustic glam."[10]

GOFF AND SAN JULE IN QUEER CHICAGO

Seeking better employment opportunities during the height of the Great Depression as well as new opportunities for creative expression, Goff moved from Tulsa to Chicago in 1934. The city would be his home—apart from a brief stint in Toledo, Ohio, in 1937—until he joined the United States Navy in 1942. De Long detailed that "with him went Richard San Jule, who had just finished his second year of college and with whom Goff was to live for most of the next decade" (fig. 28).[11] According to postmarked correspondence, 1940 census records, and Goff and San Jule's respective draft cards, the two first maintained a residence at 57 Summit Avenue in Park Ridge and then later at 1515 West Howard Street, Suite 15, in Rogers Park (fig. 29), a Chicago neighborhood far north of downtown.[12]

Scholars of modern US LGBTQ urban history have shown that the 1930s and 1940s were pivotal for emerging queer and trans subcultures across this Midwestern metropolis.[13] Despite Goff and San Jule's distance from the Near North Side epicenter of Chicago's queer subcultures, letters between the two express a keen awareness of the sexual and gender nonconformity around the city, supporting historian David K. Johnson's claim that "although this world was partly defined geographically, one did not have to live on the Near North Side to be a part of it."[14] In one 1939 letter to San Jule while his lover was away on travels, for example, Goff euphemistically recounted that "Jack and I have just returned from the lake. The 'people' are so beautiful with their sun tans, but not half so much as the one I know."[15] In another letter he sent San Jule that same year, Goff wrote, "How I miss your warmth," and recalled, "The other night when I was walking down to the COED [a Rogers Park theatre] a 'lady' passing me said 'Hello big boy.' I felt insulted as you can well imag[ine]. So you see I could have a love life if I wasn't too particular."[16] I do not think we should read his apparent affront at this cruising episode as an indication of internalized homophobia or self-closeting. Rather, I believe that, as an aspiring member of the professional classes, Goff was expressing a common middle-class gay male disdain for effeminate (often working-class) queers—sometimes called fairies in the subcultural parlance of the time—that historian George Chauncey outlined in *Gay New York*.[17] Tensions between gay men and fairies were not uncommon in pre-Stonewall queer male encounters, and Goff's remarks exemplify this social strain.

FIG. 28 Richard San Jule, Chicago, 1939. Photographer unknown. Bruce A. Goff Archive.

12. As Timothy Samuelson detailed, between 1937 and 1942 Goff "ignored the congestion of downtown Chicago in favor of a busy commercial strip at the far northern edge of the city. [He] secured a pair of irregularly shaped rooms on the second floor of a two-story, wedge-shaped commercial building . . . which he adapted as combined office and living quarters." Timothy Samuelson, "Bruce Goff in Chicago," in *The Architecture of Bruce Goff, 1904–1982: Design for the Continuous Present*, ed. Pauline Saliga and Mary Woolever (Prestel; Art Institute of Chicago, 1995), 47.

13. See Chad Heap, "The City as a Sexual Laboratory: The Queer Heritage of the Chicago School," *Qualitative Sociology* 26, no. 4 (2003): 457–87; and St. Sukie de la Croix, *Chicago Whispers: A History of LGBT Chicago Before Stonewall* (University of Wisconsin Press, 2012), 120–32.

14. David K. Johnson, "The Kids of Fairytown: Gay Male Culture on Chicago's Near North Side in the 1930s," in *Creating a Place for Ourselves: Lesbian, Gay, and Bisexual Community Histories*, ed. Brett Beemyn (Routledge, 1997), 102.

15. Bruce Goff to Richard San Jule, postmarked July 31, 1939, series I, box 20, folder 9, BGA, AIC.

16. Bruce Goff to Richard San Jule, postmarked Oct. 1, 1939, series I, box 20, folder 10, BGA, AIC.

17. See George Chauncey, *Gay New York: Gender, Urban Culture, and the Making of the Gay Male World, 1890–1940* (Basic Books, 1994), 99–127.

FIG. 29 Studio of Bruce Goff, 1515 W. Howard Street, Chicago, 1941. Photograph by Ernest Ellison. Filson History Society, Louisville, Kentucky.

What did their daily domestic life at 1515 West Howard Street look like amid these casual queer encounters? Archived photographs of the home record a hyper-stylized living space reminiscent of the Tulsa residence that Goff decorated with his former wife, Evelyn Hall, whom he married in 1928 and divorced in 1932: "Goff furnished their apartment with low, built-in couches, covered the walls with black oilcloth, and painted the floors black and the ceilings white. They evidently maintained a kind of salon for their friends, one of whom later recalled, 'It was quite exciting to be introduced to what was then 'modern' art and music.'"[18] Describing Goff and San Jule's Rogers Park environs, historian Timothy Samuelson noted a continuation of this Tulsa modernist decor: "Gold lamé curtains offered privacy while shimmering with the brilliant nighttime lights of movie theaters, restaurants, and nightclubs that surrounded the building."[19] A photograph of their space in the Bruce Goff archive confirms this description (fig. 30). Other archived images likewise feature streamlined furnishings and a wall partially painted with small squares recalling paintings by Gustav Klimt, whom Goff deeply admired (fig. 31).

Sentimental correspondence between the two—particularly San Jule's letters to Goff during the former's travels in the late 1930s and early 1940s—records the mutual fondness that this self-produced modernist space permitted them. Writing from Colorado on his way to California in August of 1939, San Jule told his lover, "Very much I miss the creative ferment of 1515 Howard, the music, the paintings, the architecture, the friendship."[20] A little more than two weeks later he

18. De Long, *Bruce Goff*, 30.
19. Samuelson, "Bruce Goff in Chicago," 47.
20. Richard San Jule to Bruce Goff, postmarked Aug. 8, 1939, series I, box 20, folder 9, BGA, AIC.

FIGS. 30–31 Interiors of Goff's Chicago studio, n.d. Photographer unknown. Bruce A. Goff Archive.

informed Goff, "In the vortex of new values, experiences, activities, none has the beauty and the richness that life had concentrated in the sanctum of 1515 Howard."[21] In July of 1942: "All the night long I was thinking of you. . . . I was remembering the soft gold flax of your hair after a washing. . . . I was remembering glimpses deep-cached, each precious and poignant now: the countless scenes and moments we have passed through together, some commonplace, some intense, but all having the quality of sympathetic and intelligent friendship and the bond of creative imagination."[22] And a few months later in October: "The rest, said so many times before but still as valid, about that special loneliness which will not be sated or soothed until I am with you again, you can see between every line I write."[23]

That love letters mailed between two men more than a quarter of a century before the Stonewall Uprising survive is itself noteworthy, but I wish to emphasize how vital their Chicago abode felt to both Goff and San Jule as they transformed a rented space into a queer "sanctum." There they fostered their collective aesthetic endeavors—in a place where their "friendship" and art making flourished amid the wider world of urban modernity that took shape in bars, on lakefront beaches, and on bustling sidewalks filled with queer life.

"THE BEAUTY OF SENSITIVITY"

Much of the creative ferment San Jule described also reflects the pair's deep affinity for queer modernism, a diverse movement that inspired their artistic productions while enabling them to express their emotional connection to each other. As noted above, Goff's interests in modernist décor traveled with him from Oklahoma to Illinois. He also launched the coedited magazine *Tulsart* in 1931, and scholars interested in Goff's musical contributions such as Benjamin R. Levy likewise remind us that he and San Jule participated in many social scenes committed to experimental aesthetics.[24]

Even before they moved in together, early writings by Goff confirm his long-standing investments in modernism as well as its queer applications. In an unpublished 1925 essay that refers to theatrical performance, Goff praised a figure he identifies as "The Modernist in the Audience." This "Modernist" is "ready to watch the new acts," and Goff claimed that his modern sensibility—the figure was gendered as male—"has perennial youth of mind, his ears can change as the art of combining sounds progresses,

21. Richard San Jule to Bruce Goff, Aug. 23, 1939, series I, box 20, folder 9, BGA, AIC.
22. Richard San Jule to Bruce Goff, July 1942, series I, box 20, folder 15, BGA, AIC.
23. Richard San Jule to Bruce Goff, postmarked Oct. 2, 1942, series I, box 20, folder 17, BGA, AIC.
24. See Benjamin R. Levy, "Material Connections: Bruce Goff, Music, and Modernism Across the Arts," *Music Theory Online* 27, no. 3 (Sept. 2021), mtosmt.org/issues/mto.21.27.3/mto.21.27.3.levy.php, for more on how Goff "cultivated modernist sensibilities across the arts" with "a committedly American modernist community"; and Arn Henderson, *Bruce Goff: Architecture of Discipline in Freedom* (University of Oklahoma Press, 2017), who argued that "Goff also learned about avant-garde art, literature, and music from reading the periodicals *Dial* and *Broom*," 25.

his sight becomes more keen as the things he sees do."[25] With this admiration for youth, novelty, and heightened perception, Goff's brief essay deployed well-known modernist tropes. Five years later in "A Declaration of Independence," published in *The Western Architect*, Goff championed a modernist perspective while placing himself squarely in the movement's queer aesthetic traditions: "All forms of artistic activity arise from man's desire to beautify this existence. And since all forms arise from that desire, we may expect a close relationship to exist between the arts and life.... This has always been so. These great thought waves surge forth. We are today living right in the midst of one of them! We call it the *Moderne Movement*." He continued: "But we cannot have a great *movement* unless all of the arts are represented." Goff went on to cite major figures in architecture, literature, and painting whom he believed contributed to modernism, including "such geniuses as" Le Corbusier and Frank Lloyd Wright; painters such as Marsden Hartley, Georgia O'Keeffe, and Paul Gauguin; and writers such as Gertrude Stein, Carl Sandburg, Carl Van Vechten, and Amy Lowell.[26]

In this fascinating piece, Goff insisted that his own modernist architectural inclinations were part of a larger movement across multiple mediums. Yet while these lines certainly confirm his modern influences, they also name-drop queer contemporaries: Lowell and Stein advanced lesbian poetics; Van Vechten promoted the queer Harlem Renaissance through his novels, photography, and collecting practice; and Hartley crafted a homoerotic male modernism in his artwork. Goff's vital relation to Wright and other architects is well-documented, but here we see him self-identify with innovators within a wider artistic world of queer painting and prose—confirming "the continuing importance of interdisciplinary artistic activity for Goff" as a young artist.[27]

San Jule likewise expressed aspirations for modernist affiliation in his writings and in several issues of *Circle* magazine that he compiled and edited.[28] Many of his poems and some of his prose are also beholden to modernist tenets. In a collection of unpublished pieces, for instance, San Jule titled one typescript draft "Poetry," writing, "Not only painting, architecture, music: / poetry too changes / from stanzas stuffy as victorian wallpaper / to the flowing vigor of free verse / unfettered metre / subtleties of modern consciousness."[29] The poem then names various queer poets who affirmed experimental style, including W. H. Auden, Hart Crane, and Lowell. In a handwritten note included among his poetic writings, San Jule also listed prominent modernist authors, including William Faulkner, T. S. Eliot, and James Joyce, as well as queer writers such as Havelock Ellis and Walt Whitman.[30]

Besides enabling them to self-characterize as "unfettered" anti-Victorians, modernism's queer movements also apparently helped Goff and San Jule realize an aesthetic that—to again quote Goff's "Declaration of Independence"—fulfilled their collective "desire to beautify this existence."[31] In these endeavors they were no different than Hartley painting *Madawaska—Acadian Light-Heavy* (fig. 32) or Van Vechten taking avant-garde photographs of nude males. San Jule infused his unstuffy modernist poems with references to such beauty that can be read as same-sex desire. "Love Song" begins: "One image everywhere One face I cannot forget / Even in the depths of loneliness or sleep—" with the subsequent stanza stating, "Wherever beauty stirs the heart, you are: / I see the soft dark-shining of your eyes / in the quiet clearness of the evening star."[32] Another proclaims

FIG. 32 Marsden Hartley (American, 1877–1943). *Madawaska—Acadian Light-Heavy*, 1940. Oil on hardboard; 101.6 × 76.2 cm (40 × 30 in.). The Art Institute of Chicago, bequest of A. James Speyer, 1987.249.

25. Bruce Goff, "The Modernist in the Audience," Jan. 10, 1925, series V, box 2, folder 27, BGA, AIC.
26. Bruce Goff, "A Declaration of Independence," *Western Architect* 39, no. 1 (1930): 17.
27. Sidney K. Robinson, "Bruce Goff and Music," in Saliga and Woolever, *Architecture of Bruce Goff*, 34.
28. See Richard San Jule, letter, Mar. 29, 1935, series I, box 32, folder 25, BGA, AIC.
29. Richard San Jule, "Poetry," n.d., series VI, box 5, folder 23, BGA, AIC.
30. Richard San Jule, note, n.d., series VI, box 5, folder 37, BGA, AIC.
31. Goff, "A Declaration of Independence," 17.
32. Richard San Jule, "Love Song," n.d., series VI, box 5, folder 32, BGA, AIC.

that "you should have known how i had starved for beauty."[33] Although these poems do not specify gender, details in an unpublished and undated experimental biographical sketch that San Jule titled "The Individual: Bruce Goff" make clear that he located such beauty within Goff's own artistic undertakings given their "desire to create an original beauty" and—as confirmed by his correspondence—within Goff himself.[34]

Poems by Goff share San Jule's interests in beauty, a concept that would form a key facet of his mature architecture theorizations and his later-life creative writing, which I briefly discuss at this essay's conclusion.[35] Their shared delight in modernist-inflected beauty, however, was never not a subcultural code for their shared queerness. Mentions of beauty's value ("mental beauty," "the beauty of life," "the beauty of things") recur across their letters, including San Jule's assertion of "the beauty and richness" of their Rogers Park apartment.[36] Take but one more citation from his letters, dated July 1942:

> It is the same feeling I had long long ago when I saw that the creative life of the imagination is worth a dozen ordinary lifetimes of shallow procreation. It is an intensive awareness of the beauty of sensitivity in human expression.... It is an unshakeable belief that such beauty is the highest and most soul-satisfying. It is a feeling that such beauty is worth all the struggle that life and environment causes to be placed in the way of its accomplishment.[37]

In almost Wildean remarks that echo Goff's "Declaration of Independence," San Jule contrasted a stultifying and familial heteronormativity ("shallow procreation") with a tacitly queer aesthetic that privileged "the beauty of sensitivity."

As Chauncey observed, *sensitivity* was sometimes used in the modern United States as a euphemism for male homosexuality. Identifying as "a 'cultured' (or 'sensitive') man," he found, "made it possible for men to try to recast gay cultural styles that might be read as signs of effeminacy as signs instead of upper-class sophistication."[38] Modernist beauty provided such possibilities for San Jule and Goff as they created queer experimental art during their time together in Chicago.

Hence when San Jule championed "the creative imagination and those in whom it lives.... the love and thankfulness I hold for [Claude] Debussy, [Katsushika] Hokusai, Goff and those sensitive others whose eyes have cleared and deepened my own vision and heart," we see how the *Moderne Movement* became a fixture of their intimate language as much as it was painted on the Vienna Secession–like walls of their Rogers Park residence or incorporated into their experimental free verse.[39] Without a doubt, modernism allowed Goff to refine his ideas about architecture as he placed himself among an all-male roster of "geniuses" such as Le Corbusier. At the same time it also gave him and his lover a way to express their desires for beauty—for male beauty and for each other—with declarations independent from normative sexual and gender social constraints. These pronouncements, I note in passing, did not cease as Goff grew older. See, for but one example, his appreciation for a Klimt drawing of a nude male that he owned and described as "remarkable" (fig. 33).[40]

"AESTHETIC ADVENTURES" AT KEBYAR

The shared investment in the queer modernist beauty that rippled through "the sanctum of 1515 Howard," their poetry, and their prose found its apogee in plans for a life together after Chicago. Sometime in 1939 a wanderlust took hold of San Jule. His letters arrived from locales such as Granby, Colorado; Reno, Nevada; and the San Francisco Bay Area, with one October 1939 letter tracking how a cross-country journey turned into a global voyage: "From Honolulu we turn south two thousand miles to Polynesia: Pago Pago in Samoa, Suva in the Fiji Islands, then angle down to Auckland, New Zealand and finally over to Melbourne and Sydney."[41] All the while he stayed in constant communication with Goff and repeatedly told him that he longed for "the circle of your friendship, its sympathy, its imagination, its infinite beauty, and there find the peace and impetus necessary to the creative life."[42] Goff, meanwhile, received his architecture license in Kentucky in July 1941.[43]

Starting that year, they both began fantasizing about continuing their queer modernism in Kentucky at a house to be named Kebyar. According to De Long, "Goff had been much taken by the natural beauty of the landscape near [client] Irma Bartman's house, and in 1941 bought property there where he hoped to build his home and studio. He wrote to Irma Bartman of his plan, saying he would call it Kebyar, 'a Balinese word meaning literally '"the sudden bursting open of a flower".'"[44] According to Kebyar's financial records, Goff purchased "property in Louisville, Kentucky, 7.89 acres more or less located on

33. Richard San Jule, untitled poem, n.d., series VI, box 5, folder 33, BGA, AIC.
34. Richard San Jule, "The Individual: Bruce Goff," n.d., series VI, box 2, folder 10, BGA, AIC.
35. See, for example, Bruce Goff, "Of Beauty and Architecture," June 24, 1961, series V, box 1, folder 13, BGA, AIC.
36. San Jule to Goff, Aug. 23, 1939 (see n. 21).
37. San Jule to Goff, July 1942 (see n. 22).
38. Chauncey, *Gay New York*, 106.
39. Richard San Jule to Bruce Goff, postmarked Nov. 5, 1942, series I, box 20, folder 17, BGA, AIC.
40. Bruce Goff to Otto Kallir, Apr. 20, 1959, series I, box 28, folder 6, BGA, AIC.
41. Richard San Jule to Bruce Goff, Oct. 18, 1939, series I, box 20, folder 10, BGA, AIC.
42. Richard San Jule to Bruce Goff, Aug. 15, 1939, series I, box 20, folder 9, BGA, AIC.
43. Goff's Kentucky architecture license is located in series XII, box 14, folder 14, BGA, AIC.
44. De Long, *Bruce Goff*, 69. To elaborate on Goff's definition, one could consult an August 1936 issue of *Theatre Arts Monthly* that is dedicated to "The Theatre in Bali," series II, box 3, folder 25, BGA, AIC. This issue was organized by Miguel Covarrubias, a Mexican artist and anthropologist well known for modernist sketches of Harlem nightlife. It includes an extensive account of Indonesian dance, including *kebyar*, which Covarrubias's *Island of Bali* (1937) further develops.

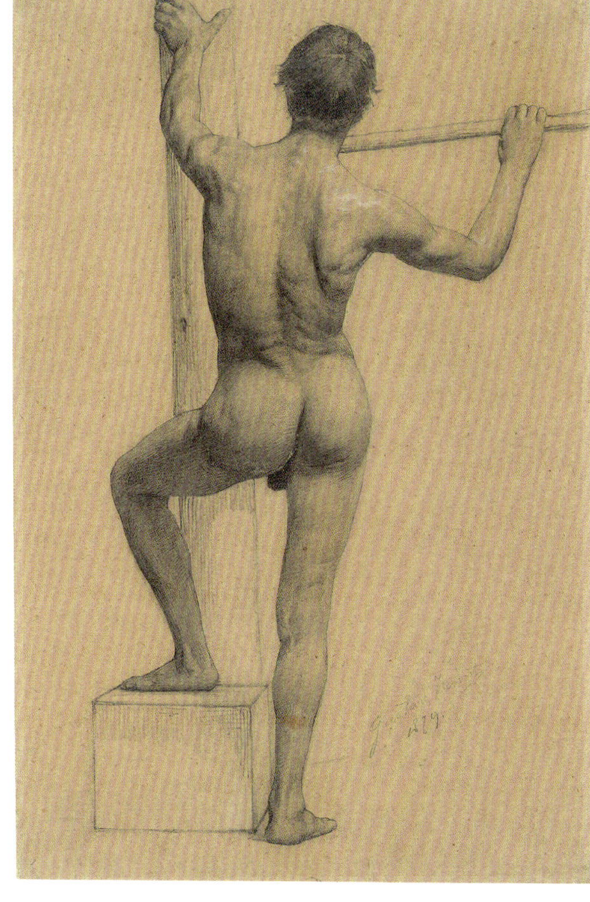

FIG. 33 Gustav Klimt (Austrian, 1862–1918). *Male Nude with Left Foot on a Pedestal*, 1879. Graphite and white heightening on paper; 40.8 × 26.7 cm (16⅛ × 10⁹⁄₁₆ in.). The Art Institute of Chicago, gift of Shin'enKan, Inc., Bruce Goff Archives, 2000.447.

OPPOSITE, FIG. 34 Goff (right) standing over the forty-foot waterfall at Kebyar's site, Louisville, Kentucky, 1953. Photograph by Charley Darneal. Published in *Louisville Courier-Journal*, Aug. 16, 1953. Bruce A. Goff Archive.

the West side of Thixton Lane between Bardstown Rd. and Cedar Creek Rd." from J. Paul Druien (fig. 34).[45] This acreage included some striking topographical features. "The property across the stream," Goff noted in the summer of 1941, "is practically inaccessible from the entrance. This can be solved by building a bridge."[46] A 1953 article for a Louisville-based newspaper later detailed at length Goff's vision for this property: "Kebyar, Goff explains, is to be a fragile-appearing thing, suspended on ¾-inch cables of stressed steel, with auxiliary bridges across the gorge."[47] The article then noted that Kebyar would feature "concealed speakers" playing "music from over five thousand records."[48]

This local newspaper report and subsequent Goff scholarship helpfully detail Kebyar. At the same time they downplay the fact that Goff and San Jule had intended to build this home expressly for the two of them. The newspaper article, for example, describes Kebyar as a future retirement home: "The spider-web home he plans to build for his own on Thixton Lane, [is] to be his home when he retires from teaching at the University of Oklahoma."[49] Decades later critics referred to the property as "his dream of gathering his own permanent group of artists" or as "an ideal studio and residence for himself."[50] Yet detailed financial records show that Goff held a "deed providing for joint ownership of Bruce, Rik, Eloise and Von Billings [that] was signed and notarized by Bruce Feb. 6, 1943."[51] Goff needed help with the property's payments as he prepared for his service during World War II, and the couple obliged.

Kebyar, which their correspondence documents, grew out of Goff and San Jule's Chicago-based appreciations of queer modernist beauty as they anticipated "a constructive and unrestrictive future" in the South.[52] While working in a Bay Area shipyard in July 1942, San Jule wrote to Goff, "For Kebyar's sake, you must make the most of the situation and try to get the best-paying job possible. That's the only reason I can keep on grinding away here—because I know that this road, however dusty, rough, steep and lonely, will join again somewhere with the road you are travelling in our mutual search for the beauty of the imagination."[53] Other communications were more explicit about joint ownership of this home: "For I feel with all intensity that the future can be fuller and richer for us than any time we have known, that we will work in surroundings appropriate to our feelings about beauty, that we will enjoy more of the things we value.... We are taking a short-cut to the good life ... and our vision of Kebyar is one of the most shining purposes of all—more eloquent than Taliesin. We must not fail. We must make it a reality."[54]

Their shared vision for a home and creative retreat was, however, never realized. Despite San Jule's delight in "the timeless aesthetic imagination I respect and love" and his wish "to return, to study and read and write again, to be a partner in aesthetic adventures once more," Kebyar was to remain a fantasy of queer modernist domesticity, its chimera archived in letters between the two.[55] On January 1, 1946, San Jule died following a surgery.[56] Unsurprisingly—given the pre–Stonewall era's homophobic climate—Goff was not mentioned in the notice; his Kebyar papers, however, confirm the date of San Jule's passing.

45. Bruce Goff with Drautman and Kohnhorst, real estate bid, July 22, 1941, series XV, box 13, folder 11, BGA, AIC.
46. Bruce Goff to Scowden Kohnhorst, July 21, 1941, series XV, box 13, folder 11, BGA, AIC.
47. Kent Previette, "With Running Water," *Courier-Journal*, Aug. 16, 1953, 34.
48. Ibid., 34.
49. Ibid., 32.
50. Robinson, "Bruce Goff and Music," 33; and De Long, *Bruce Goff*, 343.
51. Von D. Billings to Drautman and Kohnhorst, Feb. 18, 1943, series XV, box 13, folder 14, BGA, AIC. Goff again confirmed this deed in 1947.
52. Richard San Jule to Bruce Goff, postmarked June 18, 1942, series I, box 20, folder 14, BGA, AIC.
53. Richard San Jule to Bruce Goff, postmarked July 11, 1942, series I, box 20, folder 14, BGA, AIC.
54. San Jule to Goff, July 1942 (see n. 22).
55. Richard San Jule to Bruce Goff, Nov. 26, 1939, series I, box 20, folder 10, BGA, AIC. For more on "modernist domesticity," see Jeremy Braddock, *Collecting as Modernist Practice* (Johns Hopkins University Press, 2012), 80. For more on queer domesticity in the United States, see Stephen Vider, *The Queerness of Home: Gender, Sexuality, and the Politics of Domesticity After World War II* (University of Chicago Press, 2021).

QUEER BEAUTY AFTER SAN JULE

Queer beauty remained one of Goff's lifelong preoccupations in the years following San Jule's death. He never built Kebyar, and he sold the Kentucky acreage in the mid-1960s. After his career took off, however, he continued to beautify his days, not least with his shirts made of gold lamé (and polyester) fabric—perhaps recalling the gold lamé curtains that once draped their Rogers Park apartment. At the age of seventy-five, he also handwrote a poem titled "Of Beauty" (fig. 35), which reads, in part:

> Of peacocks and penises
> I prefer them to Venuses
> Both are beautiful, manly and proud
> And both are now allowed
> For more than peeing
>   screwing
>   and wooing
> They are also for beauty and viewing
> And when they rise and spread
> Across the sun
> Creation of beauty has begun![57]

Dated January 27, 1980, this lighthearted and uncharacteristically ribald piece stands as another declaration of sexual independence from heteronormativity a half century after his affirmation of queer modernists in *The Western Architect*. The homoerotic poem unabashedly idealizes "beautiful" male bodies whose uses go well beyond bodily functions or courtship ("wooing") that might result in marriage. Written in the same year that Ronald Reagan was elected US president and the Christian right ascended in American politics, Goff's lines also read like a lyrical life motto whose main theme courses through the archive of his poetry, prose, realia, and photography.

Goff has long had a reputation as a "loner" and "champion of individuality," but his interests in, affiliations with, and productions in a queer American modernism tell a different story.[58] As he and his partner put their efforts into styling themselves as queer modernists—through realized and unrealized collaborations in Chicago, including their imaginings of a dwelling in Kentucky—San Jule was central to their intimate "aesthetic adventures."[59] Their time together proved to be formative years in Goff's storied career.

Such being the case, scholars should consider letters between Goff and San Jule to be essential rather than extraneous to our ongoing appreciation of Goff's diverse artwork. Paying heed to how queerness saturates his many productions prior to his University of Oklahoma years thus reinstates San Jule's importance to Goff's aesthetic achievements across his long lifetime—a primacy that has been buried at worst or underreported at best. Let's let San Jule have the final word on that last point: "I think we both realize now that each of us is indispensable to the other and that though the world is crammed with other people, individuals all, we will never find (or need to) anyone to take the other's place. We need each other. No one else offers as much."[60]

56. De Long, *Bruce Goff*, tells us that "San Jule died unexpectedly from an embolism suffered while recovering from a routine operation," 83. See also San Jule's obituary in the *Long Beach Press-Telegram*, Jan. 3, 1946, B6. This obituary also mentions San Jule's wife Nancy (Nan). De Long, *Bruce Goff*, wrote that Goff "reunited with San Jule in Berkeley" and that Nan "left San Jule before Goff moved in," 83 and 74.

57. Bruce Goff, "Of Beauty," Jan. 27, 1980, series V, box 2, folder 51, BGA, AIC.

58. De Long, *Bruce Goff*, 301.

59. San Jule to Goff, Nov. 26, 1939 (see n. 55).

60. Richard San Jule to Bruce Goff, postmarked Nov. 29, 1940, series I, box 20, folder 11, BGA, AIC.

of Beauty

of Peacocks and Penises
I prefer them To Venuses
Both are Beautiful, manly and Proud
And Both are now allowed
For more than Peeing
Screwing
and wooing
They are also for Beauty and viewing
And when they rise and spread
Across The Sun
Creation of Beauty has Begun!
For Peacocks Too have Cocks
And use them on Their walks
And scream between Their Squaks
As other "normal people Talks!
(There are no female peacocks)

1-27-80

FIG. 35 Goff. "Of Beauty," Jan. 27, 1980. Bruce A. Goff Archive.

FIG. 36 Jerri Hodges-Bonebrake posing in front of Christmas decorations at the end of the main hall in the School of Architecture at the University of Oklahoma, 1954. Photograph by Philip B. Welch. Christopher C. Gibbs College of Architecture Collection, University of Oklahoma.

Cellophane and Seashells: The Materiality of Bruce Goff

Alison Fisher

Any survey of articles on Bruce Goff (or even their titles) points to unconventional materiality as one of the most prominent ideas used to identify (and critique) his work.[1] Despite this centrality, few writers have advanced rigorous interpretations of the physical qualities of Goff's work, including his open attitude toward new materials, his interest in joining disparate materials, or his unabashed embrace of decoration. As a result, Goff's architecture is either imperfectly lumped in with contemporary movements—organic or countercultural—or seen as exceptional. Both tendencies avoid dealing with the messiness of his mixed-media architecture, which, while certainly unusual, is not without precedent or external reference. Focusing on his most prolific genre of practice, the domestic interior, I have divided this inquiry into two categories with blurry edges: bricolage, or mixing found materials, and artificial nature. In this way, I suggest sources of inspiration in different intellectual and aesthetic genealogies—from eighteenth-century grottos to postwar kitsch—that help interpret all of the "stuff" in Goff's work.

MODERN MATERIALS

Although collage, montage, and other techniques of joining disparate material had prominent and often subversive roles in modernist art practice, the same cannot be said for mainstream modern architecture.[2] Instead, architects like Ludwig Mies van der Rohe placed material purity at the core of their modern agenda: "The long path from material through function to creative work has only a single goal: to create order out of the desperate confusion of our time. We must have order, allocating to each thing its proper place and giving to each thing its due according to its nature . . . [in] the profound words of St. Augustine: 'Beauty is the splendor of Truth.'"[3] As a leading educator and practitioner, Mies prioritized stability, order, and the pursuit of a kind of "truth" revealed through the correct, unmanipulated, and beautiful use of material.

The idea of material truth or honesty has a long history in architecture and design, which by the nineteenth century was explicitly tied to the challenges posed by industrial production.[4] Ornate furniture and clothing—once laboriously handmade and accessible only to the aristocracy and nobility—could be produced inexpensively in factories and marketed to the growing middle class. The resulting explosion in consumerism, especially in the domestic sphere, led to an aesthetic of eclectic abundance: floral rugs, overstuffed couches with turned legs, cut-glass fixtures, gilt mirrors, and velvet drapes with tassels.[5]

This shift inspired a revolt among artists and designers across Europe. Some turned to preindustrial modes of craft production, as with British writer and designer William Morris and the Arts and Crafts Movement. Others, including Austrian and German architects Adolf Loos and Hermann Muthesius, rejected ornamentation outright as a sign of unsophistication, chicanery, or even degeneracy.[6] The result was an outpouring of severe and emphatically unadorned buildings, often constructed with materials newly elevated from their industrial functions, such as concrete, glass, and steel.[7] In many ways, then, modern architecture's origins are bound up in a struggle against the negative effects of mass production, including excessive decoration and middle-class values—in short, an aesthetic chaos that had moral and social (not to mention gendered and sexual) implications.

So if modernism can be defined in opposition to middlebrow taste, how can one position Goff? Unlike Mies, he forged a career centered on the wants and needs of middle-class clients and decidedly unheroic materials sourced from mail-order catalogues and five-and-dimes. These included new products—vibrantly colored artificial lawn (AstroTurf)—and sparkly vinyl upholstery, as well as off-the-shelf materials used in unorthodox ways, such as wood roof shingles added to interior walls, further disrupting convention by scrambling the syntax of construction.

Thus, Goff's choices can be seen as a canny rejection of modern architecture's bombastic pursuit of wholeness and insistence on being set apart from the messiness of everyday life. Goff himself described a simple motivation for his departure from the modernist ethic of material truth: It often produced boring, one-dimensional architecture. "A person," he noted, "can be very honest and still be very dull, very uninteresting. Sometimes a crook is a lot more interesting."[8]

THE BRICOLEUR

Goff's work did not start out with unusual materiality. His deco projects in Tulsa for Rush, Endacott and Rush were executed in terracotta, brick, and stucco—and in Chicago he built modest modern wood houses during the late 1930s.[9] Yet by the mid-1940s, we see Goff

1. See for example "The Round House: Steel, Glass, Marbles, Copper, Rope and Coal Make a $64,000 Quonset-Hut Mansion," *Life*, Mar. 19, 1951, 70–75. Ada Louise Huxtable, "Peacock Feathers and Pink Plastic: A New Yorker Sees Bruce Goff," *New York Times*, Feb. 8, 1970, D25.
2. Although montage and collage are common forms of modernist architectural representation, with a few exceptions like Catalan architect Antoni Gaudí's, these techniques did not find a role in the matter and assembly of the buildings themselves until well into the 1960s. For more on this history, see Andreas F. Beitin, Wolf Eiermann, and Brigitte Franzen, eds., *Mies van der Rohe: Montage = Collage*, exh. cat. (Koenig Books, 2017); and Craig Buckley, *Graphic Assembly: Montage, Media, and Experimental Architecture in the 1960s* (University of Minnesota Press, 2019).
3. Ludwig Mies van der Rohe, "Inaugural Address as Director of Architecture at Armour Institute of Technology," 1938, in Philip C. Johnson, *Mies van der Rohe* (Museum of Modern Art, 1947), 194–95.
4. Scholars point to Aristotle as the origin of this ideal, which was subsequently revisited by John Ruskin, Eugène Viollet-le-Duc, and others at the height of the industrial revolution. See Fil Hearn, "Truth to the Medium: Using Materials," in *Ideas That Shaped Buildings* (MIT Press, 2003), 255–69. For another chapter in this modern history, see Reyer Banham, "The New Brutalism," *Architectural Review*, Dec. 1955, 354–61.
5. Thad Logan, *The Victorian Parlour: A Cultural Study* (Cambridge University Press, 2001), 9.
6. For a broad overview of these issues, see Alina Payne, *From Ornament to Object: Genealogies of Architectural Modernism* (Yale University Press, 2012).
7. For example, Swiss architect and Bauhaus director Hannes Meyer's 1928 manifesto "Building" features a long list of industrial materials—including reinforced concrete, wire-mesh glass, plywood, asphalt, and asbestos.

FIGS. 37–38 Goff-designed interiors at 1515 West Howard Street, Chicago, c. 1941. Photographs by Ernest Ellison. Filson Historical Society, Louisville, Kentucky.

confidently deploying a wide range of found and unconventional materials in domestic commissions, from glass ashtrays and aluminum cake pans to surplus rope, coal, and marbles.

Some of this work with ad hoc materials can be chalked up to the kind of ingenuity that often comes from limited resources. In 1934, for example, he moved to the North Side of Chicago and rented space in a non-residential building, which became a combined home, studio, and office that he shared with his partner Richard San Jule for the next five years.[10] Despite his financially precarious situation during the Depression, the descriptions and photographs of his apartment are remarkable. Windows covered with gold lamé curtains sparkle in contrast to the space's jet-black walls and wood trim. Against this backdrop hang installations of his own design (figs. 37–38), including a strand of beads and shells and an elaborate sculpture made of white string in a parabolic or "winged" shape.[11] The few extant photographs also show a ceiling with light-diffusing fabric and spare yet elegant decorations, such as a large metallic gong, Japanese prints, and a delicate arrangement of translucent dried silver dollar leaves.

Historian Timothy Samuelson has remarked that these glittering effects may have riffed off of the bright signage of many dance halls and bars in the area, but they also clearly reflect a personal, cultivated aesthetic.[12] However humble, this interior contains the seeds of an approach to materials and decoration that would define much of his mature practice, including hanging elements, dramatic color choices, and a mix of more traditional artwork and custom "installations" made from natural and manufactured objects. This foundational project also suggests that Goff came into his own architectural vocabulary from the bottom up, which is to say, through decoration rather than structure, reflecting a striking reversal of mainstream modernist values.[13]

Goff acknowledged that not every commission could nor should support such an open-ended attitude, depending on the client's finances or appetite for risk, but in his view, "If you have a client who says they would like you to experiment, then why not?"[14] By the mid-1950s Goff had completed a range of houses with different degrees of innovative zeal. Many were solid riffs on typical models—the ranch and split-level—that deployed typical building materials: laminated beams, brick, limestone, and wood siding. These houses were not terribly experimental, but they always included unexpected exterior details including tall metal masts, beams with angular finials, and woodwork finished in bold, contrasting colors (burgundy and turquoise). Inside, the Goffian "decorations" might be limited to an octagonal light fixture, a few clever built-ins, a row of embedded ashtray windows, or smaller, more ephemeral things, such as a tile mosaic or a hanging mobile of beads and glass Christmas ornaments. Although Goff was usually fairly hands off during construction, he would often come in at the very end to add this last category of finishes, which seem more like housewarming gifts than integral design elements.[15]

Between these modest projects, Goff worked with a fair share of experimentally minded clients. For these houses, largely built in the 1960s and 1970s, decoration moved from being an afterthought to an integral part of the project's architectural language. Take, for

He believed these new materials, and their association with science, technology, and economics, would facilitate the transition from architect-artist to architect-technician. Meyer, "Building," in *Programs and Manifestoes on 20th Century Architecture*, ed. Ulrich Conrads (MIT Press, 1971), 117.

8. "Honesty in Architecture," in *Goff on Goff: Conversations and Lectures*, ed. Philip B. Welch (University of Oklahoma Press, 1996), 115.

9. Goff struggled to work within the narrow criteria of Federal Housing Administration funding on these Chicago area projects. De Long, *Bruce Goff: Toward Absolute Architecture* (Architectural History Foundation; MIT Press, 1988), 63.

10. For more on Goff and San Jule's relationship and domestic sphere, see Scott Herring's essay in this volume.

11. De Long, *Bruce Goff*, 59.

12. Timothy Samuelson, "Bruce Goff in Chicago," in *The Architecture of Bruce Goff, 1904–1982: Design for the Continuous Present*, ed. Pauline Saliga and Mary Woolever (Prestel; Art Institute of Chicago, 1995), 47.

13. This approach reflects contemporary debates in which influential critics like Sigfried Giedion located the origin of modern architecture in engineering, while others, such as Nicholas Pevsner, looked to the decorative arts, thus coming to very different conclusions about the primacy of materials and ornament. Payne, *From Ornament to Object*, 1–25.

14. Goff, "Honesty in Architecture," 138.

15. Herb Greene, "Recollections of Bruce Goff as Teacher," ed. John Sergeant and Stephen Mooring, special issue, *Architectural Design* 48, no. 10 (1978): 54.

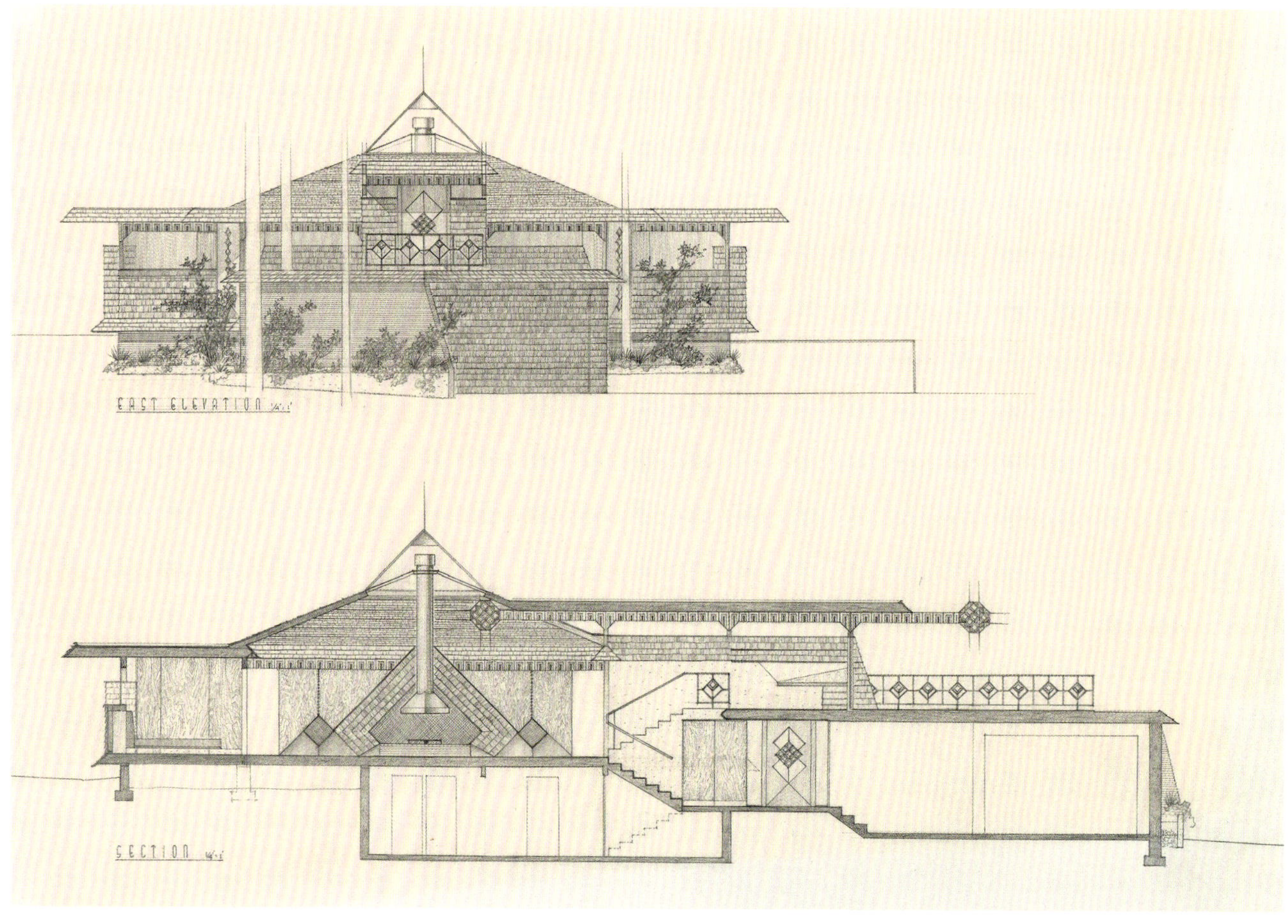

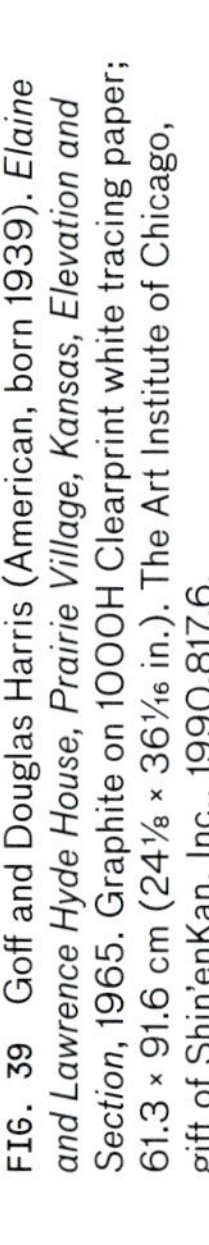

FIG. 39 Goff and Douglas Harris (American, born 1939). *Elaine and Lawrence Hyde House, Prairie Village, Kansas, Elevation and Section*, 1965. Graphite on 1000H Clearprint white tracing paper; 61.3 × 91.6 cm (24⅛ × 36¹⁄₁₆ in.). The Art Institute of Chicago, gift of Shin'enKan, Inc., 1990.817.6.

example, Goff's 1965 house for Elaine and Lawrence Hyde, inspired primarily by a color—green—and a form, the rotated square or equilateral diamond.[16] Looking at a section of the house (fig. 39), one is struck by the coherence between the overall structure and its subdivisions: triangles at the roofline and skylight dome, the elaborate angular fireplace surround, diamond details on the exterior doors and railings, and finally, elaborate, rotated-square-shaped light fixtures.

Inside, Goff added materials that soften and complicate the rigor of his geometries. Exposed beams were painted with a pattern of Josef Albers–style squares in three shades of green, light to dark, divided by glinting copper bands. Goff repeated this motif on the floor with a lush sea of shag carpeting in a similar gradient of greens. The color scheme also appears in a series of custom light fixtures attached to structural beams in the

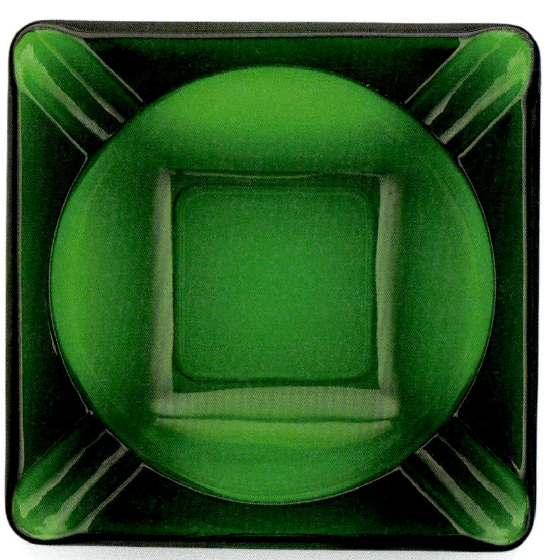

FIG. 40 Glass ashtray, n.d. Private collection.

16. Both of these aspects were highlighted in local media reports about the house. When asked if its green color reflected his own preferences, Goff replied dryly: "I don't have a favorite color." Quoted in Patricia Schin, "The House That Stops Traffic," *Kansas City Star*, Dec. 11, 1966, 2E, series VII, box 2, folder 32, Bruce A. Goff Archive, Ryerson and Burnham Art and Architecture Archives, The Art Institute of Chicago (hereafter BGA, AIC).

FIG. 41 Living room of the Elaine and Lawrence Hyde House, 1965. Photograph by Robert Alan Bowlby. Robert Alan Bowlby architectural slides. WHC M2886. American School Archive, Special Research Collections, University of Oklahoma Libraries, Norman, Oklahoma.

living room and on the exterior of the house. Each lantern was created with a rotated grid of nine mass-produced dark-green glass ashtrays (fig. 40) inset in custom-made octagonal, mint-green metal boxes, and finished with long, radiating copper rods.

As a kind of decorative crescendo, Goff created a multimedia installation surrounding a suspended metal fireplace in the center of the house (fig. 41). Behind a raised hearth of mint-green glazed tiles and sparkly green-blue vinyl sitting cushions, he designed a mural of black shingles, dark-purple mirror tile, and yellow and red accents in triangular stripes. The skylight above was decorated with the same mirrored tiles and a ring of exposed vanity-style lightbulbs, from which he hung plastic "rain"—four panels of thin, scalloped cellophane strips that sparkle in the light and move with currents of air.

It is tempting to see in this project the kind of Gesamtkunstwerk that occupied turn-of-the-century architects in Europe from Arts and Crafts to the Vienna Secession and Jugendstil. But unlike the works of Henry van de Velde or Josef Hoffmann, realized by fine craftsmen working in wood, stone, and metal, Goff's interiors were an assembly of easily obtained materials, like commercial carpeting, plywood shingles, and glass ashtrays from S. S. Kresge. In this way, his aesthetic of accumulation approaches something like the style of the age, using and celebrating the most-up-to-date materials and products. According to early twentieth-century critics like Loos, this achievement was impossible for Hoffmann and his ilk because of their retrograde reliance on custom decoration, which was increasingly out of step with trends in manufactured furnishings.[17]

Instead Goff's work is best understood as late-modernist *bricolage*, a term first defined by French ethnologist Claude Lévi-Strauss in 1962 as the practice of creating something from heterogeneous parts and working with the "collection of oddments left over from human endeavors."[18] In art history of the 1980s, *bricolage* described certain modes of early twentieth-century collage and Surrealist art in which objects from popular and consumer culture—from newspaper clippings to urinals—were integrated into compositions that radically disrupted the former ideals of naturalism and unity in painting and sculpture.[19] In place of the craftsman, then, Goff substituted the bricoleur, an expert in the inventive assembly of common materials and existing consumer goods, making do with what was at hand. Interestingly, contemporary critics interpreted Goff's improvisational impulses as a uniquely American can-do attitude that fell, in the words of an English journalist, "squarely into the folklore of Mr. Fixit and the Yankee Tinker."[20]

The unscripted feel of many Goff works and a corresponding charge of "cheapness" has been at the core of many critiques of his aesthetics. In 1970, renowned *New York Times* architecture critic Ada Louise Huxtable declared, "This is fantasy, and it is often seriously flawed. Tight budgets, cheap materials and an ingenuous and sometimes buckeye taste make it easy work to disregard. But there is also, on occasion, poetry, and glimpses of horizons beyond brashly broken rules."[21] *Buckeye* in this sense refers to something (or someone) that is cheap, of poor quality, and often showy, which—when combined with Huxtable's charge of being "ingenuous" or naive—makes for a searing assessment of Goff's material sensibility. To this we must add postmodern theorist Charles Jencks's endlessly quoted and astute, if mean-spirited,

17. See Adolf Loos's essays "The Poor Little Rich Man," in *Spoken into the Void: Collected Essays, 1897–1900*, trans. Jane O. Newman and John H. Smith (MIT Press, 1982); and "Ornament and Crime," in *Ornament and Crime: Selected Essays*, trans. Michael Mitchell (Ariadne Press, 1998).

18. Claude Lévi-Strauss, *The Savage Mind*, trans. George Weidenfeld and Nicolson Ltd. (University of Chicago Press, 1966), 19.

19. See the work of Hal Foster, in particular "The 'Primitive' Unconscious of Modern Art," *October* 34 (Autumn 1985): 45–70; and "Savage Minds (A Note on Brutalist Bricolage)," *October* 136 (Spring 2011): 182–91.

20. John Sergeant, "An Introduction to Bruce Goff," ed. John Sergeant and Stephen Mooring, special issue, *Architectural Design* 48, no. 10 (1978): 4.

21. Huxtable, "Peacock Feathers and Pink Plastic," 109.

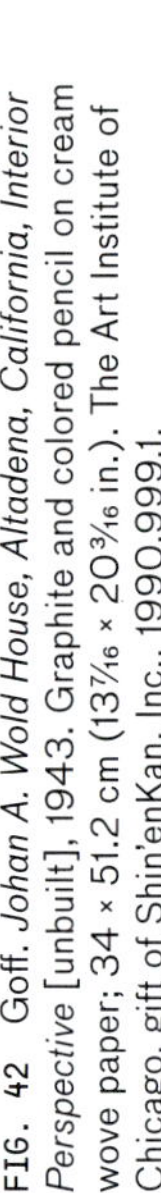

FIG. 42 Goff. *Johan A. Wold House, Altadena, California, Interior Perspective* [unbuilt], 1943. Graphite and colored pencil on cream wove paper; 34 × 51.2 cm (13 7/16 × 20 3/16 in.). The Art Institute of Chicago, gift of Shin'enKan, Inc., 1990.999.1.

article "Bruce Goff: Michelangelo of Kitsch." After taking a detour through sociologist Herbert Gans's analysis of American taste and class, Jencks advanced a theory about Goff's appeal to lower-middle-class identity. This "just arrived Mid Westerner," he believed, was attracted to Goff because they recognized in him their own (impoverished) aesthetic and intellectual ideals: "Goff has a heart of pure tinsel, pure cellophane rain-strip, pure gold-anodized metallic roof strip, pure Yyuk [*sic*]!"[22]

Although Jencks's analysis did not move much beyond class-baiting rhetoric, his article does correctly identify Goff's deep immersion in the material abundance and ingenuity of the postwar United States. This includes Goff's ready adoption of new building materials and extends to the ways he participated in the lives of his clients. Project files for the 1970–72 Glen and Luetta Harder House, for example, include a nearly endless list of possessions for which the clients required storage in their new house: crystal and glassware, garden tools, a portable hibachi, dog food, dried flowers, breakfast cereal, ribbons and gift-wrapping supplies, dress forms, jello molds, and no fewer than three fondue pots.[23] In some ways unremarkable for a wealthy family, this list has an uncanny similarity to the materials used in the typical mature work by Goff, reflecting another side of American materialism and a practice so attuned to the needs and aspirations of his clients that accumulation became both the functional precondition and the aesthetic.

Goff seemed to revel in the exercise of bringing into conversation such a wide range of objects and matter. "Many people ask," he explained in a 1979 interview, "How do you know all of these materials will look good together? . . . [I respond] How do you know that certain instruments are going to sound good together? To me, different motifs in the design can utilize different materials to clarify the effect in the composition."[24] Again, bricolage helps describe a way of working that is intentionally synthetic—that is, physically bringing together unlike things—while also suggesting the meaning created by this activity, including a kind of

22. Charles Jencks, "Bruce Goff: The Michelangelo of Kitsch," *Architectural Design* 48, no. 10 (1978): 13.
23. Luetta Harder, handwritten notes, 1974–75, series II, box 24, folder 11, BGA, AIC.
24. Quoted in Betty Leigh, "Interview: 'I Do What Comes Naturally,'" *Inland Architect* 23, no. 8 (Dec. 1979): 22.

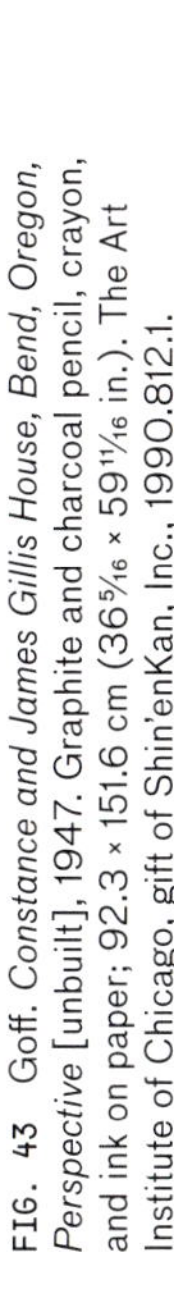

FIG. 43 Goff. *Constance and James Gillis House, Bend, Oregon, Perspective* [unbuilt], 1947. Graphite and charcoal pencil, crayon, and ink on paper; 92.3 × 151.6 cm (36 5/16 × 59 11/16 in.). The Art Institute of Chicago, gift of Shin'enKan, Inc., 1990.812.1.

realism or acceptance of the everyday that challenged modernist myths about wholeness and coherence.[25] Goff's goal, however, was not disciplinary disruption but exploration and delight, feelings he hoped to elicit from his unique blend of natural and artificial, plain and fancy, solid and ephemeral.

Instead of denying consumer culture, as middlebrow as it often was, Goff used it to its maximal effect, thus inventing a new mode that celebrated architecture's inherent connection to other cultural products. This approach also served to give maximum dignity to his clients, a stance unusual in the industry.[26] And Goff's readiness to engage with his own time, peers, and the "stuff" of the age was a radical kind of modernism that anticipated changes in the field that would arrive in the 1970s and 1980s. Jencks begrudgingly admitted as much in his description of Ivy League seminars by postmodern architects Robert Venturi and Charles Moore—"110 credit hours of Camp, Kitsch, and Schlock at Yale University"—that covered basically the same ground that Goff had in the 1950s and 1960s.[27]

THE GROTTO

Goff used another distinct idiom for several important projects, such as the Hugh Ellis and Lois Ledbetter House (1947–48) and the Eugene and Nancy Bavinger House (1950–55), as well as the unbuilt house for Constance and James Gillis (1947). Each of these houses included the prominent use of rough stone masonry combined with interior water features and plantings, which evoke natural features like caves, cliffs, ponds, and streams, and even the natural processes of weather, time, and decay.

These projects, which I am calling grottoesque, extended Goff's long-standing interest in blurring the boundaries between interior and exterior in his domestic designs.[28] He began working with this idea in the late 1930s, as seen in projects like the unbuilt Johan A. Wold House (fig. 42), designed for a client in Altadena, California, and later the Constance and James Gillis House (fig. 43). The Wold house includes Goff's first fully elaborated interior "garden," complete with

25. Foster, "Savage Minds," 182–91. Journalists have also grappled with this quality in Goff's work. See Jeremiah Sheehan, "Uniting Like and Unlike," *Building Design* 926 (Mar. 1989): 38–39.

26. Penelope Dean underscored this with a wry comparison between Mies and Goff, "Bruce accommodates: 'I just told him what I needed,' Mrs. Ford relayed; Ludwig does not: '[He] won't let me have any closets,' Dr. Farnsworth complained." Penelope Dean, "Ten Miles, Three Years, and Two Worlds Apart," *Flat Out*, Fall 2016, 63.

27. Jencks, "Bruce Goff," 13.

28. Goff stated this aim explicitly: "Glass is set so the stone wall and cedar ceiling continue uninterrupted outside. Planting inside the tall corner window, of mitered glass, further emphasizes the relationship of indoors and outdoors." Bruce Goff, "Ledbetter House, 1947," n.d., n.p., manuscript, series II, box 4, folder 22, BGA, AIC.

FIG. 44 Heinrich Breling (German, 1849–1914). *View of the Venus Grotto at Linderhof Palace in Blue Lighting*, 1881. Watercolor on paper; 22.5 × 33 cm / 23 × 33.2 cm (8 7/8 × 13 1/16 in.). Wittelsbacher Ausgleichsfonds, München, Inv.-Nr. B VIII 18.

climbing vines and a flower bed that extends under the adjacent plate glass window to join plantings outside.[29] Goff expanded this naturalistic focus in the adjacent sitting area, which features a fireplace carved out of rough stone masonry and bark-covered logs supporting the ceiling and a low coffee table.

The subtle strangeness of the Wold house—with its mixture of natural elements and highly industrial ones, including a plywood ceiling and corrugated metal wall—would be expanded in his unbuilt project for Constance and James Gillis, designed for a site in Bend, Oregon.[30] The main perspective drawing of the project presents an otherworldly scene in which the house's angular rock-and-glass facade is surrounded by a reflecting pool, craggy rocks, tall grasses, and a few leafless tree trunks. Goff designed the house as five levels, reaching from a partially excavated hollow in the earth to "a sleeping shelf with a sky window."[31] When the Gillis project was published in an architectural journal in 1948, the author described the design as an "an expression of [Goff's] belief in natural form" because of the continuous spiral design and wall of volcanic rock with irregular openings, some of which, she noted, were to be embellished with "amethyst, rose or shattered safety glass."[32]

Indeed, these descriptions of rock walls, irregular openings, and a portal to the sky seem to recall a natural—not manufactured—shelter or a cave. Of course, "shattered safety glass" is not a material found in nature, but the decorated cave *is* a human creation with a long history, beginning with ancient shrines to gods and nymphs in natural spring-fed caves. The grotto had many resurgences over the years but came to wider interest in the eighteenth century when it was included in the elaborate gardens of nobles and aristocrats, especially in England, France, and Germany.[33] Some grottos had themes, like the 1877 Venus Grotto built by King Ludwig II of Bavaria on the grounds of his Linderhof Palace (fig. 44). Modeled after the grotto featured in the first act of Richard Wagner's opera *Tannhäuser*, this grand design features a waterfall and river with novel, colored lights, thus presenting a unique synthesis of the arts, technology, and nature.[34] Other constructions were designed to display collections—for example, English poet Alexander Pope's grotto, constructed from 1720–42, contained a wide range of objects, including crystals, fossils, and moss, as well as objects with more cultural significance, such as marble from ancient Rome.[35] Thus the grotto collapses many disparate histories of the eighteenth century, including landscape design and the grand tour, ultimately serving as a potent, mystical counterpart to the Wunderkammer.[36]

I explore this idea at length because Goff's work suggests many aspects of the grotto, including the aesthetic of artificial ruins seen in the "crumbling" rock wall in the Gillis project and the facade of his Ledbetter house in Norman, Oklahoma. While more conventional in form, the Ledbetter house includes another key element of the grotto: running water. Alongside a host of unusual details—including a carport made from the roof of a grain silo and his signature glass ashtrays embedded in wood panels—Goff centered the entire house on what he called an "indoor garden room" (fig. 45).[37] This space featured a flagstone floor that began with exterior walkways and continued inside, natural light from a skylight, beds for indoor tropical plantings, a lily pool, and a plumbed "waterfall" that tumbled over ledges in the rock wall to increase its naturalistic effect.[38] All together, these features made the Ledbetter design the first of Goff's houses to fully bring the outside in, a quality that was recognized by local journalists.[39]

Goff's most well-known built project with water and plants is the Bavinger house (1950–55).[40] Designed for artist clients Eugene and Nancy Bavinger, this house was a media sensation before it was even completed, and it had a domestic interior unlike anything the American public had seen before.[41] In addition to its unique spiral shape and suspended living platforms, or pods, the house also featured elaborate "water gardens," a large network of shallow pools surrounded by plantings and flagstone paths so extensive that Goff described the interior as "a conservatory for plants and birds."[42] This feature was highlighted in a *Life* magazine photograph (fig. 46) that

29. De Long confirmed that this project was the first of its kind with "irregularly profiled masonry," which would become a prominent feature in his later work. See De Long, *Bruce Goff*, 72. However, the inside-outside garden appears a decade earlier, as seen in the 1932 design project for a "Small Inexpensive Studio and Residence" (Art Institute of Chicago, 1990.828.1–6).

30. De Long, *Bruce Goff*, 83.

31. "Pride of the Prairie: A High Priest of Individualism Is Designing in a Strikingly Regional Idiom for His Grass Roots Clients," *Architectural Forum* 88, no. 3 (Mar. 1948): 100.

32. "Pride of the Prairie," 100. This shape is the logarithmic spiral, a geometrical progression found in many natural shapes, from hurricane patterns to seashells. For more, see the classic work by mathematician Matila Ghyka, *The Geometry of Art and Life* (Sheed and Ward, 1946).

33. Laura Tradi, "Petrified Waters: The Artificial Grottoes of the Renaissance and Beyond," *Public Domain Review*, May 5, 2022, publicdomainreview.org/essay/petrified-waters/.

34. Zahra Faridany-Akhavan, "All the King's Toys," in "Essays in Honor of Oleg Grabar," *Muqarnas* 10 (1993): 297.

35. John Dixon Hunt, *Gardens and the Picturesque: Studies in the History of Landscape Architecture* (MIT Press, 1992), 92.

36. For more see Horst Bredekamp, *The Lure of Antiquity and the Cult of the Machine: The Kunstkammer and the Evolution of Nature, Art and Technology*, trans. Allison Brown (Markus Wiener, 1995).

37. Goff, "Ledbetter House, 1947" (see n. 28).

38. Ibid.

39. See "House with Backyard in Living Room," *Tulsa World*, May 2, 1948, n.p., series VII, box 1, folder 35, BGA, AIC.

FIG. 45 Garden room in the Hugh Ellis and Lois Ledbetter House, Norman, Oklahoma, 1948. Photograph by Griggs Studio. Bruce A. Goff Archive.

FIG. 46 Interior pond at the Eugene and Nancy Bavinger House, Norman, Oklahoma, 1955. Photograph by A. Y. Owen. Published in *Life*, Sept. 19, 1955.

FIG. 47 Goff and Greene. *Eugene and Nancy Bavinger House, Norman, Oklahoma, East Elevation*, 1950. Colored pencil with graphite on cream wove paper; 60.5 × 81 cm (23⅞ × 31¹⁵⁄₁₆ in.). The Art Institute of Chicago, gift of Shin'enKan, Inc., 1990.811.12.

FIG. 48 Goff and Greene. *Eugene and Nancy Bavinger House, Norman, Oklahoma, Interior Perspective*, 1950. Colored pencil with graphite on paper; 46.1 × 76.9 cm (18⅛ × 30¼ in.). The Art Institute of Chicago, gift of Shin'enKan, Inc., 1990.811.16.

shows the Bavingers' young son playing in a pool while Eugene dangles his feet in the water. Nothing about this image, from the shadowy lighting to the rough-hewn rocks and tropical plants, recalls a conventional house. What it resembles is the grotto, another fantasy interior that transfixed the public in an earlier era.

David G. De Long alluded to a connection with the past when describing Goff's colleague Herb Greene's "lush renderings" of the Bavinger house, which he believed served to "romanticize the image, distancing reality as did the picturesque drawings of the early nineteenth century."[43] *Picturesque* originally referred to the practice of creating highly manipulated gardens that mimic paintings: organized along perspectival views and populated "like stage sets," with diverse man-made features, including pavilions, winding paths, waterfalls, faux ruins, grottos, and even artificial cliffs.[44]

Although Greene's drawings are not picturesque in the original sense, his work draws out the romantic qualities of the Bavinger house and its natural setting. One elevation (fig. 47) shows the building nestled in a colorful landscape of lacy trees, rocks, and trailing vines, echoing Goff's description of the project site: "The ravine came awake and the jackoaks and the natural beauty of the site were disturbed as little as possible."[45] This natural connection was reinforced by the house's rough walls, which were built with local sandstone rocks with irregular openings for windows and doors.[46]

Yet once inside, most views of the landscape were cut off by these solid masonry walls, an inward focus that is emphasized in Greene's drawings (fig. 48). Detailed perspective views of the staircase and dining area show ledges, walls, and floors that are so densely populated with foliage and decorations that they almost appear to move. These elements included moss, purple bearded iris, spidery ferns, and giant caladium leaves, as well as more mysterious objects resembling giant shelf mushrooms, crystals, driftwood, and coral—in short, the decorations typically found in an English grotto made circa 1815 (fig. 49).[47]

Like the picturesque tradition that gave birth to both the grotto and the conservatory—the artificial cave and the artificial garden—the Bavinger house reflects civilization and wilderness, art and nature, all at once.[48] Although grottos date back to ancient times, Goff likely visited similar contemporary spaces, such as the Garfield

40. Goff proposed many houses with plantings and water features, none so dramatic as the unbuilt 1946 Don and Mildred Leidig House, a circular pavilion in which "rooms" hung from a suspended roof over a series of freeform pools, paths, and plantings. See De Long, *Bruce Goff*, 82–85.

41. "Space and Saucer House: Oklahoma Family Lives in Suspension in a Unique New Structure," *Life*, Sept. 19, 1955, 155–56.

42. Bruce Goff, "Bavinger House," n.d., brochure for tours of the house, series II, box 5, folder 3, BGA, AIC.

43. De Long, *Bruce Goff*, 106.

44. John Dixon Hunt, *Gardens and the Picturesque: Studies in the History of Landscape Architecture* (MIT Press, 1992), 114–17.

45. Goff, "Bavinger House" (see n. 42).

46. De Long, *Bruce Goff*, 107.

47. See, for example, the walls of the shell grotto on the grounds of the Duke of Bedford's Endsleigh Cottage, designed by landscape designer Humphry Repton around 1815.

48. The rococo grotto moved from Europe to the United States in the eighteenth and nineteenth centuries, including a grotto Thomas Jefferson proposed at Monticello. On the early history of American grottos, see Kerry Dean Carso, *Follies in America: A History of Garden and Park Architecture* (Cornell University Press, 2021).

FIG. 49 Endsleigh House Shell Grotto, Milton Abbot, Cornwall, England, 2016. Photograph by Homer Sykes.

FIG. 50 Fern Room at the Garfield Park Conservatory, Chicago, 1909. Photographer unknown. Chicago Public Library Special Collections, Chicago Park District Archives, Photographs, box 27, folder 18.

Park Conservatory in Chicago. Designed by landscape architect Jens Jensen in 1906, the conservatory includes a historic Fern Room (fig. 50) that features indoor waterfalls, faux rock hillocks, abundant plantings, and ponds—the height of artificial nature at the turn of the century. And even if the built version of the Bavinger water gardens was never quite so animated as Greene's drawings, the intention was achieved: to create a house that was unusually alive and filled with natural and artificial wonders. "The house," Goff wrote, "unlike most houses, will probably never be complete, because it is intended to keep growing with its occupants."[49]

CONCLUSION

Goff was well aware of the criticism aimed at his pursuit of visual (and other) sensations, of "doing things for effect."[50] He rejected this framing, arguing, "The only valid question is what effect do you want to create?"[51] And create he did, assembling diverse amalgamations of material and cultural references from across the globe to produce effects like artifice, extravagance, glamour, and sensuality.[52] These non-subtle aesthetic effects were also prominent aspects of an emerging cultural phenomenon, Camp, which was first identified in a 1967 essay by critic Susan Sontag (and later used by Jencks as one of three slurs—Camp, Kitsch, and Schlock—applied to Goff's work).[53] In this well-known text, Sontag laid out a list of qualities and values that reads in places like a chronicle of Goff's own historical fascinations: the bricolage of Antoni Gaudí and the mystery of the grotto, the decorative qualities of the Art Nouveau and the excitement of mixing of high and low.[54]

I conclude with this gesture to Camp as it brings together the most strident criticisms and celebrations of Goff's practice. We may never know exactly why Goff combined coal, glass, cellophane, and sequins, but the idea of Camp speaks to the kind of reception or effect that he hoped to (and did) achieve. Far from being trivial, Sontag argued that Camp sensibilities serve to forge connections and create communities, especially those related to queer experience: "Camp taste is a kind of love for human nature."[55] All of which is to say, material effects are one of the ways Goff's radically independent vision reached out to the broader culture, partaking in all its beauty, incoherence, and even its consumerist crutches.

49. Goff, "Bavinger House" (see n. 42).
50. "Pride of the Prairie," 190.
51. Ibid.
52. Various descriptions of Camp Susan Sontag used in "Notes on 'Camp,'" in *Against Interpretation and Other Essays* (Picador, 1990), 275–92. In addition to his diligent research and other brilliant insights, I am grateful to Craig Lee for pointing out the alignment of this essay with aspects of my argument.
53. Jencks, "Bruce Goff," 13.
54. Sontag, "Notes on 'Camp,'" 275–92.
55. Ibid., 291. For more on Goff's aesthetics and queerness, see Aaron Betsky, *Queer Space: Architecture and Same Sex Desire* (William Morrow and Co., 1997), 95–97; and Carol Mason, *Oklahomo: Lessons in Unqueering America* (State University of New York Press, 2015), 111–38.

FROM TOP, FIG. 51 Goff. *"A Modern Home of the Midwest Type," Perspective and Plans*, 1919. Ink with graphite on tan wove paper; 54.6 × 36.8 cm (21½ × 14½ in.). The Art Institute of Chicago, gift of Shin'enKan, Inc., 1990.900.1. FIG. 52 Sand dollar necklace, n.d. Bruce A. Goff Archive.

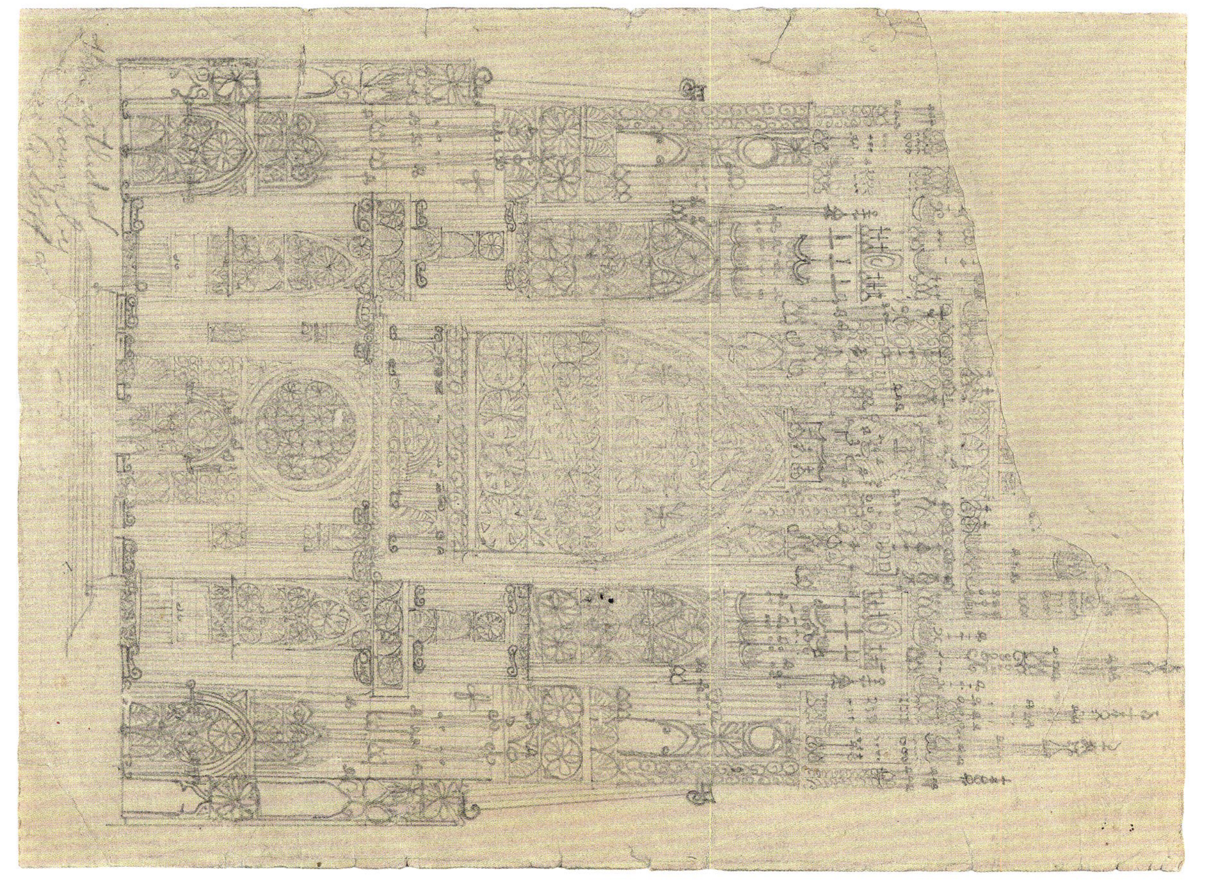

CLOCKWISE, FROM TOP LEFT, FIG. 53 Goff. *Untitled*, 1920. Graphite on cream wove paper; 30.5 × 22.9 cm (12 × 9 in.). The Art Institute of Chicago, gift of Shin'enKan, Inc., 1990.574.296. FIG. 54 Harriet Zelida York Messick (American, 1835–1924). *Untitled*, 1850. Watercolor on pith paper; 15.3 × 10.2 × 1.3 cm (6 × 4 × ½ in.). Bruce A. Goff Archive. FIG. 55 Goff. *Cathedral Sketch*, 1914. Graphite on buff wove paper; 30.2 × 22.3 cm (11⅞ × 8¾ in.). The Art Institute of Chicago, gift of Shin'enKan, Inc., RX18410/14.34.

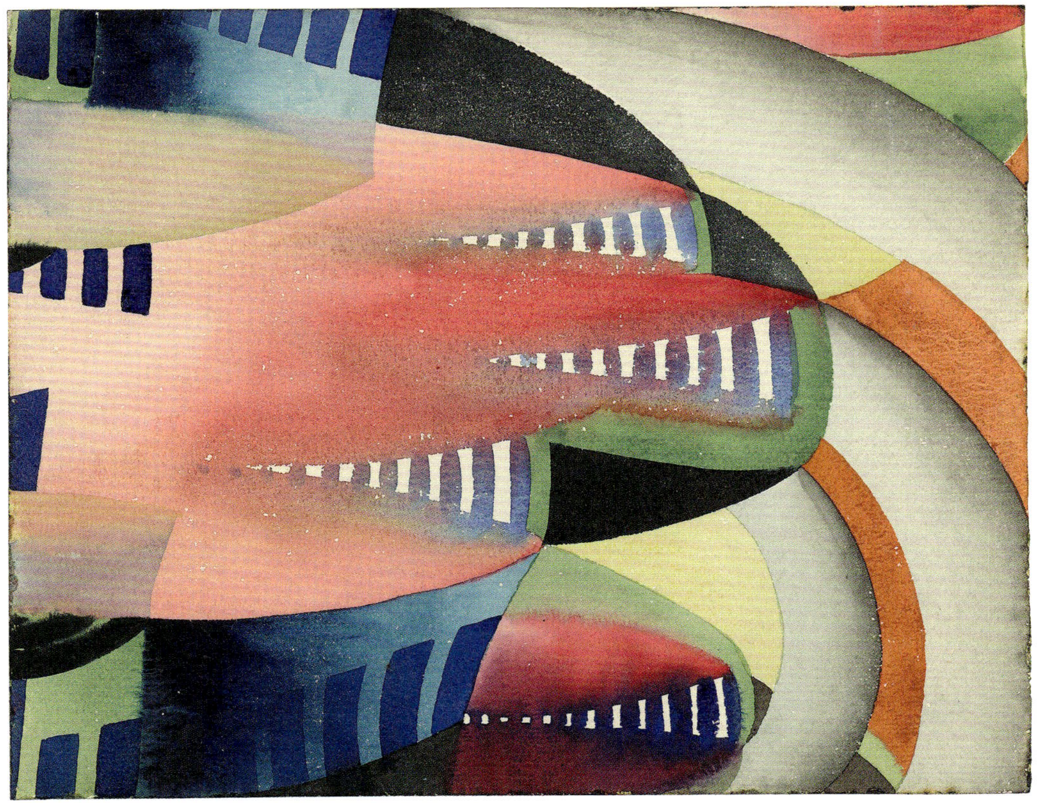

FIG. 56 Goff. *Untitled (Composition)*, c. 1925. Watercolor on cream wove paper; 29.7 × 22.9 cm (11¾ × 9⁄16 in.). The Art Institute of Chicago, gift of Shin'enKan, Inc., 1990.574.98.

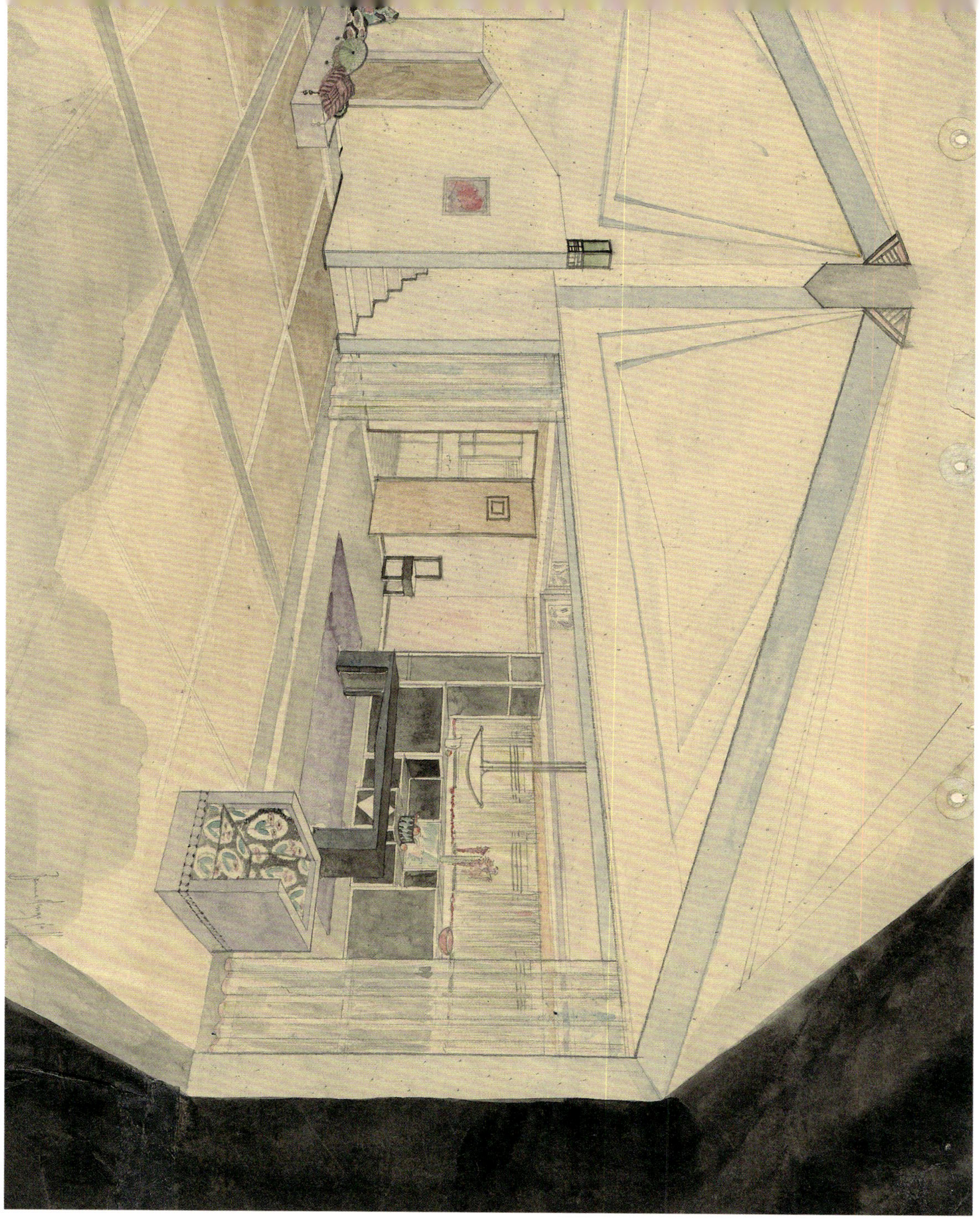

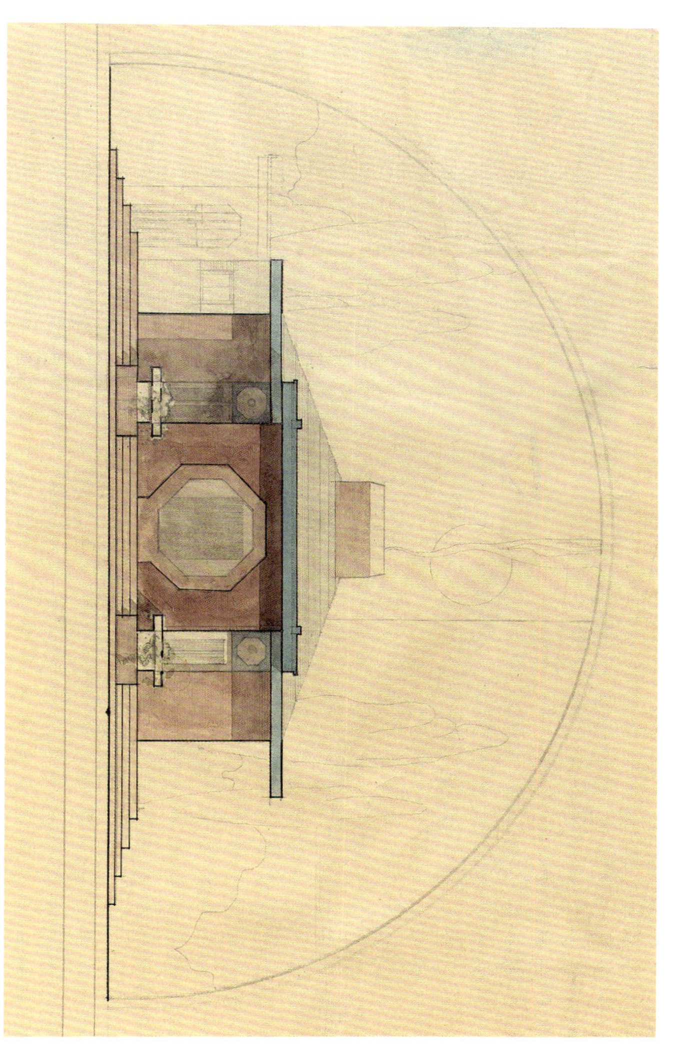

FIG. 57 Goff and Rush, Endacott and Rush, Architects. *Baughman Bungalow, Tulsa, Oklahoma, Perspective* [unbuilt], 1922. Ink and watercolor over graphite on cream wove paper; 35.2 × 46.3 cm (13⅞ × 18¼ in.). The Art Institute of Chicago, gift of Shin'enKan, Inc., 1990.573.1.

FIG. 58 Goff and Rush, Endacott and Rush, Architects. *Baughman Bungalow, Tulsa, Oklahoma, Interior Perspective* [unbuilt], 1922. Opaque and translucent watercolor and graphite on cream wove laid paper, laid down on cream board; 32.7 × 54.3 cm (12⅞ × 21⁷⁄₁₆ in.). The Art Institute of Chicago, gift of Shin'enKan, Inc., 1990.573.2.

FROM TOP, FIG. 59 Goff and Rush, Endacott and Rush, Architects. *Boston Avenue Methodist Episcopal Church South, Tulsa, Oklahoma, Perspective*, 1926. Graphite and pastel, with touches of opaque watercolor, on cream laid paper; 45.9 × 35.6 cm (18 1/8 × 14 1/16 in.). The Art Institute of Chicago, gift of Shin'enKan, Inc., 1990.891.2. FIG. 60 Auditorium of Boston Avenue Methodist Episcopal Church South, Tulsa, Oklahoma, 1946. Photograph by Matt Farrell of Richie Studio. Bruce A. Goff Archive.

FROM TOP, FIG. 61 Boston Avenue Methodist Episcopal Church South, Tulsa, Oklahoma, 1946. Photograph by Matt Farrell of Richie Studio. Bruce A. Goff Archive. FIG. 62. Goff and Rush, Endacott and Rush, Architects. *Boston Avenue Methodist Episcopal Church South, Tulsa, Oklahoma, Interior Perspective*, 1926. Graphite and pastel on cream laid paper; 45.7 × 35.5 cm (18 × 14 in.). The Art Institute of Chicago, gift of Shin'enKan, Inc., 1990.891.3.

CLOCKWISE, FROM TOP LEFT, FIG. 63 Goff. *Glass and Steel Skyscraper, Hypothetical Study*, 1929. Colored pencil on black wove paper; 47 × 29.9 cm (18½ × 11¾ in.). The Art Institute of Chicago, gift of Shin'enKan, Inc., RX18410/29.36. FIG. 64 Goff. *Hypothetical Study*, 1931. Ink on tan wove paper; 24.7 × 25 cm (9¾ × 9⅞ in.). The Art Institute of Chicago, gift of Shin'enKan, Inc., 1990.1212.1. FIG. 65 Goff. *3–Square House, Hypothetical Study*, 1931. Watercolor, graphite, and ink on gray paper-faced laminated paperboard; 33.1 × 45.8 cm (13 × 18 in.). The Art Institute of Chicago, gift of Shin'enKan, Inc., RX18410/31.36.1.

FIG. 67 Goff. *Hypothetical Study*, 1928. Watercolor and graphite on cream wove paper; 43.2 × 44.5 cm (17 × 17½ in.). The Art Institute of Chicago, gift of Shin'enKan, Inc., RX18410/28.34.

FIG. 66 Goff. *Hypothetical Study*, 1930. Ink, over traces of graphite, on cream laid paper; 55.9 × 43.2 cm (22 × 17 in.). The Art Institute of Chicago, gift of Shin'enKan, Inc., RX18410/30.35.2.

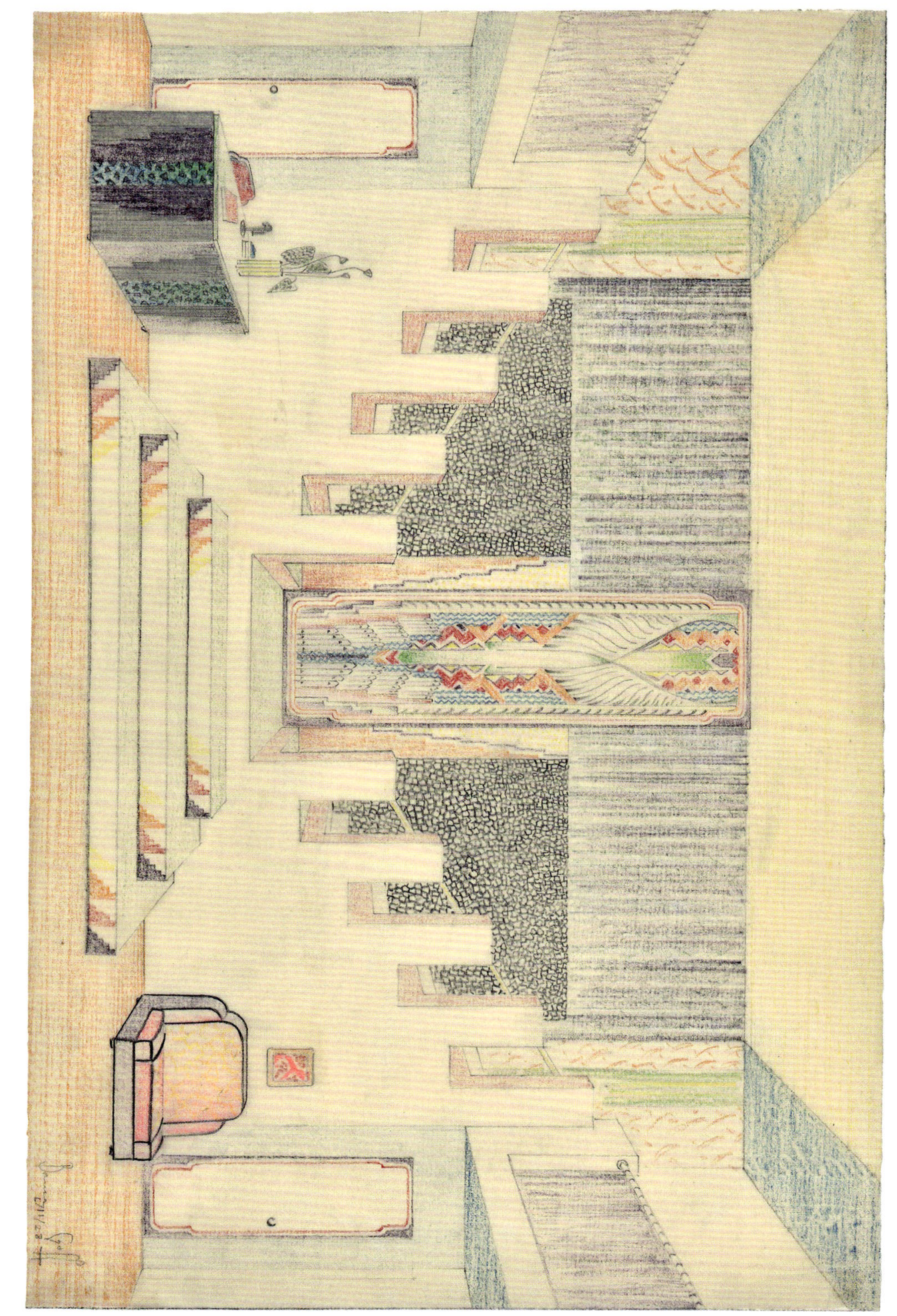

FIG. 68 Goff. *Patti Adams Shriner House and Studio, Tulsa, Oklahoma, Interior Perspective of Entrance Lobby*, 1928. Graphite and colored pencil on cream wove paper; 26.5 × 40 cm (10⁷⁄₁₆ × 15¾ in.). The Art Institute of Chicago, gift of Shin'enKan, Inc., 1990.82.6.

ABOVE, FIG. 69 Patti Adams Shriner House and Studio, Tulsa, Oklahoma, 1978. Photograph by Phillip B. Welch. Bruce A. Goff Archive.

FIG. 70 Goff. *Patti Adams Shriner House and Studio, Tulsa, Oklahoma, Perspective*, 1928. Graphite and colored pencil on cream laid paper; 53.1 × 42.7 cm (20$\frac{15}{16}$ × 16$\frac{13}{16}$ in.). The Art Institute of Chicago, gift of Shin'enKan, Inc., 1990.82.5.

FIG. 71 Goff. *Untitled (Composition)*, 1932. Opaque watercolor, over traces of graphite, on tan wove paper; 43.3 × 55.8 cm (17 1⁄16 × 22 in.). The Art Institute of Chicago, gift of Shin'enKan, Inc., 1990.574.172.

FROM TOP, FIG. 72 Goff. *Untitled (Composition)*, 1928. Watercolor and ink on cream wove paper; 29.9 × 23.2 cm (11¾ × 9⅛ in.). The Art Institute of Chicago, gift of Shin'enKan, Inc., 1990.574.208. FIG. 73 Goff and Rush, Endacott and Goff (American, 1929–1932). *Phi Beta Delta Fraternity House, Norman, Oklahoma, Perspective* [unbuilt], 1930. Graphite and colored pencil on cream wove paper; 55.8 × 76.1 cm (22 × 30 in.). The Art Institute of Chicago, gift of Shin'enKan, Inc., 1990.888.3.

ABOVE, FROM LEFT, FIG. 74 Goff. *Untitled (Composition)*, c. 1925. Watercolor and ink on cream wove paper; 28.7 × 19.6 cm (11 5/16 × 7 3/4 in.). The Art Institute of Chicago, gift of Shin'enKan, Inc., 1990.574.40.
FIG. 75 Goff. *Untitled (Composition)*, c. 1925. Watercolor on cream wove paper; 29.6 × 22.6 cm (11 5/8 × 8 7/8 in.). The Art Institute of Chicago, gift of Shin'enKan, Inc., 1990.574.218.

FROM TOP, FIG. 76 Cover of *Tulsart*, 1931. Ditto or mimeograph reproduction on tan wove paper with red gouache; 35.9 × 21.6 cm (14⅛ × 8½ in.). Bruce A. Goff Archive. **FIG. 77** Goff. *Piano Roll*, c. 1933. Cream wove paper and brown plastic scroll mount; scroll handle diam.: 5.8 cm (2¼ in.); overall h.: 30.5 cm (12 in.); paper h.: 28.9 cm (11⅜ in.). Bruce A. Goff Archive.

FIG. 78 Goff. *Ice Cream Parlor Alterations for Vitrolite, Interior Perspective* [unbuilt], 1937. Opaque watercolor, colored pencil, crayon, ink, and graphite on tan wove paper; 58.2 × 94.7 cm (22⅞ × 37¼ in.). The Art Institute of Chicago, gift of Shin'enKan, Inc., 1990.905.

FIG. 79 Reuben Haley (American, 1872–1933). *Ruba Rombic Bowl*, 1928–30. Glass; 10.8 × 31.2 × 15.9 cm (4¼ × 12¼ × 6¼ in.). Private collection.

FIG. 80 Goff. *Bradley Building for Vitrolite, Perspective* [unbuilt], 1937. Graphite, colored pencil, and watercolor on cream wove paper; 78.7 × 101.8 cm (30 15/16 × 40 1/8 in.). The Art Institute of Chicago, gift of Shin'enKan, Inc., 1990.830.2.

FIG. 81 Goff. *Untitled (Composition)*, 1932. Opaque watercolor, over traces of graphite, on tan wove paper; 43.2 × 55.9 cm (17 × 22 in.). The Art Institute of Chicago, gift of Shin'enKan, Inc., 1990.574.171.

FROM TOP, FIG. 82 Frank and Ruth Cole House, Park Ridge, Illinois, 1943. Photograph by Fons Iannelli. Published in *American Home*, May 1943. Bruce A. Goff Archive. FIG. 83 Goff. *Frank and Ruth Cole House, Park Ridge, Illinois, Perspective*, 1939. Colored pencil and graphite, with opaque watercolor, on red-orange wove paper; 43.2 × 67 cm (17 1/16 × 26 7/16 in.). The Art Institute of Chicago, gift of Shin'enKan, Inc., 1990.848.1.

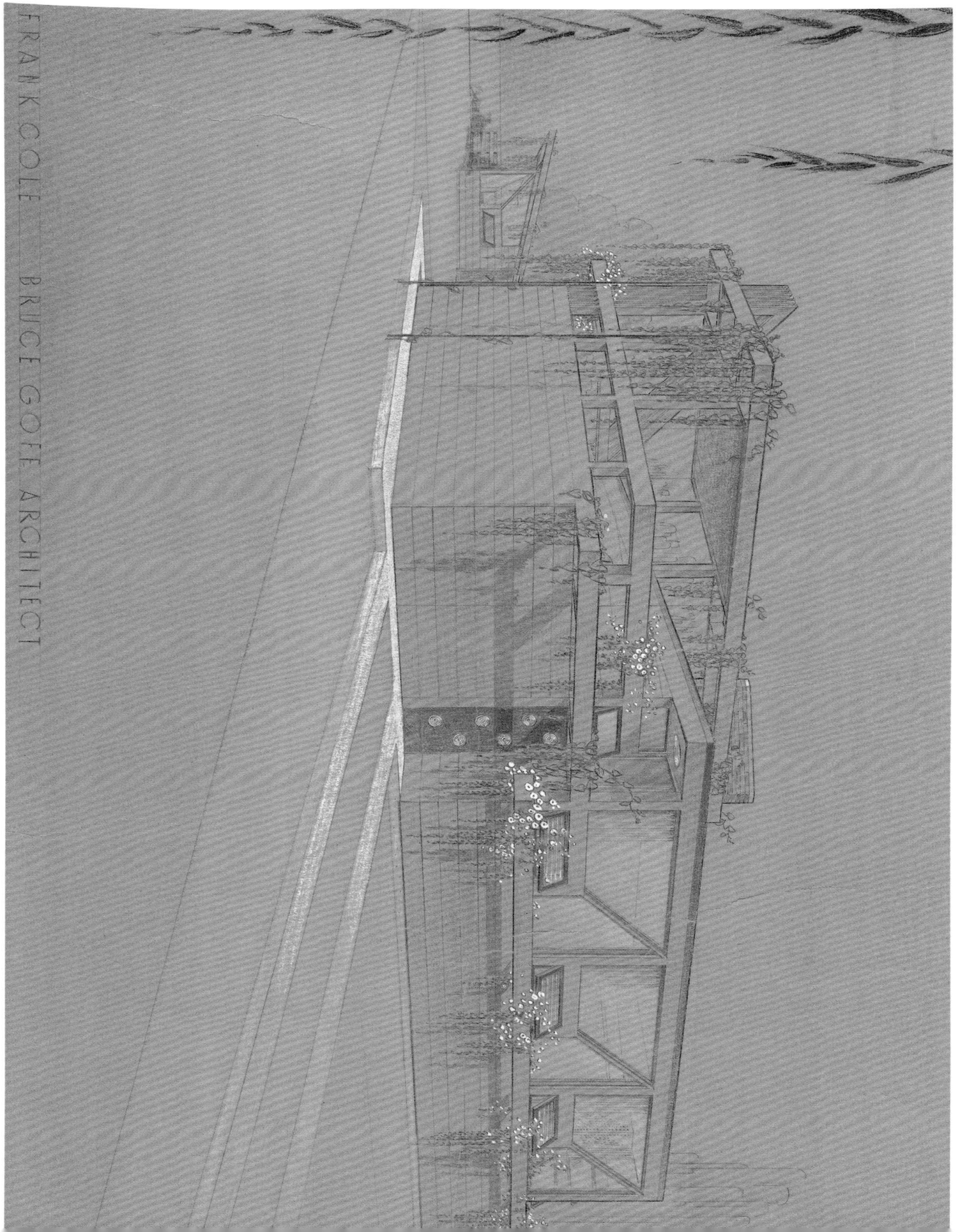

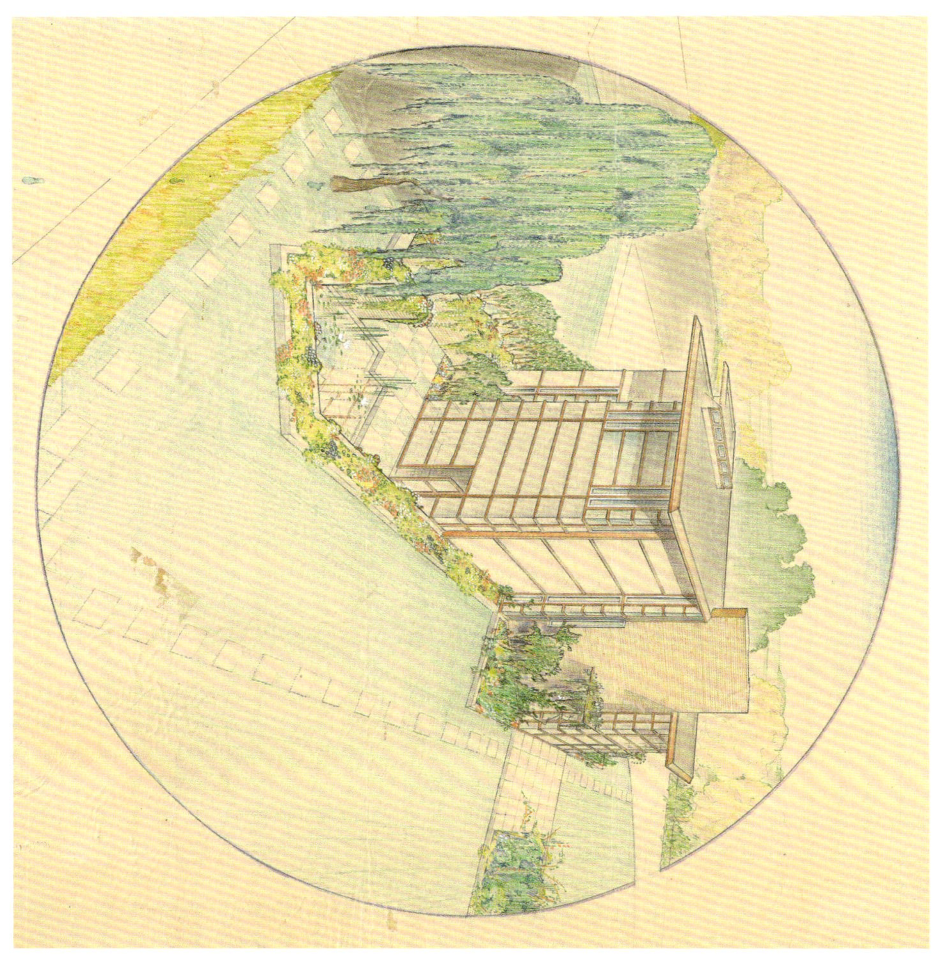

FIG. 84 Goff. *Chester and Irma Rant House, First Design, Northfield, Illinois, Perspective* [unbuilt], 1938. Colored pencil and graphite, with touches of opaque watercolor, on tracing paper, mounted to laminated paperboard; 57.6 × 55.3 cm (22 11/16 × 21 13/16 in.). The Art Institute of Chicago, gift of Shin'enKan, Inc., 1990.984.1.

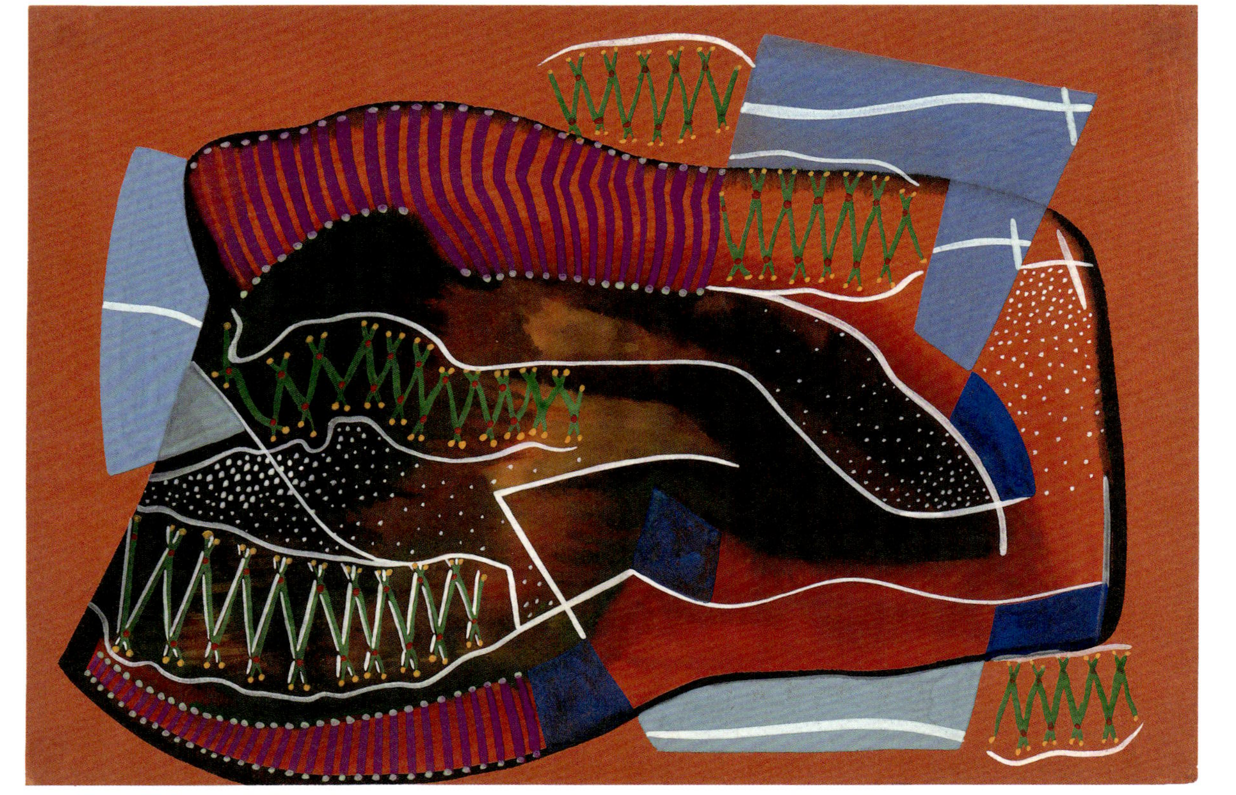

FROM TOP, FIG. 85 Wiener Werkstätte (Viennese, 1903–1932). *Aufsatz (Footed Centerpiece)*, 1920–31. Polychromed glazed ceramic; overall h.: 16.5 cm (6½ in.); bowl diam.: 24.4 cm (9⅝ in.); base diam.: 13.3 cm (5¼ in.). Bruce A. Goff Archive. FIG. 86 Goff. *Untitled (Composition)*, n.d. Opaque watercolor and ink on red-orange wove paper; 45.1 × 30.5 cm (17¾ × 12 in.). The Art Institute of Chicago, gift of Shin'enKan, Inc., 1990.574.90.

FIG. 87 Goff. *Untitled (Composition)*, 1933. Opaque watercolor, over traces of graphite, on cream wove paper; 43.2 × 53.3 cm (17 1/16 × 21 in.). The Art Institute of Chicago, gift of Shin'enKan, Inc., 1990.574.38.

FIG. 88 Goff. *Marks House, Chicago, Interior Perspective* [unbuilt], 1939. Opaque and translucent watercolor, graphite, and sand on white illustration board; 32 × 53 cm (12⅝ × 20⅞ in.). The Art Institute of Chicago, gift of Shin'enKan, Inc., 1990.878.1.

FROM TOP, FIG. 89 Goff. *Untitled (Composition)*, 1935. Opaque watercolor on turquoise wove paper; 45.1 × 30.8 cm (17¾ × 12 in.). The Art Institute of Chicago, gift of Shin'enKan, Inc., 1990.574.94.
FIG. 90 Gong, n.d. Bruce A. Goff Archive.

FIG. 91 Goff. *Untitled (Composition)*, n.d. Spray paint, opaque watercolor, and ink on cream wove paper; 110.5 × 70.5 cm (43½ × 27¾ in.). The Art Institute of Chicago, gift of Shin'enKan, Inc., 1990.574.316.

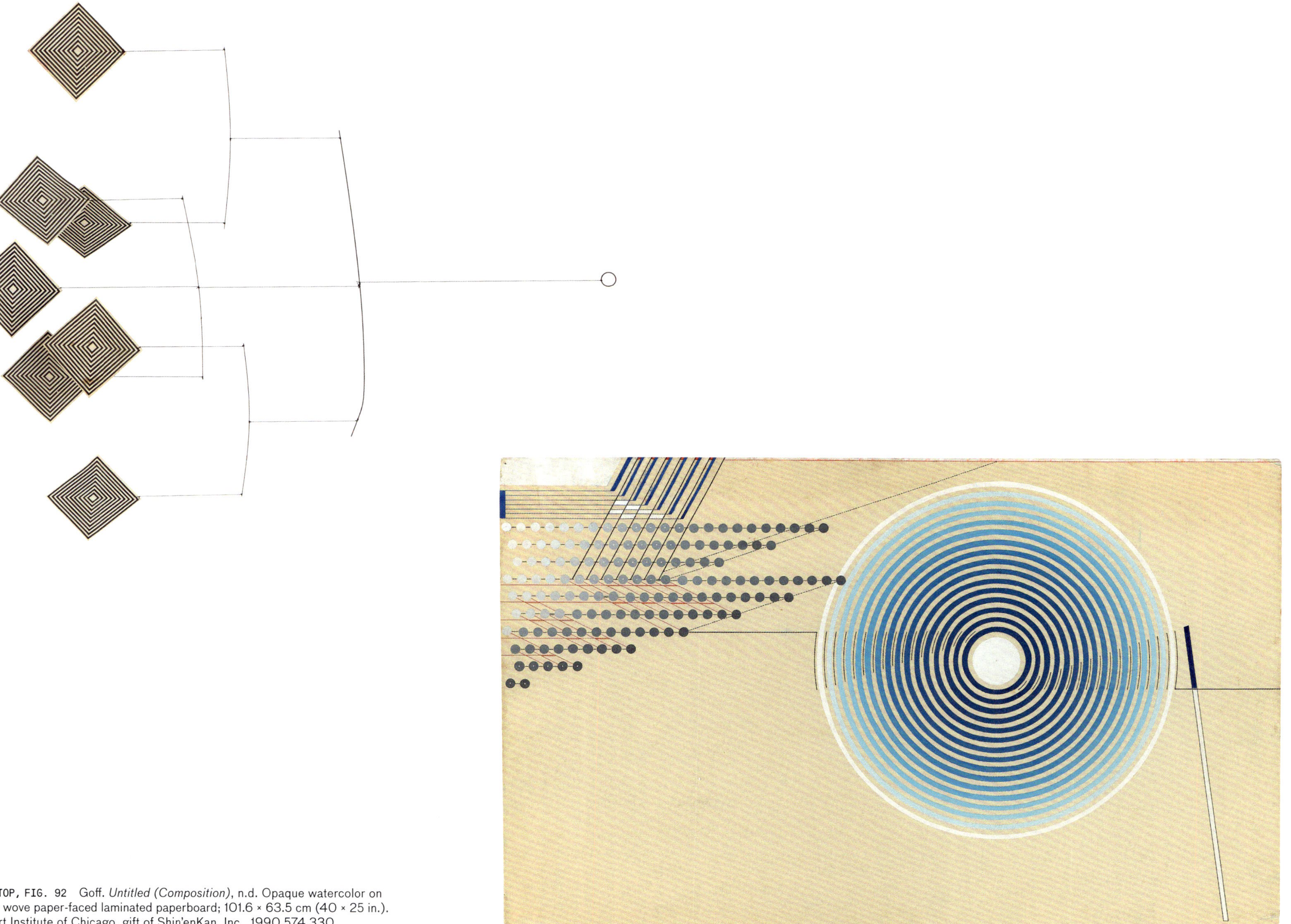

FROM TOP, FIG. 92 Goff. *Untitled (Composition)*, n.d. Opaque watercolor on cream wove paper-faced laminated paperboard; 101.6 × 63.5 cm (40 × 25 in.). The Art Institute of Chicago, gift of Shin'enKan, Inc., 1990.574.330.
FIG. 93 Mobile, n.d. Bruce A. Goff Archive.

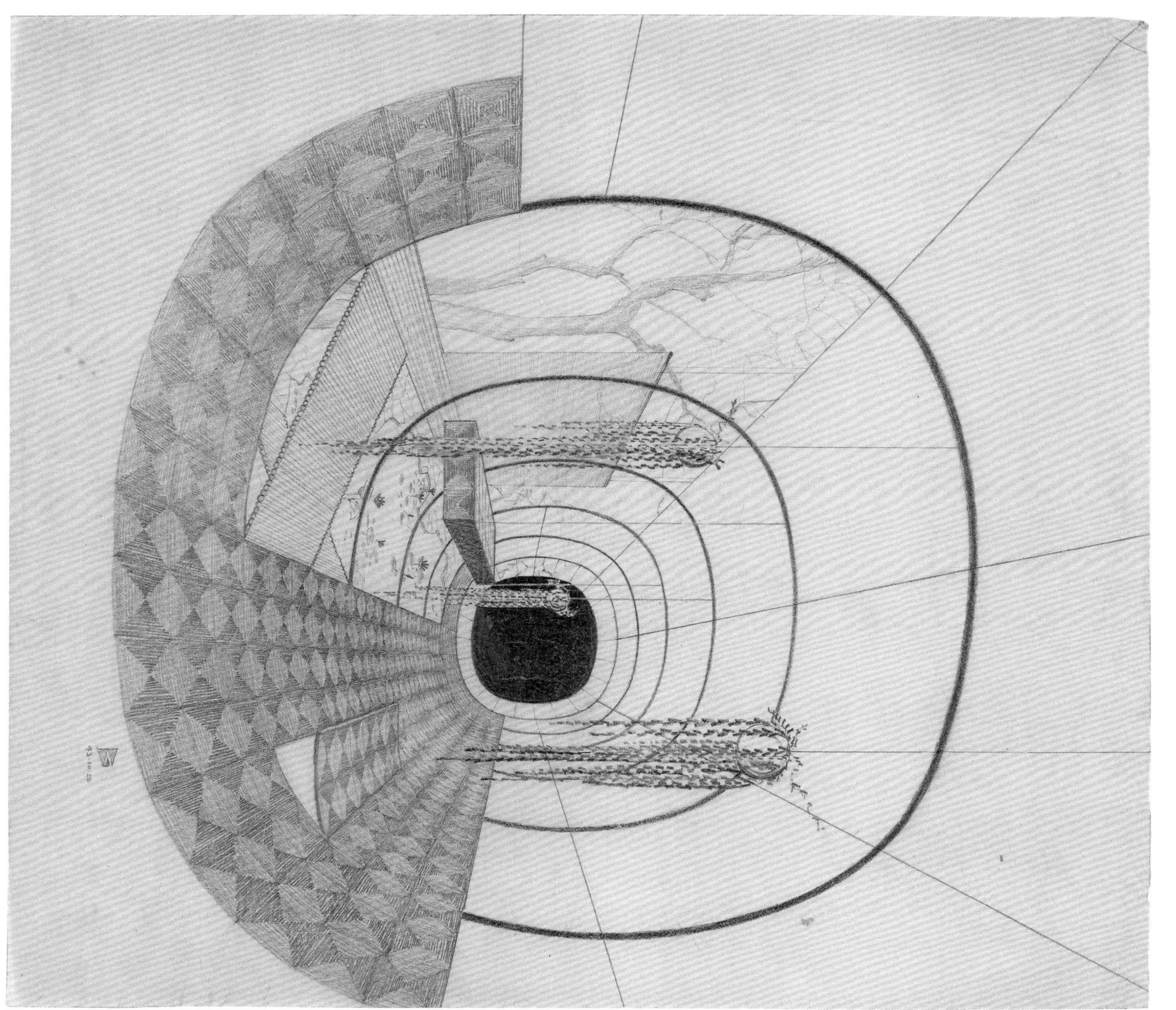

FIG. 94 Goff. *Structure Study*, 1943. Graphite on tracing paper; 47.5 × 31.2 cm (18¾ × 12 5⁄16 in.). The Art Institute of Chicago, gift of Shin'enKan, Inc., 1990.864.

FROM TOP, FIG. 95 Goff. *Untitled (Composition)*, 1927. Watercolor on cream wove paper; 28.3 × 19.1 cm (11⅛ × 7½ in.). The Art Institute of Chicago, gift of Shin'enKan, Inc., 1990.574.44. FIG. 96 Goff. *Untitled (Composition)*, n.d. Ink on cream wove paper; 30.5 × 22.9 cm (12 × 9 in.). The Art Institute of Chicago, gift of Shin'enKan, Inc., 1990.574.160.

FIG. 97 Woody Big Bow (Kiowa, 1915–1988). *Seated Southern Plains Man*, n.d. Translucent and opaque watercolor on laminated paper board; 35 × 26.1 cm (13¾ × 10¼ in.). The Art Institute of Chicago, gift of Shin'enKan, Inc., 2025.68.

In a Native Present: Bruce Goff and Oklahoma

Hadley Jerman Bruss

Bruce Goff, celebrated architect and teacher, reclines at his desk gazing into the middle distance (fig. 98). Photographed from a low angle, he appears heroic, framed against a galaxy of tumbleweeds. This interstellar quality is reinforced by five paper lanterns that orbit and illuminate his face. The photographer, Philip B. Welch, was a graduate student in architecture at the University of Oklahoma (OU), and he hinted at his professor's creative inspirations through the objects surrounding him. Peacock feathers arc into the frame at right, a memento of Goff's beloved great-grandmother.[1] The filing cabinet peeking over his left shoulder represents his role as a teacher. Just out of frame, a stack of papers near his left hand suggests a drawing practice that served as an outlet for, as fellow Oklahoma modern artist and friend Olinka Hrdy put it, Goff's "creative mind."[2] And on the dark curved walls of his office in OU's Oklahoma Memorial Stadium—surrounding those lanterns, feathers, and creative mind—hang Native American artworks: prints by Potawatomi artist Woody Crumbo depicting fantastical horses and deer and an image of Pueblo dancers. A Hopi katsina figure perches guardian-like above the architect.

Scholars often comment on Goff's wide-ranging architectural and musical influences, but rarely do they mention his interest in Native American art.[3] The omission is hardly surprising; Goff expressed admiration for non-Western art and architecture, especially Japanese, Chinese, and Javanese, and avidly collected Japanese prints, but his commentary on and collection of Indigenous art were, by comparison, meager.[4] Yet, according to Goff's biographer, David G. De Long, Goff's "strongest memories" of his Oklahoma childhood were of Cherokee dances and the "patterned and brightly colored attire" worn by Native people to which he credited his own lifelong "fascination with bright colors and geometric patterns."[5]

By midcentury Goff had collected paintings and prints by Native artists from Oklahoma and the Southwest and, as Welch's photograph reveals, surrounded himself with

FIG. 98 Candid portrait of Bruce Goff in his office at the School of Architecture at the University of Oklahoma, Norman, c. 1954. Photograph by Philip B. Welch. Bruce A. Goff Archive.

1. David G. De Long, *Bruce Goff: Toward Absolute Architecture* (Architectural History Foundation; MIT Press, 1988), 4.
2. Olinka Hrdy to Bruce Goff, Jan. 10, 1959, series I, box 11, folder 22b, Bruce A. Goff Archive, Ryerson and Burnham Art and Architecture Archives, The Art Institute of Chicago (hereafter BGA, AIC).
3. See De Long, *Bruce Goff*, 3 and 12–14; and Arn Henderson, *Bruce Goff: Architecture of Discipline in Freedom* (University of Oklahoma Press, 2017), 4.
4. "Pride of the Prairie: A High Priest of Individualism Is Designing in a Strikingly Regional Idiom for His Grass Roots Clients," *Architectural Forum* 88, no. 3 (Mar. 1948): 95.
5. See De Long, *Bruce Goff*, 4; and "Pride of the Prairie," 95.

FIG. 99 Blanket, Osage County, Oklahoma, 1920–30. Broadcloth, wool yarn, silk ribbon, and glass beads; 163.8 × 175.3 cm (64½ × 69 in.). Philbrook Museum of Art, Tulsa, Oklahoma, Museum purchase, 1976.9.2.

them. Although Goff only credited Indigenous dances and dress with inspiring his use of color and pattern over the next seventy years, his art collection and buildings demonstrate an ongoing engagement with Native art. And in select architectural designs throughout his mature career, Goff referenced Indigenous architectural forms, such as the Plains tepee. Through biographical and visual analysis, I trace Goff's relationship to Native art in Oklahoma, placing the architect within an artistic environment in which Native presence was overt, not only in the late 1920s, during his early adulthood in Tulsa, but also between 1947 and 1955, when he taught at OU. That persistent yet underrecognized Native presence, I argue, finds visual parallels and resonances in Goff's own work.

INDIAN TERRITORY

Goff first encountered Native culture when his family moved from Kansas to Indian Territory in 1906, one year before the territory merged with Oklahoma Territory and achieved statehood.[6] By 1913 he had resided in Henryetta, Skiatook, and Hominy, all located in the eastern half of present-day Oklahoma. He later recalled these towns—each with a population at, or well below, one thousand around 1907—as "dusty and featureless," with oppressive temperatures, insects, and wind.[7] They were also Native towns formed during the nineteenth century by Creek and Cherokee people forcibly removed from the Southeastern United States and by Osage

6. De Long, *Bruce Goff*, 4.
7. Goff quoted in De Long, *Bruce Goff*, 4, and 312n7 lists the towns' population and tribal affiliation.

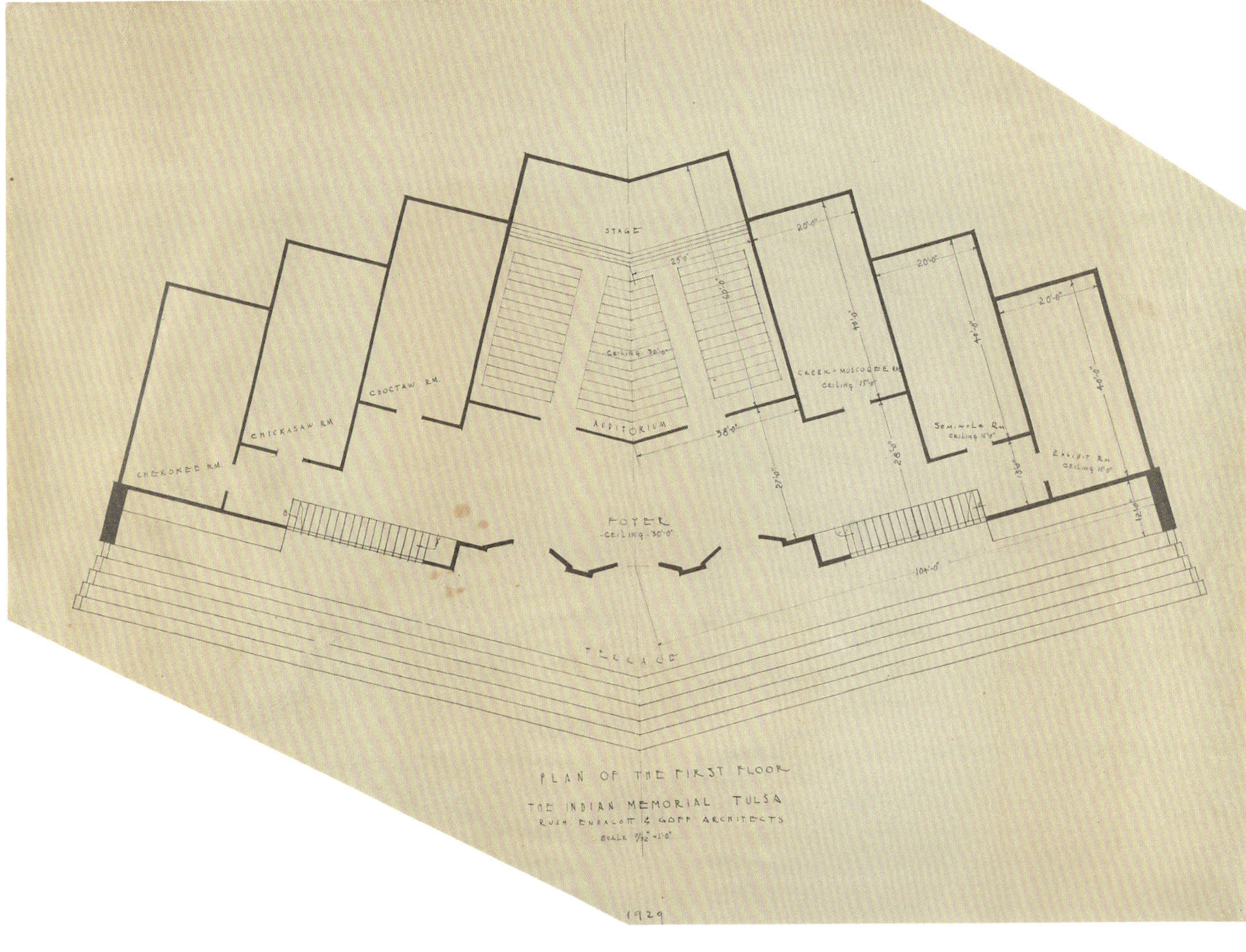

FIG. 100 Goff and Rush, Endacott and Goff. *Indian Memorial, Tulsa, Oklahoma, First-Floor Plan* [unbuilt], 1929. Photostat on cream wove paper; 41.7 × 56 cm (16 7⁄16 × 22 1⁄16 in.). The Art Institute of Chicago, gift of Shin'enKan, Inc., 1990.953.3.

FIG. 101 Goff and Rush, Endacott and Goff. *Indian Memorial, Tulsa, Oklahoma, Elevation* [unbuilt], 1929. Gelatin silver print; 14.8 × 23.5 cm (5 7⁄8 × 9 5⁄16 in.). Bruce A. Goff Archive.

people evicted from Kansas. When recalling colorful patterns worn by Native people in his childhood, Goff was likely remembering clothing made from bright strips of fabric, such as Seminole or Muscogee (Creek) patchwork or Osage ribbon work.[8]

Hominy became an important location for Osage gatherings in the twentieth century. There, at around eight years old, Goff likely saw colorful Osage appliqué, clothing and blankets (fig. 99) embellished with finger-woven sashes, and ribbon work. The latter consists of strips of rayon taffeta that have been cut, folded, and stitched together to create patterns. Zigzagging ribbons form sawtooth borders in one technique, while in another, many strips of contrasting-colored fabrics are combined to create offset layers.[9] Decades later, these textiles seem to have informed the boldly colored shirts Goff purchased and designed for himself, but well before that, in 1929, ribbon work may have influenced Goff's design for an architectural project in Tulsa, Oklahoma.

TULSA: A "WORTHY INDIAN MEMORIAL"

Tulsa boosters promoted a "Worthy Indian Memorial" as significant to the city's cultural development in the late 1920s alongside construction of a coliseum, stadium, and college of petroleum science.[10] In June 1924 Goff's former high school art teacher, Adah Robinson, for whom he had designed a home and studio in 1923, wrote to Goff about the "Indian Memorial" and requested he "help the cause."[11] Tulsa occupied Cherokee, Muscogee, and Osage lands, but the cause was neither honoring these Nations nor protesting the recent and ongoing murder of Osage people for their land and oil rights.[12] Rather, it seems to have been one of several civic efforts to memorialize *living* Indigenous cultures by Native and non-Native communities in Oklahoma at the time, and was funded not by tribes but by the local chapter of the Daughters of the American Revolution.[13] Responding to their proposal, Goff designed a three-story structure with a large auditorium on the ground floor flanked by an exhibition space and Cherokee, Chickasaw, Choctaw, Muscogee (Creek), and Seminole galleries, with Osage and Quapaw rooms on an upper level (fig. 100). Thus the project focused on tribes forcibly relocated to Indian Territory beginning in the 1830s rather than recognizing all tribes native to Oklahoma or forced to move there.[14]

Goff shared his sketch for the project's front elevation in June 1929 with Oscar Jacobson, a landscape painter and the director of the OU art department, whom he may have met as early as 1920 when competing at an interscholastic meet held at the university.[15] Like his other works from this decade, Goff's elevation reflects multiple influences but avoids a classical treatment, which both he and Jacobson considered inappropriate for modern Oklahoma.[16] Jacobson made suggestions, and by November Goff had completed a more angular version in ink (fig. 101). He added three triangular portals crowned by stepped pediments above long bands of broad and shallow steps, with landscaping and a figure wrapped in a blanket for scale.

Instead of showing the influence of specific local Indigenous architectural forms, Goff's stucco facade seems to be both self-referential and informed by a mix of Mayan and Southwestern design.[17] The plaster exterior and emphasis on vertical openings recall Goff's Art Deco design for Robinson's studio and the portal of his Boston Avenue Methodist Episcopal Church South (fig. 62) completed three years earlier in downtown Tulsa. Tile work above the memorial's doors suggests Mayan or Incan corbeled arches or the stepped mountain designs found in Diné textiles and Pueblo pottery. The narrow horizontal bands of contrasting values zigzag above these abstracted peaks, recalling an architectural version of Osage ribbon work.[18] Slim vertical bars that ascend on either side of the portal echo the pattern of windows punched into the facade of Riverside Studio, a house and studio in Tulsa that Goff constructed for piano teacher Patti Adams Shriner in 1928–29. They also suggest patterns found on finger-woven Osage sashes.[19] In Goff's drawings, branching saguaro cacti reinforce the Southwestern flavor—a peculiar inclusion given Tulsa's humid climate, which is inhospitable for this type of desert flora. In the ink drawing, Goff also inserted spindly ocotillo, a desert plant native to Arizona, New Mexico, and Texas—*not* Oklahoma—and a blanket-wrapped figure, an icon of Southwestern Indianness to non-Native viewers that was reproduced over and over in postcards and Western advertising campaigns during the 1910s and 1920s.[20]

Despite its visual references to Osage weaving, the structure gives the cumulative impression of a building informed by Native design but not Native *Oklahoman* design. Rather it appears to have sprouted from the Arizona desert, complete with xeriscapes and a stereotypical Diné figure lifted from Santa Fe Railway advertisements. Although Jacobson thought that classical and other ancient architectural forms had no business in modern Oklahoma, he apparently saw no conflict

8. For Osage clothing and ribbon work, see Daniel C. Swan and Jim Cooley, *Wedding Clothes and the Osage Community: A Giving Heritage* (Indiana University Press, 2019), 20 and 68.
9. Swan and Cooley, *Wedding Clothes*, 50.
10. "Tribune Platform," *Tulsa Tribune*, July 20, 1928, 24; "Tribune Platform," *Tulsa Tribune*, May 27, 1929, 22; and "Tribune Platform," *Tulsa Tribune*, Apr. 4, 1930, 36. *Tulsa Tribune* articles can be found at newspapers.com.
11. Adah Robinson to Bruce Goff, June 29, 1924, series I, box 19, folder 19, BGA, AIC.
12. For the Osage murders, see David Grann, *Killers of the Flower Moon: The Osage Murders and the Birth of the FBI* (Doubleday, 2017).
13. "City to Aid D.A.R. in Indian Memorial," *Tulsa Tribune*, Mar. 8, 1930, 8; for Indigenous-initiated memorials in the region, see "Creek Indian Memorial Ass'n Will Elect First Officers Since 1923," *Sunday Times Democrat*, May 29, 1927, 1; and "Choctaws Consider Sale of Coal, Asphalt Lands," *Tulsa Daily Legal News*, Oct. 23, 1930, 1. All are available at newspapers.com.
14. For tribes forcibly removed to Indian Territory, see Angie Debo, *And Still the Waters Run: The Betrayal of the Five Civilized Tribes* (1940; Princeton University Press, 2022); and Donald Fixico, "American Indians," *Encyclopedia of Oklahoma History and Culture*, Jan. 15, 2010, okhistory.org/publications/enc/entry?entry=AM010.
15. Oscar B. Jacobson to Bruce Goff, June 19, 1929, series I, box 12, folder 10, BGA, AIC. For the interscholastic meet, see "Fifteen Years Ago from the Tribune, April 29 [1920]," *Tulsa Tribune*, Apr. 29, 1935, 14. For more on Jacobson, see Anne Allbright, Janet Catherine Berlo, and Mark Andrew White, eds., *A World Unconquered: The Art of Oscar Brousse Jacobson* (Fred Jones Jr. Museum of Art, 2015); and Gunlög Fur, *Painting Culture, Painting Nature: Stephen Mopope, Oscar Jacobson, and the Development of Indian Art in Oklahoma* (University of Oklahoma Press, 2019).
16. Jacobson to Goff, June 19, 1929 (see n. 15).
17. For the influence of Mayan architecture, see Henderson, *Bruce Goff*, 13.

in appropriating Southwestern forms; he proclaimed the design "bully."[21] Goff's Southwestern approach to the memorial may have been influenced by Jacobson, whose mentorship at OU—and enthusiasm for Native art, pueblo architecture, and the newly formed art colonies of Santa Fe and Taos—led generations of art students to look to the Southwest, particularly northern New Mexico and southern Arizona, for inspiration.[22]

Goff's Southwestern approach to the memorial may have also been influenced by Olinka Hrdy, a May 1928 graduate of Jacobson's program whom he met at the university. Goff first saw Hrdy's murals on campus when he and dancer Evelyn Hall visited Norman following their wedding in early June 1928.[23] Admiring her work, he hired Hrdy to design murals for Riverside Studio, leading to their two-year collaboration in Tulsa and a lasting friendship.

The following spring, Jacobson endorsed Goff's significance as an Oklahoma modernist by opening an exhibition of his watercolors at OU on April 1. Two weeks later Goff gave an architecture lecture on campus to students barely younger than his twenty-four years.[24] On April 11 he and Hall judged costumes at the first annual El Modjii art students costume ball.[25] At the event, Goff witnessed dancing by Kiowa painters whose fame in the late 1920s well exceeded his own: Spencer Asah, James Auchiah, Jack Hokeah, Stephen Mopope, and Monroe Tsatoke (fig 102).[26]

NORMAN AND TULSA: THE KIOWA SIX AND OLINKA HRDY

These men and Kiowa woman Lois Smoky were the Kiowa Six, artists Jacobson invited to Norman in 1927 and 1928 to paint in studio space on campus. In the 1910s and 1920s, they, along with young artists from San Ildefonso Pueblo in northern New Mexico, invented an influential style that became known as "traditional Indian painting." The approach—since then more accurately described as modern—varied across cultures but is characterized by a flat application of color, stylized forms, and carefully rendered dancers and genre scenes against white or colored paper.[27] In contrast to earlier forms of Native painting that supported ceremonial and daily life, these so-called traditional paintings were made to sell to non-Native collectors. Buyers, many of whom, like Jacobson belonged to the New Mexico and Oklahoma culturati, promoted Native art throughout the country in the 1920s and 1930s.[28]

By the time Goff met the Kiowa artists in the spring of 1929, they had shown their work across the country, from San Francisco to New York, and internationally in Paris and Prague.[29] That year, the French publisher C. Szwedzicki produced a limited edition pochoir portfolio of their work titled *Kiowa Indian Art*, a sign of the keen international interest in contemporary Native American art.[30] Jacobson exhibited their paintings in the art building in mid-March 1929, just before Goff's exhibition, and a couple of months later, Goff corresponded with Jacobson about exhibiting their work at the Tulsa library.[31] Jacobson clearly hoped Goff might do more—that is, offer mural commissions to the Kiowa artists like he had with Hrdy—and wrote to Goff about Mopope's and Tsatoke's "tremendously impressive" murals, suggesting the architect "use some of this Indian talent in your work in Tulsa."[32]

Goff concurred. He envisioned three murals for the Indian Memorial project and apprised Jacobson of his plans. With characteristic paternalism and eagerness to benefit the artists, Jacobson responded in July 1929: "The Indian boys are simply made to order for this job. I hope that you will be able to give each of the five some work even if the major products are to be executed by the three best."[33] Hrdy recommended Goff employ the Kiowas who had been at OU the longest—including her friends Mopope and Hokeah—and Jacobson advised Goff to commission Auchiah, the most recent arrival, as "the most talented" of the group.[34]

Whether the Kiowa artists, who had returned home for the summer, ever learned of the potential commission remains unclear.[35] They were not mentioned when plans for the building were announced in *The Tulsa Tribune* that fall or when Goff's colleague Asbury

FIG. 102 Dr. Oscar B. Jacobson at his home with five of the renowned Kiowa Six artists, from left: Monroe Tsatoke, Jack Hokeah, Stephen Mopope, Dr. Jacobson, Spencer Asah, and James Auchiah, 1929. Photographer unknown. University of Oklahoma Photograph Collection 1107, Western History Collections, University of Oklahoma Libraries.

18. Jami C. Powell, "Osage Ribbon Work and the Expression of Nationalism: Re-Imagining Approaches to Material Culture and Nationhood" (master's thesis, University of North Carolina, 2014), 14–15.
19. For Osage finger weaving, see Swan and Cooley, *Wedding Clothes*, 80–81.
20. See Kathleen L. Howard and Diana F. Pardue, *Over the Edge: Fred Harvey at the Grand Canyon and in the Great Southwest* (Rio Nuevo; Heard Museum, 2016), 39–61.
21. Jacobson to Goff, June 19, 1929 (see n. 15).
22. See Allbright, et al., eds., *A World Unconquered*.
23. Oral history interview with Olinka Hrdy, Mar. 13–17, 1965, Archives of American Art, Smithsonian Institution, Washington, DC.
24. "Famous Art Works on Display at University," *Norman Transcript*, Feb. 17, 1929, 5; and "Goff Addresses School," *Tulsa World*, Apr. 17, 1929, 15.
25. "Costume Ball King and Queen Elected," *Oklahoma Daily*, Feb. 22, 1929, 1.
26. "Art Students Call on Supply of Ingenuity to Make First Annual Masquerade a Success," *Oklahoma Daily*, Apr. 9, 1929, 1 and 4.
27. See Julia Harth, "James Auchiah, 1906–1974," in *Kiowa Agency: Stories of the Six*, ed. W. Jackson Rushing III (Fred Jones Jr. Museum of Art, 2020), 10.
28. See J. J. Brody, *Pueblo Indian Painting: Tradition and Modernism in New Mexico, 1900–1930* (School for Advanced Research Press, 1997).
29. For more on the Kiowa Six, see Fur, *Painting Culture*, 156–158; and Rushing, *Kiowa Agency*.
30. See Jessica L. Horton and Janet Catherine Berlo, "Pueblo Painting in 1932: Folding Narratives of Native Art into American Art History," in *A Companion to American Art*, ed. John Davis et al. (Wiley-Blackwell, 2015), 267–69.
31. Jacobson to Goff, June 19, 1929 (see n. 15).
32. Ibid.
33. Ibid. Lois Smoky exhibited work with the group but had returned to her home in southwestern Oklahoma.
34. Oscar B. Jacobson to Bruce Goff, July 15, 1929, series II, box 1, folder 13, BGA, AIC.
35. Ibid.

FIG. 103 Olinka Hrdy (American, 1902–1987). Study for Tulsa Riverside Studio Murals: *Symphony of the Arts*, 1928–29. Watercolor on paper; 60.3 × 26.7 cm (27¾ × 10½ in.). Fred Jones Jr. Museum of Art, The University of Oklahoma, Norman; Gift of the artist, 1966.

Endacott convinced city leaders to donate land on Tulsa's Reservoir Hill for the memorial and museum "devoted to Indians, their history and accomplishment."[36] The project's purpose shifted by November 1929 into a museum and memorial dedicated to both American Indians *and* Oklahoma pioneers.[37] A victim of the stock market collapse if not conflicting aims, the project, and Goff's design, was abandoned by March 1930.[38] Instead, a sculpture and marker were installed in 1935—without Native input or artistic involvement—north of downtown to indicate where Cherokee, Creek, and Osage lands meet.[39]

Although Goff never acquired work by the Kiowa Six and his plan to include their murals fell through, his work demonstrates an ongoing dialogue with their champion, Hrdy.[40] The Goffs, with Hrdy in attendance, formed a salon for modern art at their apartment in Tulsa; by late 1930 Goff was hosting concerts from his music collection, a precursor to the listening sessions he would hold for OU architecture students two decades later.[41] Hrdy painted forty-six watercolors of Evelyn in 1929, which she exhibited in Tulsa and Chicago, and incorporated an abstraction of Evelyn dancing at the center of her *Symphony of the Arts* mural (fig. 103) for Riverside Studio. By Hrdy's own account, Goff inspired her "more modern" style.[42]

The influence was hardly one-sided. In 1925 Hrdy began her *Dream Falls* series, images of Turner Falls near Davis, Oklahoma, which she had not visited.[43] Her imagined falls inspired Goff's 1929 painting on silk, *Untitled (Turner Falls)* (fig. 104), which pictures an angular rush of water that plunges down gray, orange, and vermillion striated rock towers into shard-like red and black boulders. His image, like Hrdy's, depicts an imagined place, a much steeper and more Southwestern vista than the actual falls, flanked by geometric patterns and jagged zigzags. Goff's painting nods to the Art Deco borders on Hrdy's Riverside Studio murals but also to the triangular patterns found in Osage ribbon work, a source of inspiration that continued to inform his angular abstractions of the early 1930s.

As the Depression struck Tulsa and halted building projects, Goff and Hrdy left for Chicago and New York, respectively. During Goff's absence from Oklahoma between 1934 and 1946, Native art gained increasing international prominence through new schools and major exhibitions. Oklahoma's best-known artists at the time were Native artists.[44] Among them were Woodrow Wilson (Woody) Big Bow (Kiowa), Woody Crumbo, and Allan Houser (Chiricahua Apache), artists whose works Goff admired and collected at midcentury. Many attended OU or Bacone College in Muskogee under Crumbo and painted government-sponsored murals in public buildings across the state during the Depression.

36. "Plans Are Announced for Indian Memorial," *Tulsa Tribune*, Nov. 15, 1929, 6.

37. "Endacott and Goff Designed New Grand Stand at Fairgrounds," *Tulsa World*, Sept. 20, 1931, 42; and "Commission Votes for Indian Building," *Tulsa World*, Nov. 16, 1929, 6. Both are available at newspapers.com.

38. "City to Aid D.A.R. in Indian Memorial," *Tulsa Tribune*, Mar. 8, 1930, 8.

39. "Indian Monument Presented by D.A.R. Is Unveiled Here," *Tulsa World*, Nov. 17, 1935, 14.

40. Hrdy and Goff collaborated again on the interior of the Tulsa Convention Hall in 1930.

41. "Goffs Planning Series of Modern Music Programs," *Tulsa Tribune*, Nov. 9, 1930, 25; "Goff Home Reflects Unusual Temperament," *Tulsa Tribune*, Nov. 16, 1930, 20.

42. Hrdy quoted in Mark A. White, *Oklahoma Moderne: The Art and Design of Olinka Hrdy* (Fred Jones Jr. Museum of Art, 2007), 27; for Goff's influence on Hrdy, see ibid., 25–41.

43. White, *Oklahoma Moderne*, 17–20; and "Olinka Hrdy," Oklahoma Artists Manuscript, Oscar Brousse Jacobson Collection, box J13, folder 30, Western History Collections, University of Oklahoma Libraries.

44. Examples include the Kiowa Six and Allan Houser, Dick West, Acee Blue Eagle, and Woody Crumbo. After graduating from OU in 1932, Blue Eagle helped establish the art program at Bacone College. Crumbo studied at OU in 1936–37, directed the art department at Bacone after Blue Eagle, and played a pivotal role in the development of the Gilcrease Museum's collection in Tulsa. See "Art Exhibit Set Today at Bacone," *Muskogee Daily Phoenix and Times-Democrat*, May 22, 1949, 15, newspapers.com.

FIG. 104 Goff. *Untitled (Turner Falls)*, 1929. Paint on silk; framed: 188 × 101.6 cm (74 × 40 in.). Private collection.

At OU, the Kiowa artists' success and Jacobson's reputation for supporting Native art attracted Indigenous students to campus where, during the 1930s, the art school boasted more Native enrollments than any other department.[45] When Goff arrived in December 1946 to join the architecture faculty, Norman had nearly tripled in size since his visits in the late 1920s, in part due to an influx of students who, like Goff, had spent the early 1940s in military service.[46]

GOFF'S COLLECTION

Although Goff began collecting Native art almost immediately after arriving to OU in 1946—a practice that he continued until his death in 1982—in the late 1940s and early 1950s, he decorated his small North Base office with his own abstract paintings and snowflakes of translucent plastic hung from the ceiling.[47] Only after the architecture department relocated to Oklahoma Memorial Stadium in summer 1953 did he install Native paintings and reproductions.[48] This shift suggests that Goff gained exposure to Native art during his early years at OU and his appreciation grew accordingly. The artists he admired and collected were largely of his generation; many were also World War II veterans, the so-called "second generation" of Native painters. Goff's collection consists of thirty paintings on paper and numerous reproductions of works by Oklahoma, Diné, and Pueblo artists. He bought and, in some cases, matted prints of Native art from galleries, museums, and museum gift shops.[49] He clipped reproductions from calendars of twentieth-century Oklahoma Native art and likewise mounted the images to cream, muted colored, or—in the case of reproductions of two works by fellow Oklahoman Allan Houser—reflective gold matboard. That Goff treated these ephemera like artwork worthy of matting is consistent with his repurposing and recycling of feathers, scrap metal, and ashtrays in building designs. He viewed it all, as Welch's photograph implies, as fodder for creativity.

Goff's focus on Oklahoma and Southwestern Native art paralleled Oklahoma museum collecting at the time, including that of the OU art museum. In fact, he seems to have emulated Jacobson's curatorial practice, purchasing original paintings by the same Native artists the museum acquired in the late 1940s, as well as by artists who won awards at the Philbrook Annual, a yearly exhibition of Native art at Tulsa's Philbrook Museum of Art that began in 1946.[50] In 1947 Jacobson acquired three paintings by Harrison Begay (Diné) for the OU museum.[51] Two depict Diné riders galloping across country above the splayed arms of spiny ocotillo. Goff was drawn to similar compositions, acquiring paintings and reproductions of Begay's images of Diné horsemen, galloping horses, and women weaving and tending flocks. In each of these works, Begay indicated distance by painting undulating lines with a gradation of three or four tints underneath that represent receding ridges, a technique Goff adopted in his own architectural renderings.

45. Fur, *Painting Culture*, 233.
46. Larry O'Dell, "Norman," *Encyclopedia of Oklahoma History and Culture*, okhistory.org/publications/enc/entry?entry=NO006.
47. Philip B. Welch, ed., "Introduction," in *Goff on Goff: Conversations and Lectures* (University of Oklahoma Press), 9.
48. Jimmy Abe, "Architecture School Moves to Stadium," *Oklahoma Daily*, Sept. 15, 1953, 1 and 16, newspapers.com.
49. Native art collections grew in the same cities where Goff lived. In Tulsa, the Philbrook Museum of Art opened in 1939 and the Gilcrease Museum opened in 1949. In Norman, the University of Oklahoma's art museum (now the Fred Jones Jr. Museum of Art) was instituted in 1936. In Bartlesville, Frank Phillips's Woolaroc Museum opened in 1929. Goff's prints of Crumbo's *Rainbow Horse*, *Peyote Ceremony*, and *Peyote Bird* have Gilcrease Museum captions, which suggests he purchased them from the gift shop.
50. Native artists with work represented in Goff's collection and the OU museum's collection that Goff acquired during his years at OU include Harrison Begay (Diné), Woody Big Bow, Woody Crumbo, Oliver Phillips (Lakota), Theodore Suina (Cochiti), Carl Sweezy (Arapaho), Andrew Tsihnahjinnie (Diné), and Thomas Vigil (Tesuque). Karen Bowles, email to the author, Aug. 18, 2024.
51. In 1947 the museum acquired *Two Horsemen* (n.d.), *Navajos Going to a Dance* (1946), and *Ye-Be-Cha Dancer* (n.d.). *Horses*, already in the collection, was acquired in 1937.

FROM LEFT, FIG. 105 Woody Big Bow. *Southern Plains Dancer*, n.d. Opaque watercolor, over graphite, on laminated paper board; 25.4 × 19.7 cm (10 × 7¾ in.). The Art Institute of Chicago, gift of Shin'enKan, Inc., 2025.67. FIG. 106 Beatien Yazz (Diné [Navajo], 1929–2021). *Diné Warriors on Horseback*, 1955. Opaque watercolor, over traces of graphite, on green wove paper-faced laminated board; 55.9 × 81.3 cm (22 × 32 in.). The Art Institute of Chicago, gift of Shin'enKan, Inc., 2025.45.

The most works Goff acquired from a single Native artist are nine paintings by the prolific Kiowa artist Woody Big Bow, who gained notoriety in Oklahoma City for his artwork and business acumen in the 1940s; there he maintained a studio, participated in arts fairs and community events, and supported his family by selling his paintings.[52] Jacobson collected Big Bow's work for the museum throughout the 1940s, and the subjects of paintings in Goff's collection echo those that Jacobson purchased: single Kiowa dancers (fig. 105), individuals or pairs of figures in pebbly landscapes, and in a painting nearly identical to *Conference* (acquired by the OU art museum in 1949), three Kiowa men conversing, seated amid abstracted forms that resemble stones and yucca. That Goff's collection so closely resembles the museum's suggests that he followed the museum's lead or sought advice from Jacobson; no midcentury correspondence, however, exists between the two men. This relationship aside, Big Bow's palette of black, brown, crimson, and sage green must have appealed to the architect's color sense; in 1956 Goff painted an abstract watercolor (fig. 189) with the same striking colors and crisp edges. Goff's acquisitions suggest that he was attracted to representational images of figures in motion, paintings containing fine detail, bright colors, visual rhythms, and strong patterns composed of abstracted natural forms.

Perhaps the most striking works in Goff's collection are two paintings by Diné artist Beatien Yazz, both dated 1955, Goff's final year at the university. In one, six Diné men gallop across the desert with their rifles and lances held high (fig. 106). Yazz rendered details with specificity—patterned shirts, concho belts, silver-studded headstalls, and stands of gold and green chamisa. His realistic representation contrasts with a blue horse at center, mysterious plant forms, and a looping line above that suggests clouds and frames the riders. In Yazz's painting of four deer bounding through a forest at night (fig. 147), the artist similarly treated the flora and fauna as decorative patterns. The deer soar in parallel diagonals, their golden hides vibrant against the dark paper, and abstracted tufts of grass form ridges that appear to recede into space. The otherworldly quality of Yazz's abstracted landscapes parallels Goff's own inclusion of ambiguous forms and decorative patterns in detailed renderings of buildings.

THE "TEPEE" CHURCH, 1947–1951

Native culture's most obvious influence on Goff's work is in his buildings that reference Indigenous forms, beginning with his incongruous pueblo-like design for Tulsa's Indian Memorial. In central Oklahoma, in 1947, almost immediately after joining the OU faculty, he designed a church from repurposed oil-field materials based on Plains tepee design, which, given Norman's proximity to

52. Nan Sheets, "Kiowa Paintings on Display," *Daily Oklahoman*, June 3, 1945, 35, newspapers.com.

HOPEWELL BAPTIST CHURCH
OKLAHOMA

Plains communities, Goff could have seen firsthand.[53] The conical structure was his solution to Pastor D. B. Hoskins's request for an inexpensive building that could be fabricated by oil-field workers in the congregation.[54] Hopewell Baptist Church (fig. 107), referred to by the public and press as the "tepee" church, occupies a shallow rise on the edge of Deer Creek, northwest of Oklahoma City. In contrast to Plains tepees, in which hide or canvas is stretched around poles, the sanctuary's shell is suspended *inside* twelve poles made of oil-field trusses. At the top, a pyramidal window resembles the opening at a tepee's apex, which allows smoke to escape. The sanctuary originally featured vents around the baseboards that opened to create airflow to the window high above, much like tepee covers were rolled up from the ground to create a breeze. Each truss attaches to the ground with bolts on a hinge, a visual reminder of the portability of Plains tepees.

In colored pencil, Goff drew the church beneath a blue dome of sky. The atmospheric arc, which transitions from deep to light blue, reprises Yazz's and Begay's linear gradations suggesting clouds or ridges of earth. It also resembles the rainbowlike yé'ii figures—protective supernatural beings—that Begay often painted above scenes of children and young animals (fig. 108). In Goff's elevation a golden V shape interrupts the sky, echoed by a smaller gray V at the lower right. These forms recall abstracted birds in flight or Art Deco devices in Pueblo paintings of the 1930s and 1940s but elude easy explanation.

The tension between the mystical (ambiguous flying forms) and the prosaic (architectural elevation) in Goff's drawing exists in Hopewell's sanctuary. Architecture historian Arn Henderson recalled, "Looking upward one loses the sense of both scale and distance in an endless space reaching to the clouds"; yet everyday objects—a chandelier of fluted cake pans, for example—reference "the reality of everyday life."[55] Terry Ward, pastor of the current congregation that meets adjacent to Goff's building, attended Hopewell Baptist Church since childhood. His earliest memories are of looking up at the glass prisms suspended high above the sanctuary: "The strings would twist and turn, and like a pendulum, turn back the opposite direction and I [was] captivated. It was just an amazing sight."[56] As Goff's interior combines sacred and mundane to create a contemplative yet "amazing" space, his drawing of the church likewise expresses an aura of mystery even as it serves an "ordinary" architectural purpose.

FIG. 108 Reproduction of a painting by Harrison Begay (Haashké yah Níyá) (Diné [Navajo], 1917–2012), n.d. Bruce A. Goff Archive.

Even in his T square (fig. 20), Goff merged this sense of mystery and the everyday. He embellished the tool with pumpkin, teal, and mirrored silver triangles, in effect mimicking coral and turquoise inlay on Zuni silverwork. In modifying his T square, Goff demonstrated an awareness of—and borrowed from—the Indigenous practice of beautifying one's tools with symbols and patterns that communicate cultural values. As a result the tension between the supernatural and prosaic was always before him as he worked.

Perhaps this dialogue, expressed in a style as precise and intentional as that found in architectural renderings, is what attracted Goff to midcentury Native art. The figurative paintings and prints he collected depict dancers, weavers, riders, flora, and fauna with exacting detail. They are, in a sense, like Goff's architectural drawings in their precision of line and representational subject matter. Yet through abstraction, surreal coloration, references to heavenly or supernatural beings, and carefully designed negative spaces, they allude to the spiritual. As historian Donald Fixico (Shawnee/Sac and Fox/Creek/Seminole) wrote, in Oklahoma, "Native logic is guided by the knowledge that the metaphysical and physical forces both operate in life, by thinking from a communal perspective, and also by thinking in a circular pattern."[57] These concepts resonated with Goff, whose own works merged the ordinary and the mysterious, and who understood creativity as existing in a "continuous present."[58]

OPPOSITE, FIG. 107 Goff and William H. Wilson (American, 1919–1997). *Hopewell Baptist Church, Edmond, Oklahoma, Perspective*, 1948–49. Graphite, colored pencil, and opaque watercolor over diazo print on cream wove paper; 124 × 92.3 cm (48⅞ × 36⅜ in.). The Art Institute of Chicago, gift of Shin'enKan, Inc., 1990.866.2.

53. Native OU students also erected tepees annually during homecoming and, after its opening in 1948, on the grounds of the university's Stovall Museum. Ed O'Brien, "Tom Toms Roll Tonight for Saturday Tilt," *Oklahoma Daily*, Oct. 31, 1947, 1; and Larry Stephenson, "Dr. Stovall Gets His Museum," *Sooner Magazine*, Mar. 1948, 14.

54. Henderson, *Bruce Goff*, 136. The building is in disrepair and at risk of vandalism. To contribute to its preservation and restoration, visit goff-hopewell.com.

55. Henderson, *Bruce Goff*, 137 and 142.

56. Terry Ward, phone call with the author, July 8, 2024.

57. Fixico, "American Indians."

58. The "continuous present" is a concept borrowed from the writings of Gertrude Stein. See David G. De Long, "Bruce Goff Reconsidered," in *The Architecture of Bruce Goff, 1904–1982: Design for the Continuous Present*, ed. Pauline Saliga and Mary Woolever (Prestel; Art Institute of Chicago, 1995), 29–30.

FIG. 109 Goff. Monogram logo for Evelyn Hood piano recital program, 1930. Bruce A. Goff Archive.

The Modernist in the Audience: Bruce Goff's Music and Domestic Theaters

Nolan Vallier

On May 29, 1931, Bruce Goff, Ernest Brooks, and Olinka Hrdy recorded a series of atonal and polyrhythmic pieces of music in Goff's home in Tulsa, Oklahoma. Although this was not Goff's first recorded performance, it is emblematic of his lifelong dedication to shaping communal spaces for musical experience. This essay explores Goff's interactions with music first as a composer and then as an architect. I argue that he approached musical composition, discourse, and design as a constantly evolving and collaborative enterprise, placing audio-recording technology at the heart of his epistemology of music.[1] For Goff, the acts of listening to and composing for audio-recording media structured his understanding of music and the spaces for performing and appreciating it.

MUSIC AND THE MODERN ARCHITECT

Many modern architects were fascinated with listening to and making music. Frank Lloyd Wright, for instance, was an avid piano player and organized weekly amateur parlor concerts and an annual summertime concert series at Taliesin, his home and studio in Spring Green, Wisconsin.[2] Others—including Claude Bragdon, Walter Burley Griffin, Dwight H. Perkins, and Louis Sullivan—not only participated in amateur music performances but also wrote essays constructing homologies between music and architecture.[3]

Goff participated in amateur performances like Bragdon, Sullivan, and Wright, but of these architects, he was the only one to showcase his own compositions at such events.[4] Largely between 1930 and 1934—a period in which he had few architectural clients—Goff composed six scores for piano (one was a collaboration [fig. 110]), two libretti without scores, nine hand-cut compositions for player piano, and twenty two-minute compositions on phonograph records, half of which were collaborations.[5] Previous studies of Goff's musical interest by architectural historian Sidney K. Robinson and music theorist Benjamin R. Levy have examined his written manuscript scores and downplayed his collaborative approach to composing, but this focus is misleading; Goff's predominant compositional medium was the audio recording, and a large number of his compositions were collaborations.

Goff also stands out among modern architects for his penchant for listening to records. As he noted in a 1980 interview with Robert Morris, "I have about two dozen recorded interpretations of Debussy's *La Mer* and every time I listen to any one of them I hear something new."[6] Goff clearly used records to educate himself about modern music through experiential and repetitive listening. As we shall see, he also approached listening to records as a communal activity, sharing his favorite records with close confidants and testing his knowledge about music in intimate environs.

One of my primary goals is to explore Goff's engagement with modernist music through the lens of collaborative composing and communal listening. I begin with an overview of the early pieces he composed with Ernest Brooks between 1925 and 1936 and the salon they established in Tulsa in 1926. I also discuss Goff's work with different technologies for audio recording, reflecting a polymath firmly entrenched within multiple modernist traditions. Finally, I consider Goff's approach to designing two domestic theaters: the Patti Adams Shriner House and Studio (also known as Riverside Studio) in Tulsa, Oklahoma (1928–29), and the Evelyn and John Garvey House in Urbana, Illinois (1954–55).

EMBRACING MODERN MUSIC

Goff once stated, "I used to hate music. It is hard to realize now that there ever was a time when I did hate it."[7] His appreciation for music, particularly modernist music, began after his Central High School classmate Ernest Brooks introduced him to the "shocking" work of Maurice Ravel.[8] Brooks's taste in music was initially quite conservative because of the education he received as a piano and composition major at Drury College in Springfield, Missouri.[9] Goff took credit for bringing Brooks around on the composer—and secured a musical collaborator for the next decade—noting, "Because of his having had a musical education, it [Ravel's music] bothered him considerably. It took some time for him to learn to like it.... I think I had a lot to do with his education in music indirectly by getting him to listen to the music as I was able to get the records."[10] Goff described this evolution in an essay he wrote shortly after they graduated from high school, entitled "The Modernist in the Audience." In this work Goff glorified his own inclinations as a listener and alluded to Brooks's gradual acceptance of modernism: "For he [the modernist] has perennial youth of mind, his ears can change as the art of combining sounds progresses."[11] As a young modernist,

1. Ethnomusicologist Steven Feld would later call this "acoustemology," or a joining of acoustics with epistemology. See Steven Feld, "Acoustemology," in *Keywords in Sound*, ed. David Novak and Matt Sakakeeny (Duke University Press, 2015), 12.

2. Nolan Vallier, "Sacred Sounds and Natural Grounds: Designing Acoustic Communities Within Prairie Style and Organic Architectural Spaces" (PhD diss., University of Illinois Urbana-Champaign, 2021), 107–34; see also Jack Quinan, "Frank Lloyd Wright's Intuitive Sound Modernity," *Journal of Architecture* 23, no. 6 (2018): 961–72.

3. Vallier, "Sacred Sounds," 44–81; see also Mark Clague, "Chicago Counterpoint: The Auditorium Theater Building and the Civic Imagination" (PhD diss., University of Chicago, 2002), 193–208.

4. See Vallier, "Sacred Sounds," 44–81.

5. Sidney K. Robinson, "Bruce Goff and Music," in *The Architecture of Bruce Goff, 1904–1982: Design for the Continuous Present*, ed. Pauline Salida and Mary Woolever (Prestel; Art Institute of Chicago, 1995), 33–46; and Benjamin R. Levy, "Material Connections: Bruce Goff, Music, and Modernism Across the Arts," *Music Theory Online* 27, no. 3 (Sept. 2021), mtosmt.org/issues/mto.21.27.3/mto.21.27.3.levy.php.

6. Robert Morris, "Autobiography in the Continuous Present: An Interview with Bruce Goff," *Cite* 3 (Spring 1983): 7. See also Bruce Goff, "Goff on Debussy," in *Goff on Goff: Conversations and Lectures*, ed. Philip B. Welch (University of Oklahoma Press, 1996), 277–78.

7. Bruce Goff, "Music and Architecture," in Welch, *Goff on Goff*, 227.

8. Ravel's use of non-functional harmonic progressions was innovative for the time. Robinson, "Bruce Goff and Music," 32.

9. *The Sou'wester: Drury College Yearbook* (Hugh-Stephens Printing, 1922), 18, 28, and 56.

Goff firmly believed that exposure to new sounds was fundamental to learning music.

In 1926 the pair began working on two pieces of music. Brooks composed the music and Goff wrote the libretto for both the one-act opera *The System of Dr. Tarr and Professor Fether*, which was based on the short story by Edgar Allan Poe, and the seven-scene "Musical-Moral" *A Woman's Trick*, which was based on *One Thousand and One Nights*.[12] Although Goff did not set these libretti to music himself, this experience was Goff's first attempt at composing a collaborative piece of music.

This early phase of collaboration paused in 1927, when Brooks left Tulsa for Chicago to study orchestration with American composer Leo Sowerby, the first fellow at the

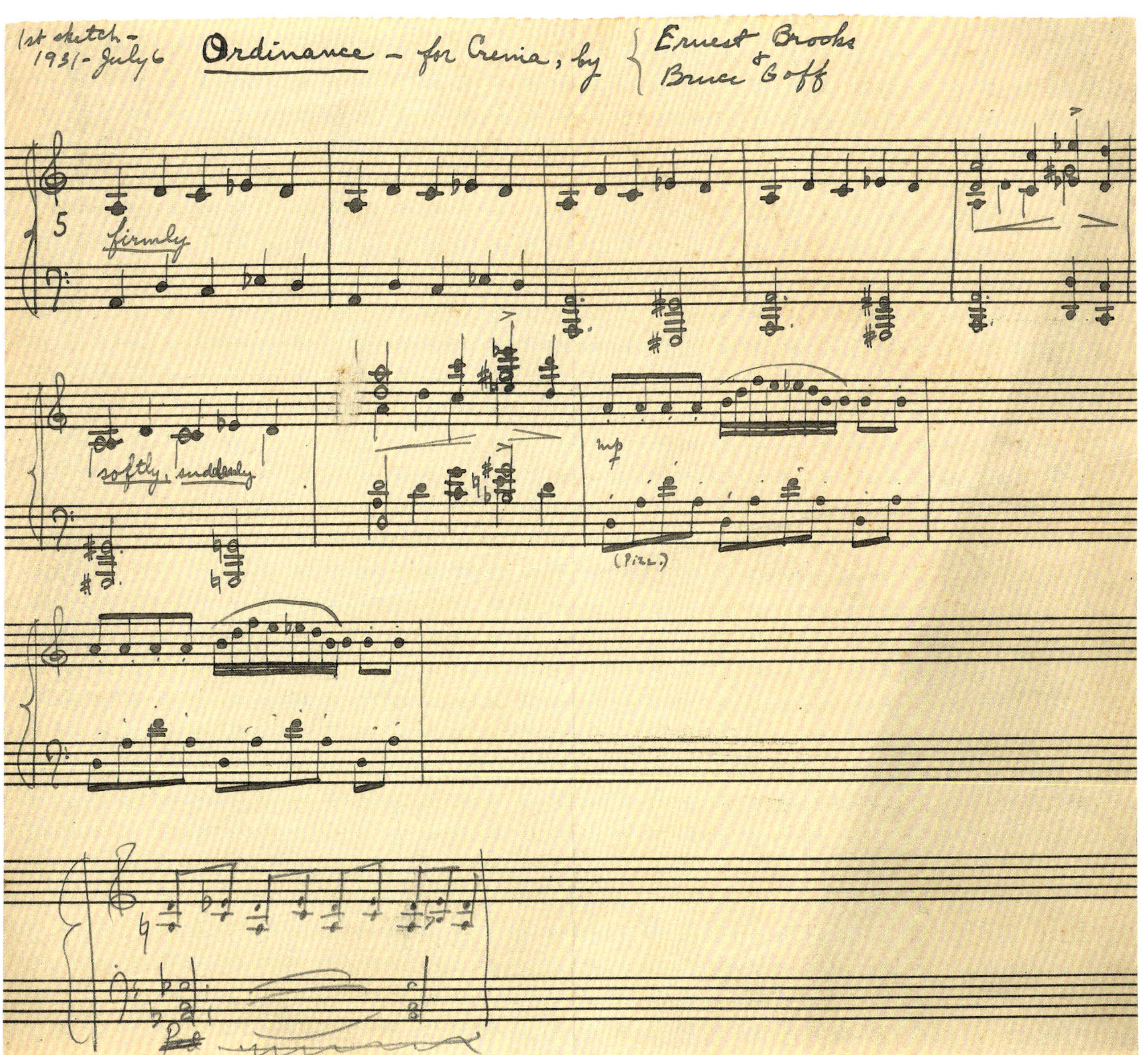

FIG. 110 Goff and Ernest Brooks (American, 1908–1980). "Ordinance" score, July 6, 1931. Bruce A. Goff Archive.

10. Goff, "Music and Architecture," 231.
11. Bruce Goff, "The Modernist in the Audience," Jan. 10, 1925, series V, box 2, folder 27, Bruce A. Goff Archive, Ryerson and Burnham Art and Architecture Archives, The Art Institute of Chicago (hereafter BGA, AIC).
12. *The System of Dr. Tarr and Professor Fether, a Music-Drama in 3 Scenes*, 1926, by Bruce Goff and Ernest Brooks, series V, box 2, folder 52, and *The Woman's Trick, a Music-Moral*, c. 1926, by Ernest Brooks, series V, box 2, folder 53, both BGA, AIC. Brooks's scores for both pieces are lost. List of compositions, series V, box 1, folder 12, BGA, AIC.

American Academy in Rome. In his absence, Goff and his wife, dancer Evelyn Hall, began studying piano and music theory with the gifted pianist Evelyn Hood, who was completing her graduate studies at the University of Tulsa and likely appealed to Goff because of her interest in Claude Debussy.[13] Given his later comments about music, these embryonic music studies likely included some discussion of Western music theory.[14]

By May 1930 Goff reached a new level of musical proficiency and gave his first-known public performance at Hood's spring studio recital. He performed his original composition "Machinery" and Debussy's *First Etude*: *Pour les cinq doigts après Czerny*, a piece that begins with simple finger patterns and gradually introduces complex time signatures and modulations. "Machinery," presumed lost, is likely one of the partial scores in a folder of piano manuscripts preserved in the Art Institute of Chicago's Bruce Goff archive.[15] One partial score is untitled and features a notation for a mechanistic arpeggio: "Use same finger for each note." Like his later works for player piano, "Machinery" embraced modern mechanical processes and—like the Debussy piece Goff paired it with—would have represented a drastic rupture within the conservative local music scene. For many audience members, Goff's performance would have been their first engagement with Debussy, but they would have likely been more surprised by Goff's original composition.[16]

In the spring of 1931, Brooks abandoned his study with Sowerby and returned to Tulsa to collaborate with Goff. The reunited pair composed with new creative fervor over the next four years. Brooks completed no fewer than twenty-seven new works and revised five others.[17] Goff began to shift from composing for piano to composing for mechanical recording media, purchasing an at-home recording kit for direct-cut Victor discs and a player piano for these purposes.[18] Between May and July of 1931, the duo composed at least one piano piece, entitled "Ordinance" (fig. 110), and ten other works for at-home recording. "Ordinance" is in 5/4 time—an asymmetrical, or uneven sounding, meter—and it features a tritone-spanning ostinato, a repeating bass-line pattern of A – D – C – E flat – D, which attempts to avoid a clear tonal center.[19] Goff's use of mixed meters and tritones may have been seen as unsophisticated or outmoded by other modernist composers of the period, but these techniques, which recall Brooks's compositions, suggest that Goff's style was influenced as much by his collaborator as it was by famous composers such as Debussy.

THE TULSA SALON

Goff and Brooks launched their most interesting collaboration in the summer of 1931, when they began inviting close friends to listen to and discuss their compositions. The Tulsa salon began as a series of musical soirees in Bruce and Evelyn's home devoted to making, listening to, and discussing modern music, with guests such as artist Olinka Hrdy; poet Richard San Jule; artist Adah Robinson; writer Luada Boswell; and pianists Nelle Gubser, Blaiselion Montandon, and Tom Ryan. Like many contemporary twentieth-century salons in the United States and elsewhere, this Tulsa salon served as the primary vehicle for promoting Goff's and Brooks's compositions. Brooks's *Caprice* (1926) for piano, for example, survives in a draft of the single issue of *Tulsart*, their coedited magazine. The piece ends with a jarring non-functional resolution in traditional tonal music (A major to A-flat dominant seventh). Compared to the innovative works Brooks and Goff were producing in 1931—which obfuscate any sense of a tonal center or key and abandon traditional structures like ABA—Brooks's 1926 composition merely dips its toes into modernist methods.

Beyond highlighting their own compositions, *Tulsart* offered Goff a platform for comparing the chamber music recitals given by members of his salon to those performed in the larger Tulsa music scene.[20] Montandon, Gubser, and Ryan performed within local concert clubs and societies throughout the year, but like those of many Midwestern cities, Tulsa's cultural scene dried up in the summer. As Goff noted, "We have always been used to 'all quiet' on the musical front during summer periods, tho [*sic*] this has been no arbitrary situation."[21] Likely responding to uninspired performances at forums such as the Tulsa Harmony Club and the lack of concert opportunities, Goff intended to bring attention to modernist music in Tulsa during this offseason.

Goff's record collecting served as an extension of this salon. In 1931 his impressive array of modernist music—beyond the numerous recordings of Debussy—included rare recordings by John Alden Carpenter, Ernst Krenek, Harry Partch, Alexander Scriabin, and Edgard Varèse.[22] He played many of these in a series of Sunday salon programs in August 1931.[23] For other newly released recordings, Goff provided his own reviews.[24] His collection of LPs would eventually exceed more than 7,600 unique recordings, including rare recordings by American experimental composers; albums of early twentieth-century African American jazz bands, such

13. "Evelyn Hood to Give Recital in Y. W. Auditorium Friday," *Tulsa Tribune*, Oct. 12, 1930, 25. See also "Tulsa University Recitals," *Tulsa Daily World*, May 25, 1930, 4; and the Second Division of the Harmony Club in "Musicgraphs," *Tulsa Tribune*, Oct. 20, 1929, 5-C, all available at newspapers.com.
14. Goff "Music and Architecture," 237–40.
15. "Music Manuscripts for Piano," c. 1930, series IX, folder 1, box 7, BGA, AIC.
16. The Hyechka Club, a private women's music society founded in 1904, presented the first concerts of Debussy's music in Tulsa in 1914. See Sara Davidson, "City Social Affairs, Hyechka Club," *Tulsa Democrat*, Dec. 14, 1914; and "Wonderful Music in Tulsa Tonight," *Tulsa Daily World*, Dec. 13, 1918.
17. List of compositions (see n. 12).
18. Victor marketed its DIY record blanks in the early 1920s. See Eleanor Patterson, *Bootlegging the Airwaves: Alternative Histories of Radio and Television Distribution* (University of Illinois Press, 2024), 46.
19. The tritone, or the interval of an augmented fourth, is significant to modernist music for its obfuscation of tonal systems. See William Drabkin, "Tritone (Lat. *Tritonus*)," *Grove Music Online* (2001).
20. Bruce Goff, "About Tulsa," *Tulsart*, Aug. 1931, series XIII, box 1, folder 5, BGA, AIC.
21. Ibid.
22. Musicians lists, series V, box 2, folder 60, BGA, AIC.
23. Bruce Goff, untitled record programs, *Tulsart*, Aug. 1931 (see n. 20).
24. Bruce Goff, "Reviews: Recent Recordings," *Tulsart*, Aug. 1931 (see n. 20).

as The Savoy Bearcats, led by Leon Abbey, and Bennie Moten's Kansas City Orchestra; and many early ethnographic field recordings—obtained when the public demand for modernist music and ethnographic recordings was low and their distribution was limited. He would continue to host listening parties long after the dissolution of the Tulsa salon.[25]

While teaching at the University of Oklahoma, Goff hosted album-listening soirees for his students and faculty, and he later continued this practice in his architectural office. These guests were treated to themed recording concerts featuring a veritable smorgasbord of different styles, composers, and musical traditions.[26] In this way Goff shared his cosmopolitan record collection with others, educating them about modern music from the comfort of his home.

FIG. 111 Recording of *Piano Trio*, May 29, 1931. Composed by Goff, Brooks, and Hrdy. Bruce A. Goff Archive.

MAKING MECHANICAL MUSIC

Tulsa's relative cultural isolation led Goff to seek out material modalities of culture, namely audio recordings. Mechanically reproduced music offered him crucial access to modern ideologies, and this inspired him to create compositions through the medium of the audio recording itself—including the series of complex atonal recordings Goff recorded at home with Brooks and Hrdy in 1931. Among them are the four-movement composition *Piano Trio* (fig. 111); an exoticized Indianist piece called "Orientale"; and a composition called "Voice of the Wilderness," featuring the voices of Hrdy and Hall.[27] Each of these recordings features a tom-tom beat; prepared piano techniques, which involved placing something in the piano to deaden the vibration of the strings; and a mix of pentatonic, chromatic, and whole-tone melodies. In at least one movement of *Piano Trio,* they quoted several popular tunes of the 1920s, including Mort Dixon's "I'm Looking over a Four Leaf Clover" and George Gershwin's *Rhapsody in Blue*. Although these works sound improvised, the compositions on the recordings were partially notated and rehearsed, and at least one existing sketch of transcribed tom-tom rhythms taken "mainly from the Osage and Cherokee" suggests that the group performed from sheet music.[28]

Goff's interests in audio recording technologies also led him to compose for the player piano, likely the Ampico foot-powered pneumatic system.[29] Like most audio recording mediums of the period, this system (which came in both foot-powered and electric variants) only played its own products. To create these propriety recordings, performers usually worked in real time, pumping the bellows to produce a vacuum and thereby coordinating the striking of each key with the act of punching holes in an unperforated piece of paper.[30] This method requires precise rhythmic interpretation because such machines are unforgiving. Goff could not play in time while using the foot pedals, so he created a pitch template, taking a straight razor to blank player piano rolls and laboriously cutting predetermined chords, cluster chords, pitch constellations, chords in parallel motion, and uniquely visual patterns. Cutting by hand, therefore, allowed Goff more creative freedom when composing using this medium.

In his player piano compositions, Goff frequently relied on chord planing, or chord movements in parallel motion, a technique used by Debussy and Ravel; X-shaped and V-shaped scales, supported by additional chords or scales; and pointillistic melodies, which were derived from Brooks's style. In *Outline*, Goff even paid homage to the composer Johann Sebastian Bach—who famously incorporated his name into several of his pieces using the notes B – A – C – H (*H* signifies B natural in German)—by notating a stylized *G* for Goff (fig. 112). Tellingly, having trained as a visual artist and architect, Goff was drawn toward visual aspects of music notation as much as the

25. See jazz records list, series V, box 2, folder 60, and Bruce Goff, record inventory list, both BGA, AIC. See Henry Cowell, "Music of and for the Records," *Modern Music* 8 (Mar.–Apr. 1931): 32–34, reprinted in Timothy D. Taylor, Mark Katz, and Tony Grajeda, eds., *Music, Sound, and Technology in America: A Documentary History of Early Phonograph, Cinema, and Radio* (Duke University Press, 2012), 104–7.

26. Henderson, *Bruce Goff*, 98–99. See also Bruce Goff, "The School of Architecture at Oklahoma, 1947–1956," *Architecture and Urbanism, A+U* 134 (Nov. 1981): 15.

27. Bruce Goff, Ernest Brooks, and Olinka Hrdy, "Piano Trio (I and II)," series IX, box 3, folder 14; Bruce Goff, Ernest Brooks, and Olinka Hrdy, "Piano Trio (III and IV)," series IX, box 3, folder 15; and Bruce Goff, Ernest Brooks, and Olinka Hrdy, "Orientale—Voice in the Wilderness," series IX, box 3, folder 13, all BGA, AIC.

28. See "Tom Tom Rhythms," c. 1931, series IX, box 1, folder 1, BGA, AIC. Hrdy grew up hearing Osage drum patterns. See Oral history interview with Olinka Hrdy, conducted by Betty Hoag, Mar. 13–17, 1965, Archives of American Art, Smithsonian Institution, aaa.si.edu/collections/interviews/oral-history-interview-olinka-hrdy-12581.

29. See Ampico label on "Charade," series IX, box 4, no folder, BGA, AIC. Goff, however, may have used a different player piano system when composing. It is clear that he used a non-electric system with manually operated foot pedals.

30. See Arthur W. J. G. Ord-Hume, *Pianola: The History of the Self-Playing Piano* (George Allen and Unwin, 1984), 182.

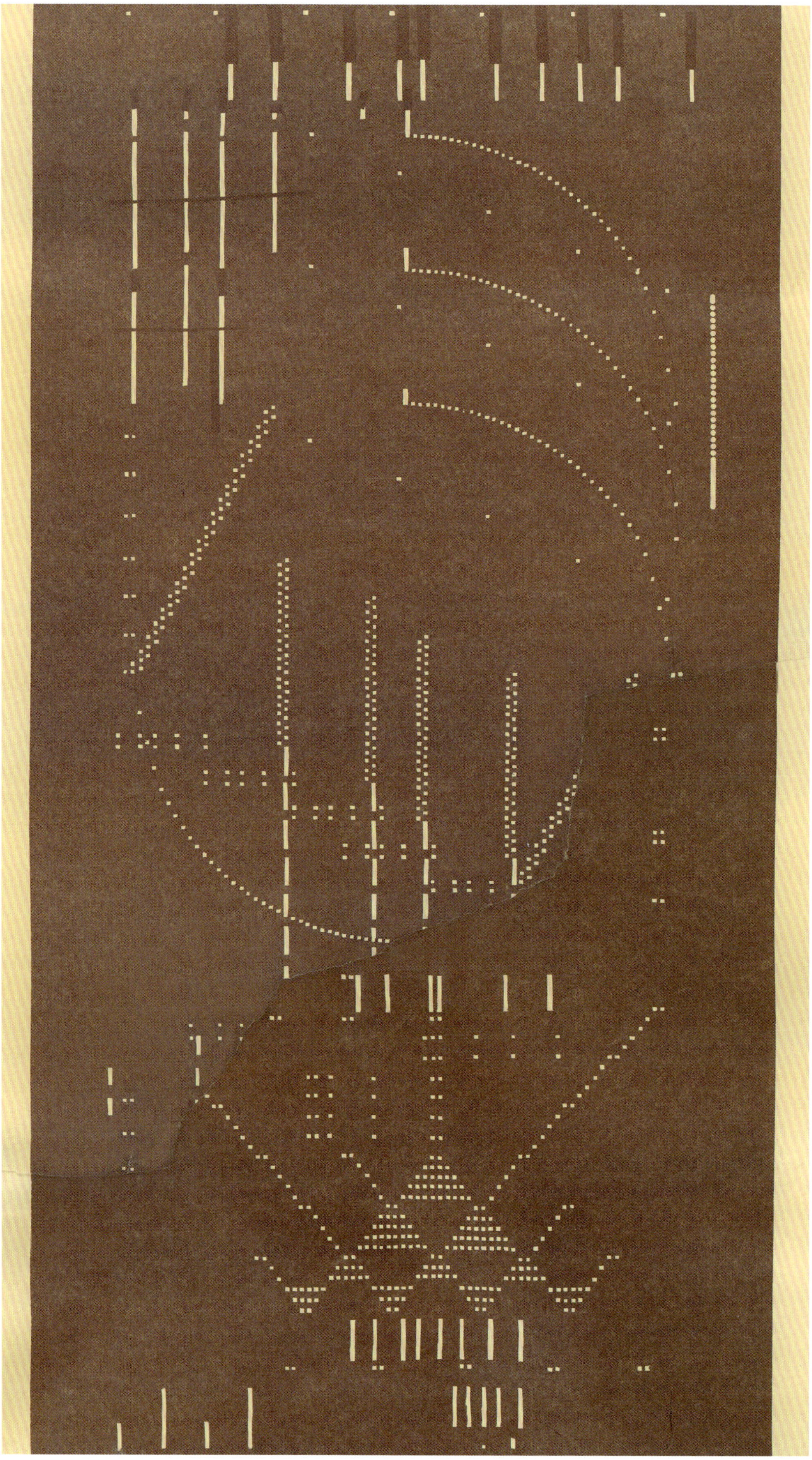

FIG. 112 Goff. Ozalid print of player piano roll of *Outline*, 1932. Bruce A. Goff Archive.

resultant sound of the composition, which led to a unique listening experience.

Still, it seems Goff did not understand the full nuances of the system with which he was working. Conlon Nancarrow—whose technique of composing music for the player piano, according to Sidney Robinson, closely relates to Goff's—offers a useful point of comparison.[31] Nancarrow outstripped Goff by incorporating all eighty-three tone holes available on the Ampico system as well as the seven bass and eight treble tracker holes—each of which controlled the ability to crescendo and diminuendo at varying speeds—mimicking the different foot pedal effects of a traditional piano, and altering the tempo.[32]

Goff compensated for his rudimentary training in music theory and composition—likely learning theory from Brooks and Hood—by engaging directly with the medium of recording and by creating works with individuals with musical training. Except for one monophonic piece, Goff's player piano compositions are densely polyphonic, involving many melodies and countermelodies. In some, had the rolls been cut by a live performer, they would have required two or more players. There is also evidence that Goff constructed these works in collaboration with Brooks. For instance, *Composition No. 6* contains orchestration notes that were likely annotated by Brooks. The circled tone holes indicate specific instruments for certain melodic lines.[33] Given the date of this composition, it quite possibly developed in the collaborative setting of the Tulsa salon. Shortly after composing this piece, Goff moved to Chicago in 1934 (Brooks left for Taliesin in Wisconsin the year before), bringing an end to this high moment for the Tulsa salon.

CHICAGO: NEW MUSICAL HORIZONS

After spending eleven months with the Fellowship, Brooks left Taliesin following several disagreements with Wright over the music programming. Eager to reassociate himself with like-minded individuals, Brooks moved in with Goff and San Jule in 1935, and the pair once more entrenched themselves in music, joining the Chicago Composers' Forum. This subsidiary of the Works Progress Administration's Federal Music Project provided work for struggling composers during the Depression. Organized by music critic Albert Goldberg, the forum took place predominantly in Lyon and Healy Hall, located in the Chicago Loop, and other participants included Hazel Felman, Heniot Levy, Nathan Lupu, and David Sheinfeld.[34] Compared to its New York–based sister collective, which featured performances by well-known composers such as Aaron Copland, Charles Ives, George Gershwin, and Ruth Crawford Seeger, the Chicago collective seems to have been a much smaller operation.[35]

During this period Goff appeared alongside Brooks in the premiere performances of the latter's *Three Dedications* and *Scherzo* sometime between 1934 and 1936.[36] Goff also performed three of his own works, including *Outline*, *Three Exaggerations*, and *Toccata*—all for player piano—on July 14, 1936, at the Lyon and Healy Recital Hall. *Three Exaggerations* consists of three contrasting movements: "Going," a fast 4/4 movement with an F – F-sharp – G – C-sharp motive that outlines a tritone; "Going," a slow waltz; and "Gone," a syncopated melody with fast scalar runs. In his introduction to the program notes, Goff made an apt comparison between his player piano compositions and organic architecture, noting, "In the case of these pieces the medium is part and parcel of the scheme."[37]

After Goff's premiere an intense discussion took place among the gathered audience in the hall about Goff's medium-driven compositional approach. Some thought his use of the player piano was ill-conceived because it highlighted the instrument rather than the music performed on it. Reviews of the event struggled to define Goff's pieces, calling the melodies "angular" and rhythmically "baffling."[38] Brooks, Hood, and San Jule were in attendance supporting Goff, but it appears that the criticism his performance received turned him away from music composition entirely. It is also possible that Goff realized the precariousness of earning a steady income as a composer of modernist music and instead chose to keep his more lucrative day job as an architect, exploring his interest in music by other means.

This short period in Chicago offered Goff a moment to explore the life of a composer by performing pieces in public that were originally intended for his private salon. Following his foray into the spotlight, Goff continued to participate in the act of musicking, attending concerts, discussing music in his architectural courses at the University of Oklahoma, expanding his record collection, and later hosting record programs in his home. In other words, he never fully gave up on the Tulsa salon; he merely integrated it into his architectural practice.

31. Robinson, "Bruce Goff and Music," 36.
32. See Jürgen Hocker, *Encounters with Conlon Nancarrow* (Lexington Books, 2012), 10–11 and 130–37. See also Kyle Gann, *The Music of Conlon Nancarrow* (Cambridge University Press, 1995), 8–10 and 28–32.
33. See *Composition No. 6*, series IX, box 4, no folder, BGA, AIC, and DVD of player piano performances, 16:12–18:34, series IX, box 2, no folder, BGA, AIC.
34. "Sixth Concert, Composer's Forum," July 14, 1936, concert program, series IX, box 1, folder 28, BGA, AIC.
35. Goff was likely not paid for performing his work at the forum. See Melissa de Graaf, *The New York Composers Forum Concerts, 1935–1940* (University of Rochester Press, 2013), 39.
36. Program included in a letter from Ernest Brooks to Richard San Jule, Jan. 27, 1941, series I, box 32, folder 12, BGA, AIC.
37. "Sixth Concert, Composer's Forum" (see n. 34).
38. "Compositions for Mechanical Piano by Bruce Goff Heard at Loop Forum," *Park Ridge Herald*, July 17, 1936, series VII, box 3, folder 2, BGA, AIC.

FIG. 113 Patti Adams Shriner House and Studio, Tulsa, Oklahoma, 1929. Photograph by Ginter. Bruce A. Goff Archive.

DOMESTIC THEATER: RIVERSIDE STUDIO AND THE GARVEY HOUSE

The Riverside Studio and the Evelyn and John Garvey House represent Goff's two clearest attempts at blending his passion for music with his architectural practice. In the cases of Patti Adams Shriner's home and studio and the Garvey family home, Goff's interest in modern music had a direct impact.

Goff began working with Shriner in 1928. She was a pianist from Texas who studied with the Polish piano virtuoso Moritz Moszkowski in Paris in 1910; she founded the Patti Adams Piano School after moving to Tulsa in 1926.[39] Shriner wanted a space that would not only function as her personal home but also serve as a working music school replete with practice rooms and a recital hall.[40] Goff's first rendering of the building was a cathedral-like structure with a second-floor recital hall and balcony capable of seating two hundred and fifty audience members, six practice rooms, and a living space for Shriner on the ground-floor basement.[41] It also had a record library, mostly likely Goff's suggestion, which was cut from the second design. The first project sketches may have been abandoned since the design would have required two separate pianos on each floor or because the sheer size of the facility may have proved too costly.

For the second, smaller design, Goff leaned into the function of the commission with an intricate facade (fig. 113) featuring windows that paid homage to music through an arpeggio motif consisting of the notes F – A – C – E, or the spaces of a treble clef staff.[42] The interior featured four practice rooms and a recital hall with a stage wide enough for two grand pianos.[43]

39. Scott Pendleton, "The Piano Player," *This Land*, June 9, 2016.
40. "River Side Studio Brochure," series VII, box 28, folder 13, BGA, AIC.
41. See architectural drawings (Art Institute of Chicago, 1990.801.1–9) for "Patti Adams Shriner House and Studio, First Design, Tulsa, Oklahoma," 1928, Architecture and Design, Art Institute of Chicago.
42. The key to this motif can be seen in the architectural drawing *Patti Adams Shriner House and Studio, Plan, Tulsa, Oklahoma*, 1928 (Art Institute of Chicago, 1990.82.10).
43. Bill E. Peavler, "Bruce Goff's Riverside Music Studio," in *Of the Earth: Oklahoma Architectural History*, ed. Howard L. Meredith and Mary Ellen Meredith (Oklahoma Historical Society, 1980), 241–61.

Although the building was eventually realized according to his design, Goff recalled Shriner was difficult to work with and often interrupted construction to change plans and give advice to the builders.[44] Shriner also took offense with Goff's collaborations with Hrdy, whom he commissioned to paint eight music-inspired murals.[45]

Despite this friction, Hrdy realized the murals in the main recital hall, hanging them in two rows where they would be visible to both the audience and performers (fig. 114). Taking a closer view, it is clear that these compositions were a product of her and Goff's long-standing engagements with modern music. Following their shared tastes, the eight mural panels are dedicated to subjects like Modern American Music (fig. 115a), which features "prophetic" jazz rhythms on the right side of the image; Music of the Future, which depicts a cascade of phonographic discs; and Piano Music (fig. 115c), which presents a "great glissando" of piano hammer mechanisms.[46] Hrdy's progressive representations of music reflected Goff's interest in modern music, focusing on the visual characteristics of the medium rather than depicting the music or sound.

Goff would have a second opportunity to give physical form to his utopian salon in May 1952, when the University of Illinois' resident Walden String Quartet came to the University of Oklahoma.[47] Sometime during the quartet's weeklong stay in Norman, Goff met with violist John Garvey, who commissioned Goff to design his family home. Like Goff's musical works, which emphasized the materials of modernism, his first design for Garvey's house was an experimental utopia, incorporating as many unusual materials as possible (fig. 116). Designing an exterior made from a semi-translucent plastic, Goff planned for the building to change with the natural landscape. This exterior encircled a garden and lily pool and could, according to Goff, effectively

FIG. 114 Interior view of Goff's Riverside Studio recital hall seen from stage left with four of Olinka Hrdy's eight murals, from left: *Modern American Music*, *Vocal Music*, *Piano Music*, and *String Music*, c. 1929. Photograph by Paul Stithem. Bruce A. Goff Archive.

44. Ibid., 257.
45. Ibid., 248.
46. "Artistic World Interested in Modernistic Tulsa Mural," *Tulsa Daily World*, Nov. 10, 1929, series VII, box 1, folder 11, BGA, AIC.
47. Goff likely attended the first program on May 16, 1952. See Bound Programs of the School of Music, 1951–1952, box 2, file 7, Western History Collection, University of Oklahoma.

OLINKA HRDY

OLINKA HRDY

FROM LEFT, FIGS. 115A–D Hrdy. Studies for Tulsa Riverside Studio Murals: *Modern American Music*, *Vocal Music*, *Piano Music*, and *String Music*, 1928–29. Watercolor on paper; each: 45.8 × 11.5 cm (18 × 4½ in.). Fred Jones Jr. Museum of Art, The University of Oklahoma, Norman; Gift of the artist, 1966.

FIG. 116 Goff. *Evelyn and John Garvey House, First Design, Urbana, Illinois, Interior Perspective* [unbuilt], 1952. Graphite on white tracing paper; 71.2 × 79.6 cm (28 × 31⅜ in.). The Art Institute of Chicago, gift of Shin'enKan, Inc., 1990.860.3.

FIG. 117 Evelyn and John Garvey House, Urbana, Illinois, 1957. The central living room includes a stage and audience seating. Photograph by Philip B. Welch. Bruce A. Goff Archive.

transition with the Midwest seasons.[48] However, the first design did not adequately take into account Garvey's desire for a dedicated performance space within the home. Goff did include a music room, but it was isolated and hidden under the ramp to the second floor, and he proposed acoustically deadening materials for the space, including cork baffling, which would have resulted in little or no reverberation.[49] Although Goff's first design perfectly encapsulated his avant-garde ideals, it did not reflect his experience as a composer.

Goff claimed to abandon the first iteration in 1954 after a manufacturer of a plastic material could not guarantee that their product—intended to construct the translucent walls of the home—would function as a structural element.[50] It is just as likely, however, that Garvey was dissatisfied with the design of the music room.[51] The space needed to function as both a living room and a venue for parlor concerts. Because of their demanding tour schedule, the string quartet frequently rehearsed off of university property, and it would have been a boon for Garvey to practice at home. In addition, Evelyn Garvey was a gifted accompanist and piano teacher, and she required a space large enough to work with her students.

In the fall of 1954, Goff redesigned the home, adding revolving doors like those used in theaters, stage curtains to dampen the sound of rehearsals from the home's living spaces, and a performance stage within the sunken living room. Most importantly for the Garveys, Goff used a resonant wood ceiling and a flat concrete floor to allow music to reverberate within the space (fig. 117). This second design also more closely aligned itself with the Garveys' intentions for the home, because it now functioned as a hybrid living room and performance space. Moreover, when Goff relocated the music room to the heart of the home, he also transformed the space into *the* ideal modernist salon, directly embedding the materials of modern music venues and creating a space that would maximize an audience's ability to listen to the music performed therein. Unlike Riverside Studio, which simply juxtaposed private and public space, the Garveys' living room combined the private with the public, promoting the type of communal focused listening Goff introduced to his Tulsa salon and to his engagement with audio recordings.

CONCLUSION

In "Music and Architecture," Goff noted that the most compelling music was that which "doesn't give up its secrets so easily and sometimes requires quite a few hearings to really understand."[52] This type, he continued, existed "for the musical impulse itself—the musical idea as it is expressed through the material and through the medium."[53] Goff's compositions were governed by this epistemology. It was not enough for him to embrace the stylistic features of musical modernism: The medium of a recording was central to its compositional structure.

Collaboration was also key. Goff did not listen to recordings nor compose music in a vacuum; he sought out others with whom he could share both his listening experiences and his philosophy of sound. Whether performing for the Tulsa salon or Chicago Composers Forum or designing architecture to facilitate music making, Goff demonstrated a lifelong desire to educate others, foster discourse, and broaden all intrepid listeners' appreciation for modern music.

48. Goff, "The Idea in Architecture," in Welch, *Goff on Goff*, 289.
49. Much like Frank Lloyd Wright, Goff was not formally trained in acoustic design; his method for designing sonic spaces was therefore intuitively driven. See Quinan, "Frank Lloyd Wright's Intuitive Sound Modernity," 61–72.
50. David G. De Long, *Bruce Goff: Toward Absolute Architecture* (Architectural History Foundation; MIT Press, 1988), 120.
51. Only one extant piece of correspondence documents Garvey's relationship with Goff. See John Garvey to Bruce Goff, Apr. 16, 1953, series II, box 2, folder 5, BGA, AIC.
52. Goff, "Music and Architecture," 233.
53. Ibid., 251.

FROM TOP, FIG. 118 Ruth and Sam Ford House, Aurora, Illinois, 1950. Photograph by Eliot Elisofon. FIG. 119 Goff. *Ruth and Sam Ford House, Aurora, Illinois, Elevation*, 1947–49. Graphite on tracing paper; 44.4 × 86.2 cm (17½ × 33$^{15}/_{16}$ in.). The Art Institute of Chicago, gift of Shin'enKan, Inc., 1990.809.15.

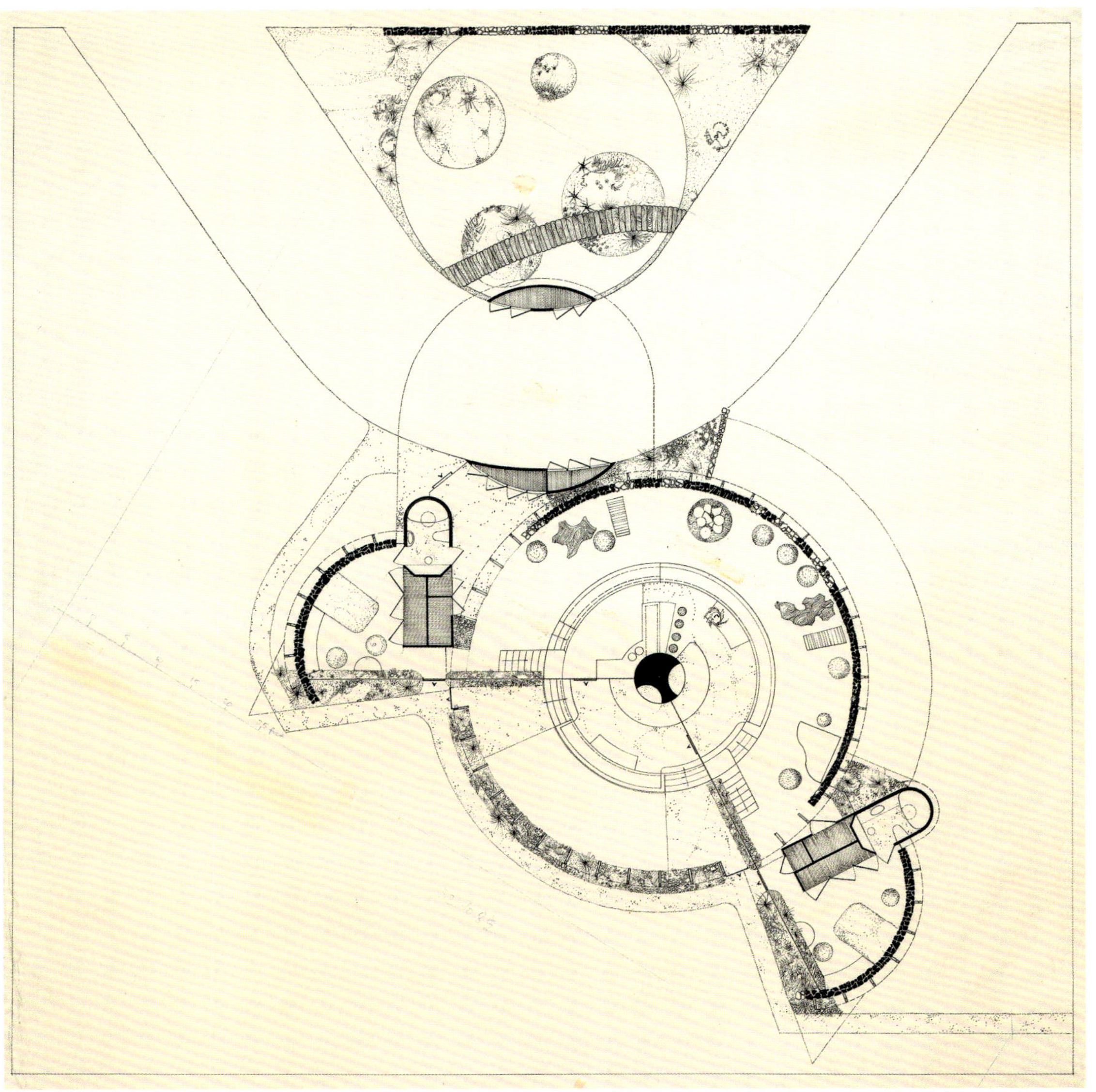

FIG. 120 Goff. *Ruth and Sam Ford House, Aurora, Illinois, Floor Plan*, 1947–49. Ink, with traces of colored pencil and graphite, on tracing paper; 89.3 × 94.2 cm (35⅛ × 37 1/16 in.). The Art Institute of Chicago, gift of Shin'enKan, Inc., 1990.809.1.

FROM LEFT, FIG. 121 Goff. *Ruth and Sam Ford House, Second Design, Aurora, Illinois, Perspective* [unbuilt], 1948. Graphite on tracing paper; 92 × 147.5 cm (36¼ × 58⅛ in.). The Art Institute of Chicago, gift of Shin'enKan, Inc., 1990.808.5. FIG. 122 Quonset hut ribs in construction of Ruth and Sam Ford House, Aurora, Illinois, 1950. Photograph by Wayne K. Williams. Bruce A. Goff Archive.

FIG. 123 Goff. *Untitled (Composition)*, n.d. Opaque watercolor and synthetic fur on brown wove paper; 60.8 × 91.3 cm (23 15/16 × 36 in.). The Art Institute of Chicago, gift of Shin'enKan, Inc., 1990.574.390.

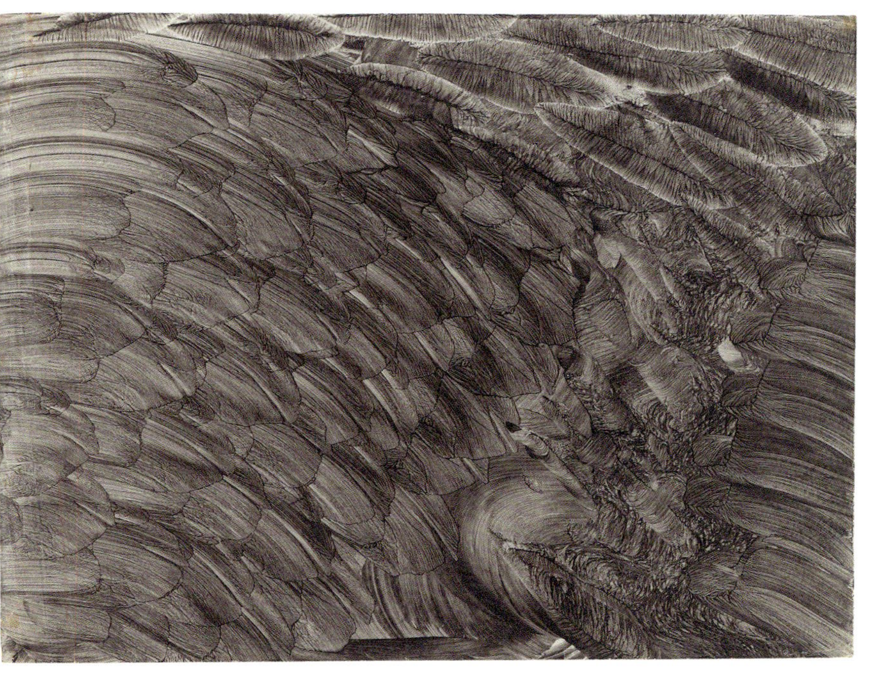

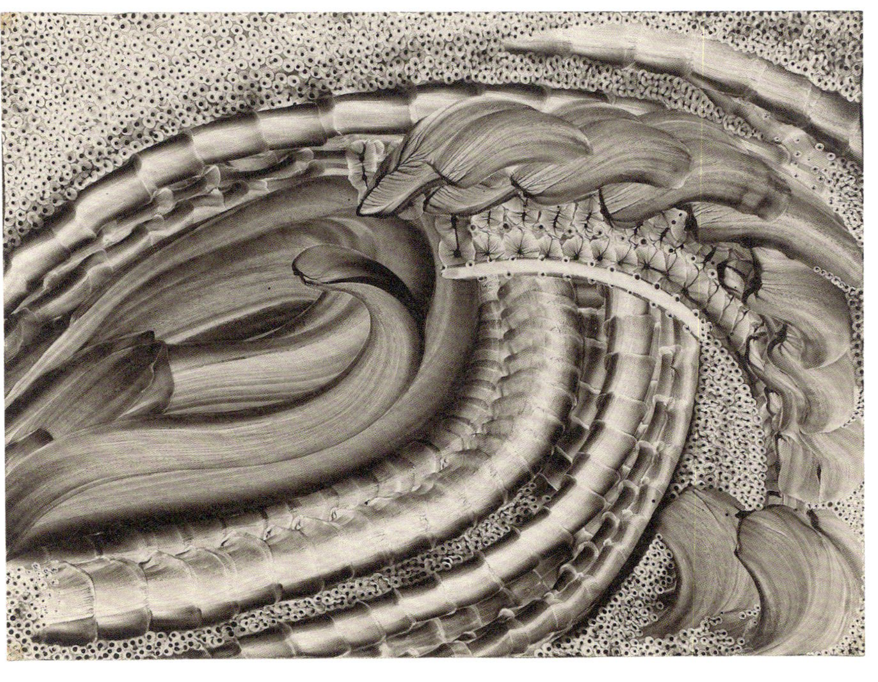

FROM TOP, FIG. 124 Goff. *Untitled (Composition)*, n.d. Ink and starch paste on cream paste paper prepared with white ground; 63.5 × 48.3 cm (25 × 19 in.). The Art Institute of Chicago, gift of Shin'enKan, Inc., 1990.574.227.
FIG. 125 Goff. *Untitled (Composition)*, n.d. Ink and starch paste on cream paste paper prepared with white ground; 63.9 × 48.4 cm (25$\frac{3}{16}$ × 19$\frac{1}{16}$ in.). The Art Institute of Chicago, gift of Shin'enKan, Inc., 1990.574.201.

FIG. 127 Goff. *Untitled (Composition)*, n.d. Opaque watercolor on mauve wove paper; 90.9 × 61 cm (35¾ × 24 in.). The Art Institute of Chicago, gift of Shin'enKan, Inc., 1990.574.434.

FIG. 126 Goff. *Untitled (Composition)*, n.d. Opaque watercolor, over traces of graphite, on blue wove paper; 91.5 × 61 cm (36 × 24 in.). The Art Institute of Chicago, gift of Shin'enKan, Inc., 1990.574.433.

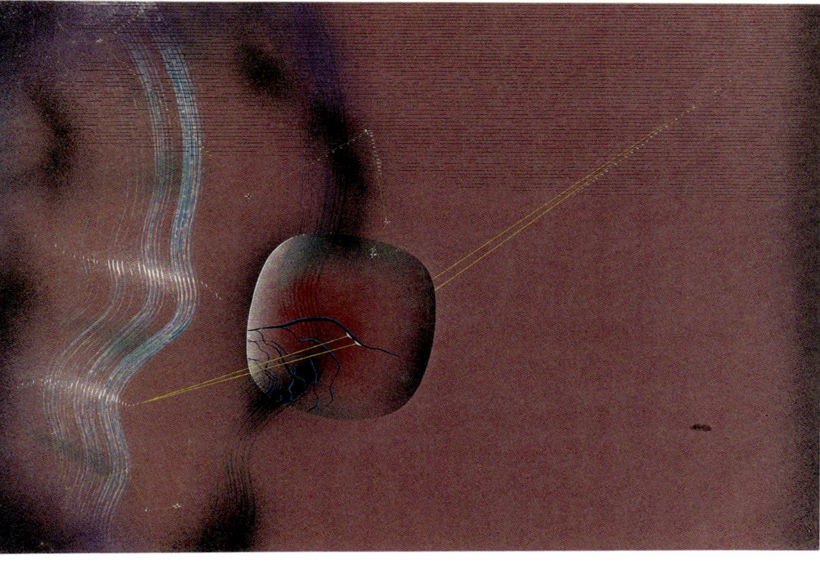

FIG. 128 Goff. *Untitled (Composition)*, c. 1935. Translucent and opaque watercolor and ink over graphite on cream Japanese paper; 67 × 102 cm (26 7/16 × 40 3/16 in.). The Art Institute of Chicago, gift of Shin'enKan, Inc., 1990.574.328.

FROM TOP, FIG. 129 Paul Purington (American, 1910–1995). *Mounted Butterflies*, 1972. Butterflies and plastic; 25.4 × 25.4 × 7.7 cm (10 × 10 × 3 in.). Bruce A. Goff Archive. FIG. 130 Amethyst crystal, n.d. Bruce A. Goff Archive. FIG. 131 Dog tags, by 1942. Bruce A. Goff Archive.

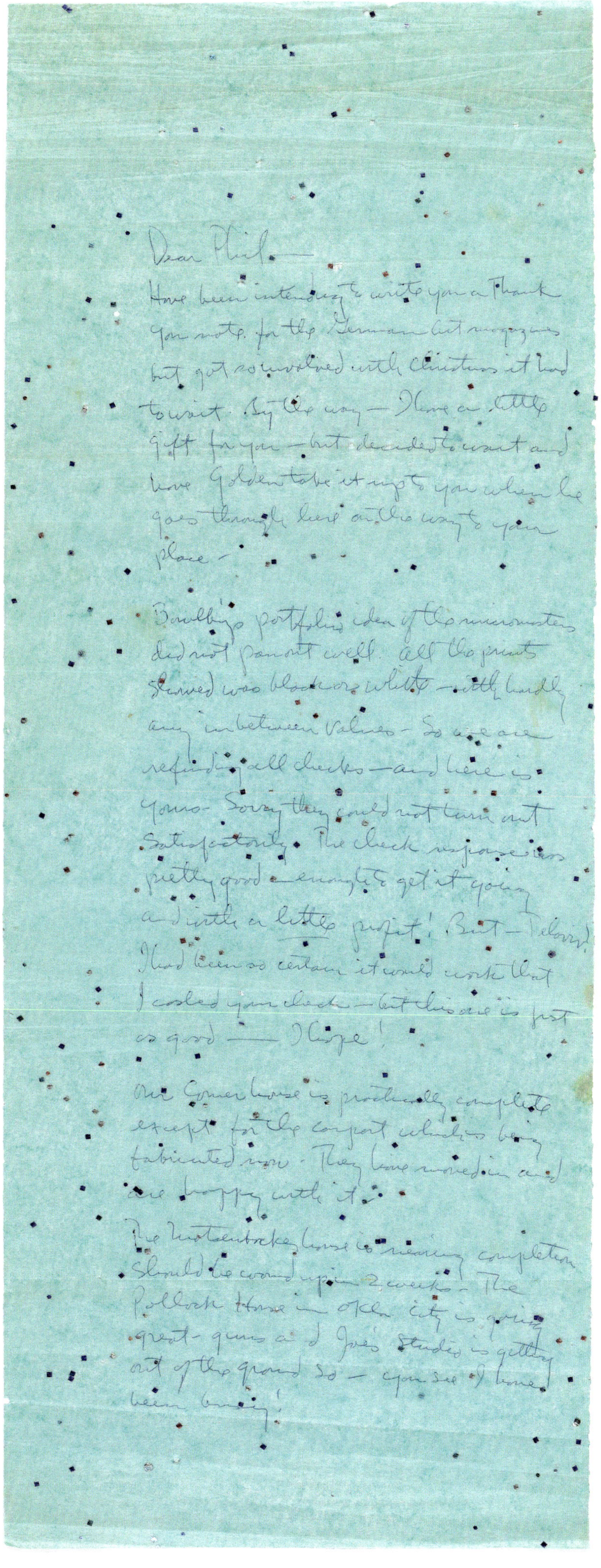

Dear Philo—

Have been intending to write you a thank you note for the German art magazines but got so involved with Christmas it had to wait. By the way — I have a little gift for you — but decided to wait and have Golden take it up to you when he goes through here on the way to your place—

Bowlby's portfolio idea of the micromasters did not pan out well. All the prints showed was black or white — with hardly any in between values — So we are refunding all checks — and here is yours — Sorry they could not turn out satisfactorily. The check response was pretty good — enough to get it going and with a little profit! But — Delivery! I had been so certain it would work that I cashed your check — but this one is just as good — I hope!

Our Gamer house is practically complete except for the carport which is being fabricated now. They have moved in and are happy with it.

The Motsenbocker house is nearing completion. Should be coming up in 2 weeks — The Pollock House in Okla City is going great — guns and Joe's Studio is getting out of the ground so — you see I have been busy!

FIG. 132 Goff. Letter on glitter paper, 1958. Bruce A. Goff Archive.

FROM TOP, FIG. 133 Goff and Greene. *Eugene and Nancy Bavinger House, Norman, Oklahoma, Plan of Lower Level*, 1950. Colored pencil with graphite on tracing paper; 67 × 66 cm (26⅜ × 26 in.). The Art Institute of Chicago, gift of Shin'enKan, Inc., 1990.811.9. FIG. 134 Nautilus shell, n.d. Private collection.

FIG. 135 Eugene and Nancy Bavinger House, Norman, Oklahoma, 1961. Photograph by Julius Shulman. Julius Shulman photography archive. © J. Paul Getty Trust. Getty Research Institute, Los Angeles (2004.R.10).

FROM TOP, FIG. 136 Interior of Eugene and Nancy Bavinger House, Norman, Oklahoma, 1955. Photograph by A. Y. Owen. FIG. 137 Goff. *Bavinger House Door*, c. 1955. Douglas fir, steel, and stainless steel; 220 × 154 cm (86½ × 60½ in.). Collection of Mark Fletcher and Tobias Meyer.

FIG. 138 Goff and Greene. *Eugene and Nancy Bavinger House, Norman, Oklahoma, Interior Perspective*, 1950. Colored pencil with graphite on tan wove paper; 58.9 × 53.9 cm (23³⁄₁₆ × 21³⁄₁₆ in.). The Art Institute of Chicago, gift of Shin'enKan, Inc., 1990.811.17.

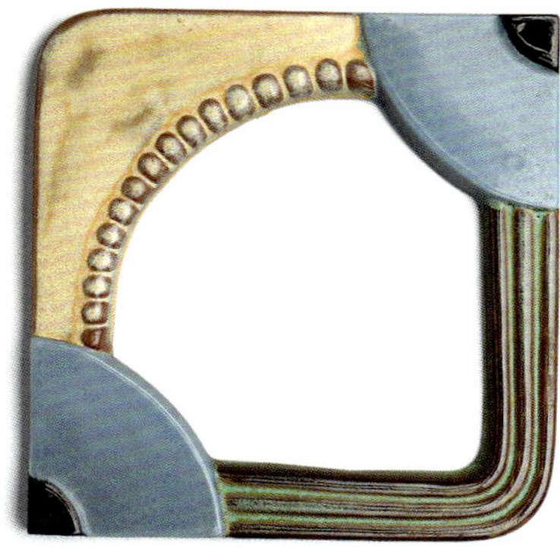

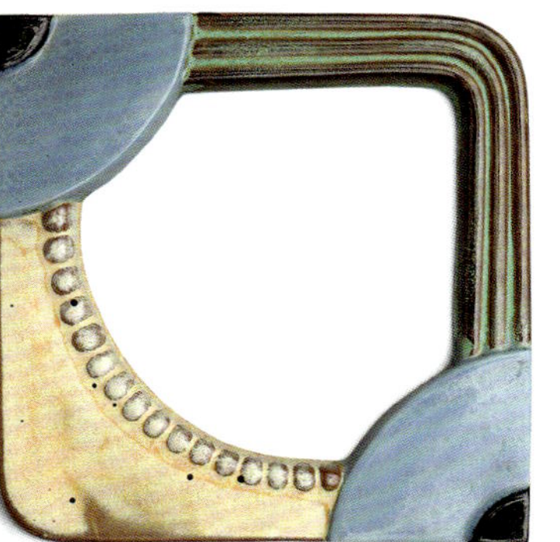

FROM TOP, FIG. 139 Ceramic tiles, c. 1955. Made by Frankoma Pottery (American, 1933–2010). Bruce A. Goff Archive. FIG. 140 Goff. *Grace Lee and John Frank House, Sapulpa, Oklahoma, Perspective*, 1955. Graphite and colored pencil on tracing paper; 70.8 × 118 cm (27⅞ × 46½ in.). The Art Institute of Chicago, gift of Shin'enKan, Inc., 1990.827.1.

FRANK HOUSE
SAPULPA, OKLA.
BRUCE GOFF ARCHITECT

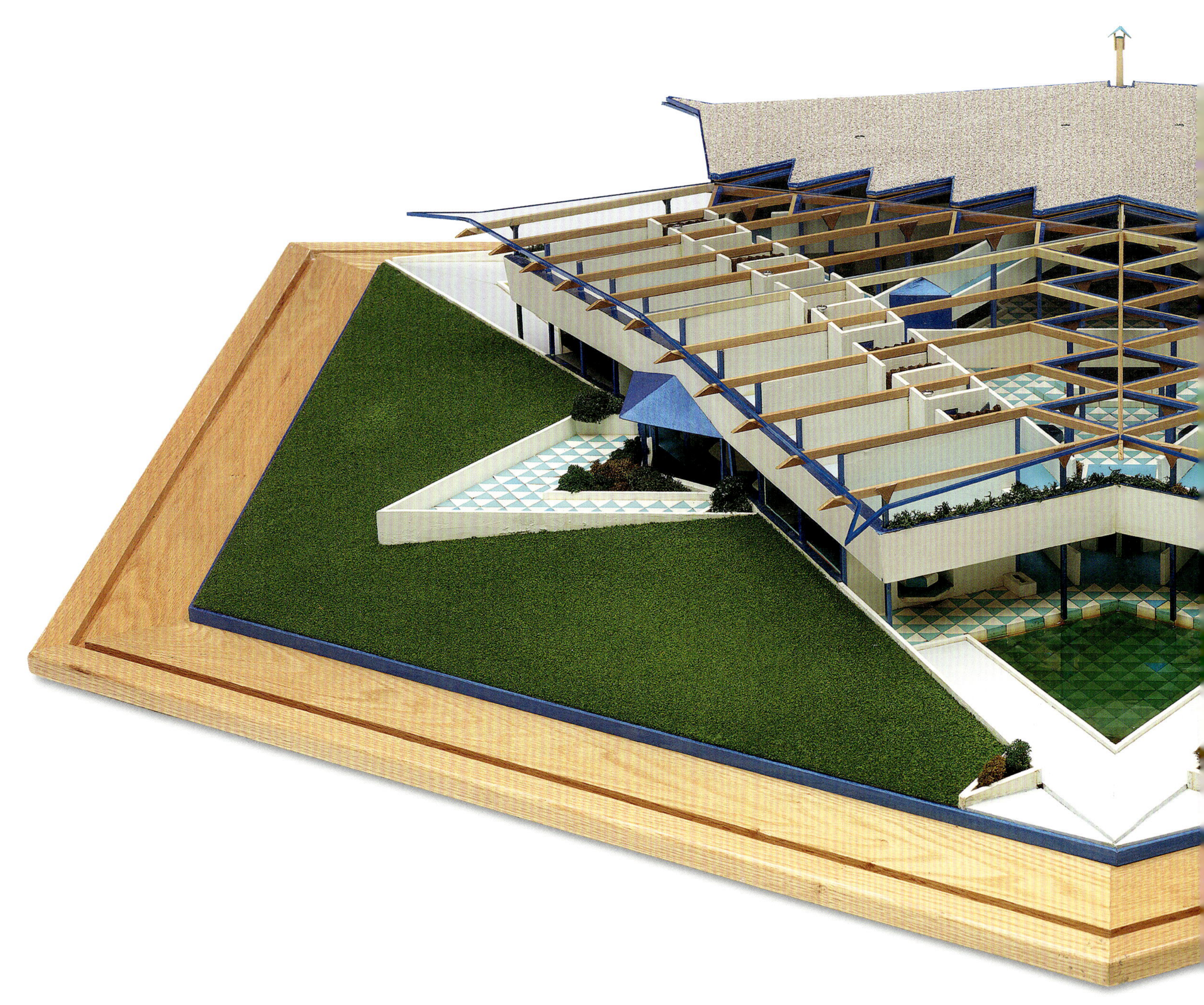

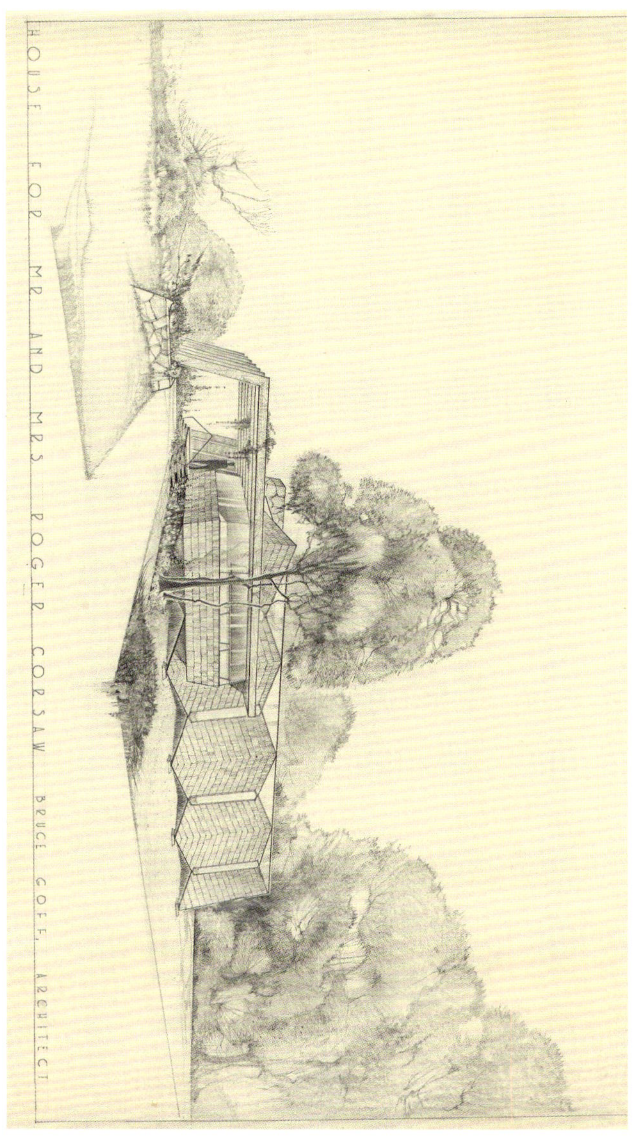

FROM LEFT, FIG. 141 Goff, Robert L. Faust (American, 1932–2020), and Norman Froelich (American, born 1932). *Pi Lambda Phi House Model*, c. 1955. Painted wood, cardboard, colored paper, and mixed media; 130.2 × 146.1 × 21.6 cm ($51\frac{1}{4}$ × $57\frac{1}{2}$ × $8\frac{1}{2}$ in.). The Art Institute of Chicago, gift of Vincent Mancini, 2005.131. **FIG. 142** Goff. *Roger and Wilma Corsaw House, Norman, Oklahoma, Perspective*, 1952. Graphite on tracing paper; 47 × 75.2 cm ($18\frac{9}{16}$ × $29\frac{5}{8}$ in.). The Art Institute of Chicago, gift of Shin'enKan, Inc., 1990.1050.4.

FROM LEFT, FIGS. 143A–D Polyester shirts and one cotton shirt, n.d. Bruce A. Goff Archive.

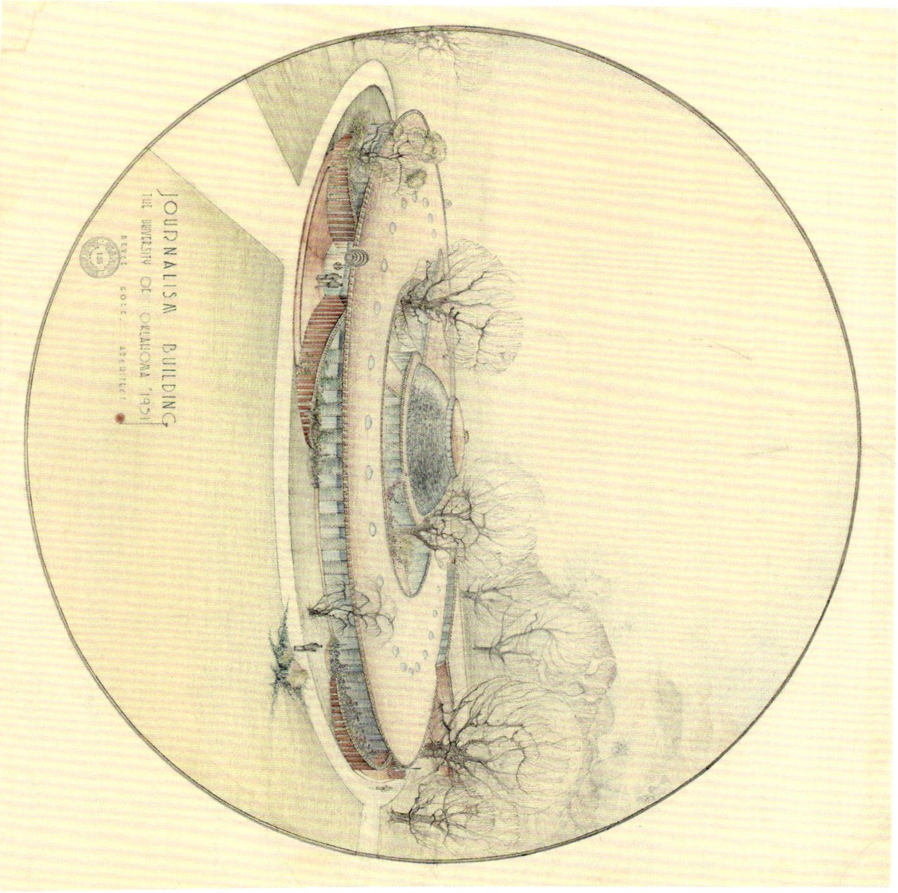

FIG. 145 Goff. *University of Oklahoma Journalism Building, Norman, Oklahoma, Perspective* [unbuilt], 1951. Graphite and colored pencil on tracing paper; 95.5 × 92.1 cm (37 9/16 × 36 1/4 in.). The Art Institute of Chicago, gift of Shin'enKan, Inc., 1990.858.1.

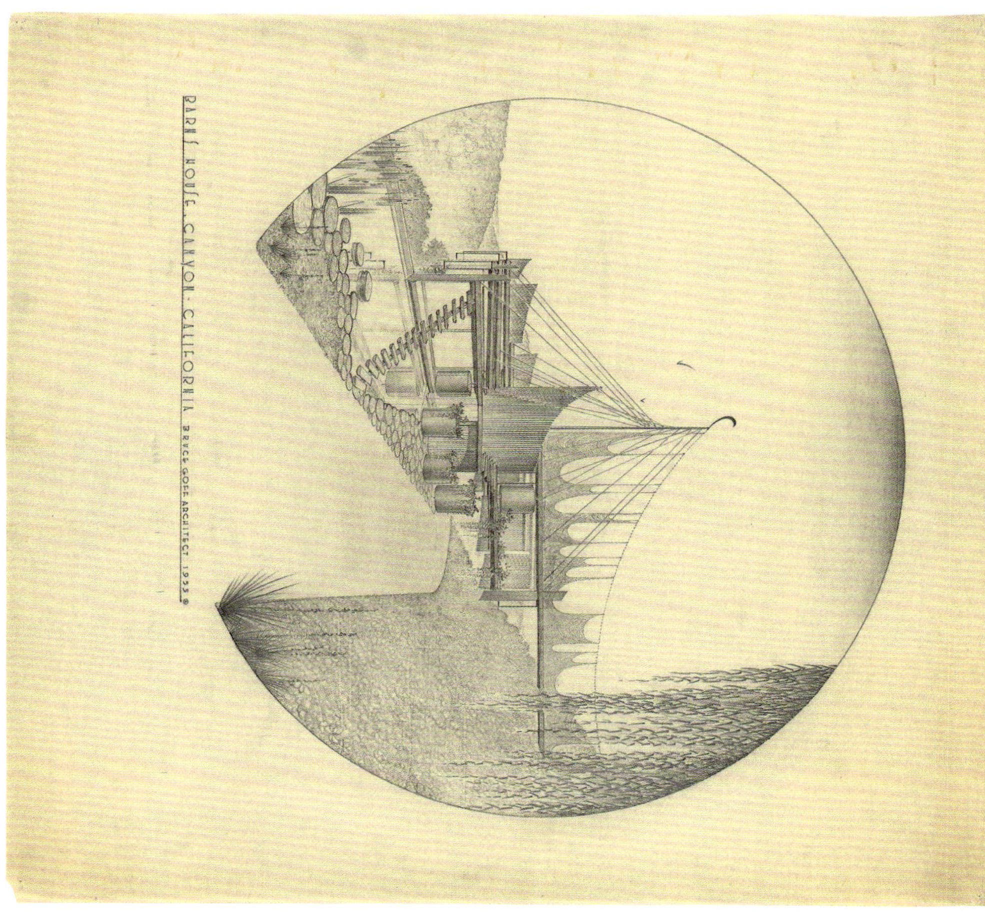

FIG. 144 Goff. *Bob and Doreen Barns House, Canyon, California, Perspective*, 1955. Graphite on tracing paper; 67 × 60.6 cm (26 7/16 × 23 7/8 in.). The Art Institute of Chicago, gift of Shin'enKan, Inc., 1990.936.3.

FIG. 146 Goff. *Circle Apartments, Bartlesville, Oklahoma, Perspective* [unbuilt], 1957. Graphite on tracing paper; 146 × 87 cm (57 7/16 × 34 1/4 in.). The Art Institute of Chicago, gift of Shin'enKan, Inc. 1990.896.1.

FROM TOP, FIG. 147 Yazz. *Deer in the Moonlight*, 1955. Opaque watercolor, over traces of graphite, on black wove paper-faced laminated board; 51.5 × 40.7 cm (20¼ × 16 in.). The Art Institute of Chicago, gift of Shin'enKan, Inc., 2025.44. FIG. 148 D. Humetewa (Hopi, 1935–2018). *Katsina in Dance*, n.d. Opaque watercolor, over graphite, on cream wove paper; 39.8 × 33.1 cm (15¹¹⁄₁₆ × 13 in.). The Art Institute of Chicago, gift of Shin'enKan, Inc., 2025.48.

FROM TOP, FIG. 149 Kamares-style stoneware pitcher, n.d. Private collection.
FIG. 150 Heishi bead necklace, n.d. Bruce A. Goff Archive.

FIG. 151 Goff and Greene. *Al and Jean Dewlen House, Amarillo, Texas, Perspective* [unbuilt], 1956. Colored pencil, with opaque watercolor and graphite, on cream wove paper; 58.5 × 86.5 cm (23¹⁄₁₆ × 34¹⁄₁₆ in.). The Art Institute of Chicago, gift of Shin'enKan, Inc., 1990.867.2.

FIG. 152 Goff and Harris. *Al and Jean Dewlen House, Amarillo, Texas, Interior Perspective* [unbuilt], 1957. Colored pencil, graphite, and ink over diazo print on tan wove paper; 46 × 74 cm (18⅛ × 29³⁄₁₆ in.). The Art Institute of Chicago, gift of Shin'enKan, Inc., 1990.867.5.

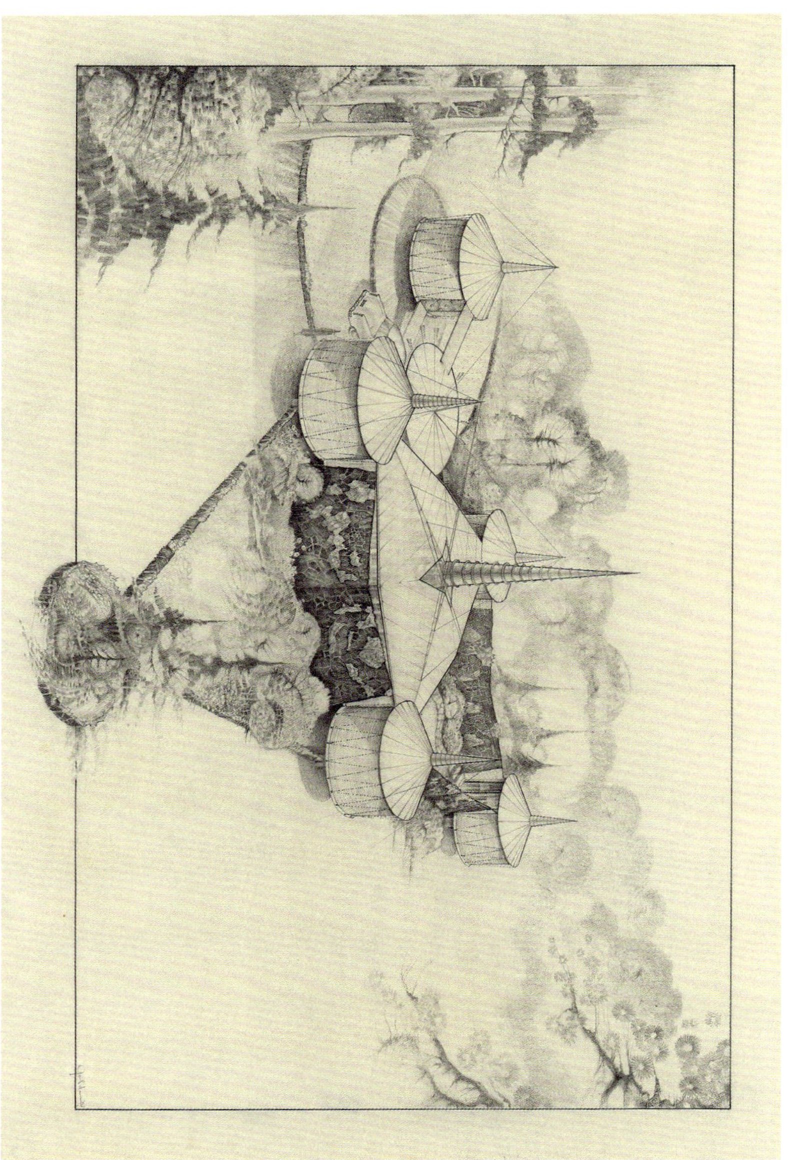

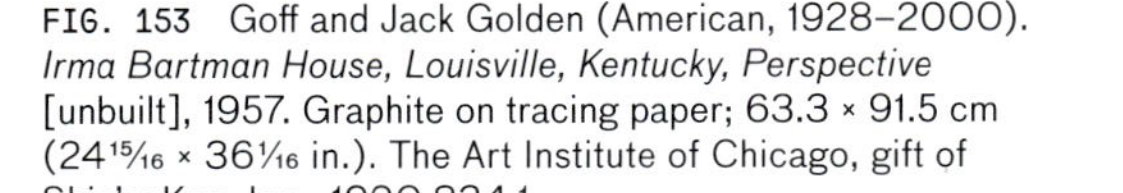

FIG. 153 Goff and Jack Golden (American, 1928–2000). *Irma Bartman House, Louisville, Kentucky, Perspective* [unbuilt], 1957. Graphite on tracing paper; 63.3 × 91.5 cm (24 15/16 × 36 1/16 in.). The Art Institute of Chicago, gift of Shin'enKan, Inc., 1990.834.1.

FIG. 154 Goff and Harris. *Irma Bartman House, Louisville, Kentucky, Interior Perspective* [unbuilt], 1957. Colored pencil, with graphite and opaque watercolor, over diazo print on cream wove paper; 56.2 × 77.7 cm (22$\frac{3}{16}$ × 30$\frac{5}{8}$ in.). The Art Institute of Chicago, gift of Shin'enKan, Inc., 1990.834.6.

FIG. 155 Goff and Takenobu Mohri (Japanese, 1925–2019). *Andrew and Elaine Kozak House, First Design, Marin County, California, Perspective* [unbuilt], 1946. Colored pencil and graphite over diazo print on cream wove paper; 45.4 × 123.2 cm (17⅞ × 48$\frac{9}{16}$ in.). The Art Institute of Chicago, gift of Shin'enKan, Inc., 1990.852.38.

FIG. 156 Goff and Grant Gustafson (American, born 1955). *Ignacio Perez House, Caracas, Venezuela, Perspective* [unbuilt], 1979, after a 1953 graphite drawing by Rex Slack (American, 1925–2013). Ink on tracing paper; 76.3 × 106.5 cm (30 1/16 × 41 15/16 in.). The Art Institute of Chicago, gift of Shin'enKan, Inc., 1990.857.1.

FIG. 157 Goff. *Don and Mildred Leidig House, Hayward, California, Plan* [unbuilt], 1946. Graphite and colored pencil on tracing paper; 63.1 × 38.4 cm (24⅞ × 15⅛ in.). The Art Institute of Chicago, gift of Shin'enKan, Inc., 1990.876.1.

FROM TOP, FIG. 158 Betty and James Nicol House, Kansas City, Missouri, c. 1967. Photographer unknown. Bruce A. Goff Archive.
FIG. 159 Goff and Harris. *Betty and James Nicol House, Kansas City, Missouri, Interior Perspective*, 1966. Colored pencil and graphite on cream wove paper; 76.2 × 101.6 cm (30 × 40 in.). The Art Institute of Chicago, gift of Jamie Nicol Bowles, 2021.416.

FROM TOP, FIG. 160 Goff and Harris. *Betty and James Nicol House, Kansas City, Missouri, Perspective*, 1966. Colored pencil over diazo print on cream wove paper; 60.5 × 92.1 cm (23⅞ × 36$^{5}/_{16}$ in.). The Art Institute of Chicago, gift of Shin'enKan, Inc., 1990.840.10. **FIG. 161** Goff. *Stool for the Nicol House*, c. 1967. Metal, vinyl, and synthetic cushion; 45.8 × 40.7 cm (18 × 16 in.). Collection of Rod Parks.

FROM TOP, FIG. 162 Erwine Laverne (American, 1909–2003) and Estelle Laverne (Amrican 1915–1997). *Lily Chair*, designed 1957, used in the Betty and James Nicol House, Kansas City, Missouri. Lucite and vinyl; 92.8 × 61 cm (36½ × 24 in.). Collection of Rod Parks. FIG. 163 Children's bedroom in the Betty and James Nicol House, Kansas City, Missouri, c. 1967. Photographer unknown. Bruce A. Goff Archive.

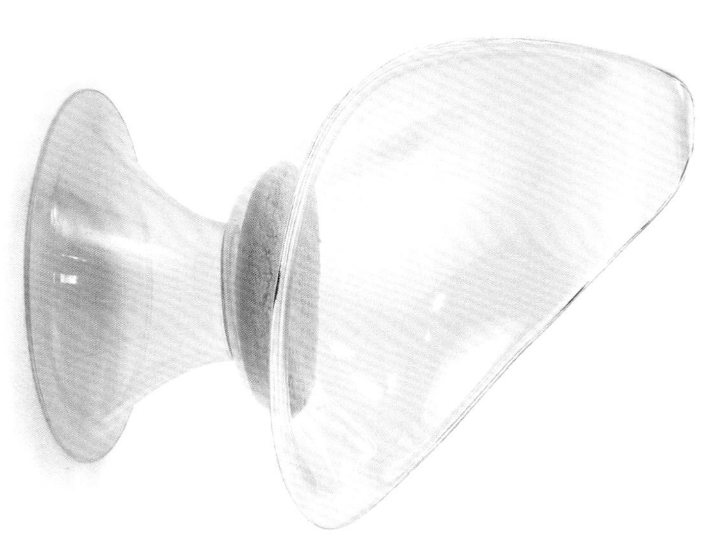

FROM TOP, FIG. 164 Betty and son Bruce sitting in the Betty and James Nicol House, Kansas City, Missouri, c. 1967. Photographer unknown. Bruce A. Goff Archive. FIG. 165 *Zebra-Print Upholstery*, n.d., used in the Betty and James Nicol House, Kansas City, Missouri. Polyester; 142.3 × 226.1 cm (56 × 89 in.). Private collection.

FIG. 166 Goff. *Untitled (Composition)*, 1938–40. Opaque watercolor with collage of cut-and-painted paper on brown wove paper; 90.9 × 60.2 cm (35¾ × 23$\frac{11}{16}$ in.). The Art Institute of Chicago, gift of Shin'enKan, Inc., 1990.574.363.

Compositions, Exercises, Improvisations: A Practice in Painting and Abstraction

Craig Lee

Painting in one form or another occupied Bruce Goff for most of his life (fig. 167). By age six or seven he "was always drawing or painting something," his mother recalled, and his great-grandmother, herself a self-taught painter, exposed him to watercolors.[1] In adulthood he was prolific and efficient—he made paintings in a single sitting, usually on Sundays, and he kept nearly all of them. The importance of this practice is reflected in the plans he designed for his homes in Kansas City, Missouri, and Tyler, Texas, each of which included dedicated workspaces to paint and closets and drawers for storing works. What began as an innate interest—in a medium that he watched his great-grandmother use to paint birds—developed into a serious, parallel practice that kept pace with his architecture: Goff painted as many abstract compositions as he designed architectural projects—that is, more than five hundred.

FIG. 167 Bruce Goff carrying paintings, Tulsa, Oklahoma, c. 1925. Photographer unknown. Bruce A. Goff Archive.

These comparable numbers, however, do not reflect a direct correlation. Goff did not use painting as a tool for architectural design, but an activity that he described as primarily "for relaxation."[2] It was a medium unto itself with which he could develop his ideas about abstraction and modern creative expression. Although his paintings are among his now lesser-known areas of work, over the course of his career the notoriety of Goff's architecture and the relative acclaim for his abstract paintings went hand in hand. Goff showed them in more than thirty exhibitions, ranging from informal displays accompanied by speaking engagements to formal exhibitions at galleries and art museums, and publications regularly featured his compositions alongside his architectural projects.[3] These bodies of work also existed side-by-side in his home and studio (fig. 168)—reflecting how seamlessly he considered them part of the same creative practice. This essay examines Goff's approach to painting across various areas of engagement to illuminate the critical role it played in his career and outlook. In particular, I explore his early education and writing, exhibiting, teaching, and painting practice, all of which connected him to key people and ideas related to modern and abstract art. In reconsidering Goff as a painter, I argue that his work in this medium was fundamental to his construction of individuality and creativity across the arts.[4]

EARLY INFLUENCES AND OPPORTUNITIES

Goff's exposure to modern art and abstract painting came early in life, as a combination of self-directed and formal pursuits, much like with modern architecture and modern music. He recalled later that, before entering high school in the fall of 1918, he encountered a sepia-toned reproduction of Gustav Klimt's *The Kiss (Lovers)* (1908–9; Belvedere, Vienna), which affected him so greatly, he subsequently ordered the large, expensive art portfolio *Das Werk von Gustav Klimt* (1918) from a New York bookseller.[5] Klimt remained an artistic touchstone for the rest of Goff's life, reaching a high point in the 1950s when he acquired a Klimt drawing and two Klimt paintings—including the landscape *Park at Kammer Castle* (1909; Neue Galerie, New York)—which he proudly displayed in his home.[6]

At Central High School in Tulsa, Goff flourished in the arts. He received encouragement from artist and art teacher Adah Robinson, who previously taught high school– and college-level arts in Oklahoma City,

1. Bart Prince, "Bruce Goff, Friend and Teacher," *Triglyph* 1 (Fall 1984): 35. Both Goff's great-grandmother Harriet Zelida York Messick (1835–1924) and his maternal grandmother, Lille Furbeck (1861–1921), were self-taught painters. See David G. De Long, *Bruce Goff: Toward Absolute Architecture* (Architectural History Foundation; MIT Press, 1988), 4; and Paul Nicolaides, "Bruce Goff and His Architecture" (master's thesis, Kansas State University, 1960), 19–20.
2. For "for relaxation," see "Goff's Non-Objective Art Is Displayed at University," *Norman Transcript*, Jan. 19, 1947.
3. Bruce Goff issue of *Baukunst und Werkform*, July 1953, 328–84; and Takenobu Mohri, *Bruce Goff, Architect* (Kenchiku Planning Center, 1970), 202–4.
4. For other writings on Goff's paintings, see Mark Andrew White, "'Steadily to the Ideal': The Paintings of Bruce Goff," in *Bruce Goff: A Creative Mind*, ed. Scott W. Perkins (Fred Jones Jr. Museum of Art, University of Oklahoma; Price Tower Arts Center, 2010), 93–105; Sidney Robinson, "Compositions: The Abstract Paintings of Bruce Goff," *Friends of Kebyar Journal* 28.2, no. 78 (Winter 2013); and Arn Henderson, *Bruce Goff: Architecture of Discipline in Freedom* (University of Oklahoma Press, 2017), 27–35.
5. Betty Leigh, "Interview: I Do What Comes Naturally," *Inland Architect* 23, no. 8 (Dec. 1979): 18.
6. Goff sold the paintings in 1981. See Yagna Yass-Alston, "The Provenance of *Park at Kammer Castle*," in *Klimt Landscapes*, ed. Janis Staggs (Prestel, 2024), 272–83.

FIG. 168 *Untitled (Composition)* (Art Institute of Chicago, 1990.574.354) and Al and Jean Dewlen House drawing (fig. 151) in Goff's studio at Price Tower, Bartlesville, Oklahoma, c. 1957. Photographer unknown. Bruce A. Goff Archive.

where she was also involved in the local art scene.[7] Goff earned "excellent" marks in Robinson's classes and in a mechanical drawing course and won several statewide awards in pencil drawing and poster design.[8] He also participated in the school's art club, Chiaroscuro, which assisted with local art exhibitions—including shows of historically significant sixteenth- to eighteenth-century European paintings and etchings—where the students delivered short gallery talks.[9] In the group's yearbook photo of more than fifty members, Goff is the only person holding a sketchbook, likely indicating his position as the group's official club artist. Routinely designing school posters, he was well known in high school for his creative output and artistic inclination, so much so that his 1922 senior year portrait listed "futuristic art" as his "chief accomplishment."[10]

"Futuristic art" likely referred to the abstract, non-objective paintings Goff began making in 1921—just a year after he started painting in earnest. His artistic output during this period was varied: studies of flowers and trees in pencil and pastel, landscapes and still lifes that show the influence of French Post-Impressionist Paul Cezanne and Cubism, and scenes of "Oriental" subject matter—and then a quick turn to abstract compositions in loose watercolor. These latter works on paper demonstrate his budding interest in Expressionism and Symbolism, as he explored using abstract forms and shapes with intense color to convey feelings rather than depict a subject. Although he did not usually sign, date, or title his work—a tendency throughout his life—one signed and dated 1921 composition (fig. 169) illustrates this early moment. In the work, a silhouetted figure at the bottom center stands dwarfed by mountain faces rendered in black and mottled colors, all against a blue-and-white-streaked sky. In addition to evoking an atmospheric mood through contrasting colors and forms, the work transitions from dense areas of paint to thin, blended areas flecked with pointed daubs, demonstrating Goff's adeptness in various techniques.

Goff continued to make modestly sized abstract watercolors throughout the 1920s. Although some works depict a subject, ranging from haunting figures in dramatic landscapes to spectral masklike forms, the vast majority are "pure" abstractions composed of colors and forms. He was reluctant to call these works paintings even in the beginning and instead referred to them as "composition in color."[11] For Goff, *composition* was a looser term, more indicative of process and a

FIG. 169 Goff. *Untitled (Composition)*, 1921. Translucent and opaque watercolor on cream laid paper; 19.4 × 14.7 cm (7⅝ × 5¾ in.). The Art Institute of Chicago, gift of Shin'enKan, Inc., 1990.574.14.

7. She had taken courses at the Chicago Art Institute and in New York and Provincetown, Massachusetts. For more on Adah Robinson's background, see Therese Holder, *That Damn Art Woman: Adah Robinson, Bruce Goff and the Controversy Behind the Design of the Boston Avenue Methodist Episcopal Church* (Oklahoma State University, 2019), 6–23.

8. "Tulsa County Goes After Cup at State Fair," *Tulsa World*, Sept. 17, 1916, 1; newspaper clipping, "Just Thirty Years Ago," Sept. 22, 1948, series VII, box 3, folder 4, Bruce A. Goff Archive, Ryerson and Burnham Art and Architecture Archives, The Art Institute of Chicago (hereafter BGA, AIC); and "Art Contests," *Sooner State Press*, May 7, 1921, 3.

9. Holder, *That Damn Art Woman*, 23–24.

10. *Tom Tom* (Central High School, Tulsa, 1922), 52; and De Long, *Bruce Goff*, 7.

11. Calvin Good, "Art Exhibits Held in Norman," *Sooner Magazine*, July 1929, 330.

FIG. 170 Goff. *Untitled (Composition)*, 1927. Gouache on white cardboard; 29.6 × 23 cm (11 11/16 × 9 1/16 in.). Deutsches Architekturmuseum.

way of thinking about abstraction that released Goff to explore—even luxuriate in—the effects of color, shape, and their various combinations.

These works as much as Goff's architecture caught the attention of Chicago designer Alfonso Iannelli, who visited Tulsa in summer 1927 to oversee an ecclesiastical stained-glass commission. Impressed by the rising construction of the Boston Avenue Methodist Episcopal Church South, he sought out the architect—Goff—later recalling, "I cancelled my reservations to return to Chicago and stayed in Tulsa for two or three days to look at other works of his. I also went to his home and saw his paintings which were delightful."[12] Iannelli at the time was head of the design department at the School of the Art Institute of Chicago and was so taken with the architect and his abstract paintings that the following year he featured about fifty of them in a solo exhibition from December 1928 to spring 1929.[13] Although we have no record of the works he displayed, we can see a representative composition from this period in an abstract painting Goff sent to Iannelli (fig. 170). Goff's first painting exhibition was soon followed by a solo exhibition in the Fine Arts Building at the University of Oklahoma (OU).[14]

FREEDOM IN ABSTRACTION

Around 1930 Goff transitioned from creating loose, transparent watercolors—like those that featured in his breakthrough exhibitions in Chicago and Norman—to working at a slightly bigger size and with opaque watercolor paint. By this time making solely formal abstractions, Goff used the additional space and new medium to explore not only color and form but also layering (rather than blending), pattern, and decoration. This paint offered Goff more control in delineating hard edges and creating repeated geometries or chromatic bands of color, which he tried out in numerous compositions (fig. 171). Other works became studies in asymmetry and the balance of color, line, and shape, reflecting his changing focus from subjective explorations of emotional atmosphere to intuitive formal studies of compositional elements.

Goff's shift at this moment can likely be attributed to a productive creative exchange with artist Olinka Hrdy, an OU graduate he met while visiting the university. She moved to Tulsa in 1929 at Goff's invitation to complete a series of abstract murals related to music for the interior of the Patti Adams Shriner House and Studio (see figs. 114 and 115a–d). To match his modernist architectural design, Hrdy's mural program embraced greater abstraction than her previous work in Norman and Oklahoma City.[15] With a lush sense of color, Hrdy painted the Shriner murals in an Art Deco or moderne style, with its characteristic hard edges, repeated geometries, and swooping lines in a dynamic, abstract composition that captures the subject of different kinds of music (fig. 172)—an important commission in her artistic development. Before Hrdy left Tulsa for New York in 1931, she worked with Goff on another project, painting a stage curtain of a machine-age abstraction that hung as the centerpiece of Goff's 1930 interior renovation of the Tulsa Convention Hall.[16] Although this period lasted only two years, during this time they each transformed the other's work: Goff's architecture affected Hrdy's approach to greater abstraction, which, in turn, influenced his own paintings.

Around this time, Goff published his earliest text on modern and abstract art, an essay titled "Pure and Representative Art," in *Tulsart*, a journal he coedited with

12. Alfonso Iannelli, memorandum, n.d., Collection of Tim Samuelson, Chicago.
13. Iannelli likely held the exhibition in a classroom or other school space; there are no records of this exhibition in the museum's papers. See "Drawings of Tulsan in Chicago Art Institute," *Tulsa Tribune*, Dec. 14, 1928; and "Bruce Goff, '22, Now an Architect, Has a Lot of Interesting Ideas," *Tulsa Tribune*, Dec. 19, 1928.
14. Good, "Art Exhibits Held in Norman," 330.
15. Mark Andrew White, *Oklahoma Moderne: The Art and Design of Olinka Hrdy* (Fred Jones Jr. Museum of Art, University of Oklahoma, 2007), 20–36.
16. They also worked together on an abstract painting on silk that Goff designed and Hrdy executed. See undated photograph, series III, box 22, folder 7, BGA, AIC.

OPPOSITE, FIG. 171 Goff. *Untitled (Composition)*, 1930. Opaque watercolor and colored pencil on cream wove paper-faced laminated paperboard; 71.2 × 55.9 cm (28 × 22 in.). The Art Institute of Chicago, gift of Shin'enKan, Inc., 1990.574.293.

FIG. 172 Hrdy's "Symphony of the Arts" mural at the Patti Adams Shriner House and Studio, Tulsa, Oklahoma, 1929. Photograph by John D. McCurry. Museum of Tulsa History, 2017.113.043.

his friend, composer Ernest Brooks. The one-issue publication aimed to "present personalities and philosophies in a comprehensive integrality with truth, glorified in art as abstraction."[17] The fact that abstraction across the arts was the organizing principle of their project highlights how central the subject was to Goff. In his apartment in Tulsa, he designed built-in furniture that harmonized with an abstract composition that he painted on his bathroom door (fig. 173). In the essay, Goff is at his most strident when calling for a modern art of "pure" abstraction—meaning free of representation—a stance reflecting recent developments in his painted compositions. He declared, "Cubism was the most radical step to rid the parasite [of representation]," and in it, he continued, "composition, color, beauty of line and material asserted themselves more aggressively than ever before."[18] In highlighting these elements of abstraction, he also acknowledged Rembrandt van Rijn, Paul Cezanne, Gustav Klimt, Pablo Picasso, and Japanese printmakers for their advancements as "man grows steadily to the ideal of ABSTRACTION."[19] Goff's reference to these artists highlights the depth and range of his artistic knowledge and the focus of his appreciation.

In an essay he wrote the following year relaying a similar sentiment, Goff used the term "absolute" art and cited other forms of stylistic development to illustrate the ultimate progression for painting and drawing toward abstraction to fulfill its intents and purposes: "[Painting and drawing are] still struggling with representation . . . stumbling thru Impressionism, stumbling thru cubism, stumbling thru sur-realisme . . . trying to realize more than the 'subject,' trying to escape its demands and limitations, trying to find conscious color and composition, trying to start anew with elementals . . . to realize art purely by and for itself."[20] Goff understood abstraction as an amalgamation of modern styles drawn from Post-Impressionism, Cubism, Expressionism, Symbolism, and Surrealism, filtered through Japanese art and European painting traditions and techniques, such as chiaroscuro. It offered the means and the formal ("elemental") qualities of color, composition, line, and material needed to achieve his ideal: a "pure" and "absolute" art.

Goff's efforts to promote modern art and abstraction seemed to mirror those of his contemporary Le Corbusier, a fellow architect painter. Corbusier, with French painter Amédée Ozenfant, founded Purism in 1918 as a rejection of an increasingly decorative tendency in Cubist art. They sought to return modern art to a rational, orderly visual logic based on machine-made objects. To spread these ideas, they launched the publication *L'esprit nouveau* (1920–25), and others such as artists Fernand Léger and Juan Gris joined the movement. Where they diverged, however, is in their conclusions about abstraction. Whereas Purist art reduced subjects to their formal elements and emphasized visual aesthetics, Goff's abstraction was influenced by the spiritual, affective direction of Expressionism and Symbolism. It was inner-directed, rather than referential, as the artist combined formal elements into the final composition.

In Goff's early 1930s writings, he laid out the foundational and lasting ideas that would guide his painting practice. From this point onward, despite creating larger

17. Bruce Goff, "Pure and Representative Art," in *Tulsart*, Aug. 1963, 1, series XVIII, box 1, folder 6, BGA, AIC.
18. Ibid., 9.
19. Ibid.
20. Bruce Goff, "About Absolute Art," Aug. 23, 1932, series V, box 1, folder 2, BGA, AIC. A few years later, Goff returned to the subject, publishing "Drawing and Painting," *Circle*, Oct.[?] 1935.

abstract compositions and integrating new techniques of paint and media application, he stayed constant in his attitude toward abstraction. Goff later summarized his approach in a 1948 profile—one of the earliest published statements describing his mature, abstract working method:

> My paintings are all improvisations, which start with the size, shape, color and texture of the paper itself. Then I use ideas generated into elements of design characteristic of the medium employed to form a sense of order for each composition. There is no intention of representation, symbolism, or extraneous subject matter. They are spontaneous and usually completed at one sitting, and are, for me, exercises in imaginative solutions of problems created by the organic growth of the composition.[21]

FIG. 173 Composition Goff painted on a bathroom door in his apartment, Tulsa, Oklahoma, 1928. Photographer unknown. Bruce A. Goff Archive.

In effect, as an "exercise in imaginative solutions," painting was a release. In painting—in abstraction—there was freedom.

TEACHING BY DOING

In 1934, five years into the Great Depression, Goff moved to Chicago in search of better professional opportunities. He continued to compose music and devoted even more time to painting. In letters to his partner Richard San Jule, Goff described the progress he had been making in his abstract compositions and dedicated a series to him.[22] During this period, he taught architecture and interior design at the Chicago Academy of Fine Art, where he integrated abstract painting into his curriculum by taking students to exhibitions of his work. This included two presentations at the academy in the spring of 1935 and in March 1936—reviewers described them as "rhythmic abstractions"[23]—and another in the summer of 1936 at the Davis Store, a discount department store, a joint exhibition of photography by Clyde T. Brown and architectural work and paintings by Goff. The last of these featured twenty-four of his paintings, including three works recorded as "Interpretation of Debussy's La Mer" and twenty-one other abstract "colour compositions."[24] In addition to bringing his students to look at his abstract works, Goff instructed them to try their hand at abstract painting. This became known as the "Friday group," an informal, extracurricular club. In the next exhibition of his work, at the Paul Theobald Gallery in September 1940, sixteen of Goff's paintings and nineteen photographs featuring four architectural works were displayed alongside fifteen "color compositions" created by four of his students.[25] In a photograph of student Kenneth Bartman holding up one of his paintings (fig. 174), the work's style of abstraction reflects Goff's influence.[26] Goff's encouragement of another student, Marguerite Hohenberg, who enrolled in Goff's interior design course in spring 1936, led her to pursue a successful practice in non-objective painting.[27]

When he joined the faculty of the University of Oklahoma in 1946 and soon after became chairman of the School of Architecture, Goff continued to teach through his paintings and exhibit them in a more extensive fashion: including fifty abstract compositions in an exhibition at the University of Oklahoma's art building (opening January 1947), fifty at the Philbrook Art Center in Tulsa (opening March 2, 1948), and seventy at the

21. Nan Sheets, "Art," *Daily Oklahoman*, May 16, 1948.
22. Richard San Jule to Bruce Goff, [Oct. 2–Nov. 28], 1942, series I, box 20, folder 17, BGA, AIC.
23. "Joins Academy Bruce Goff," *Tulsa Tribune*, June 24, 1935; and C. J. Bulliet, "Around the Galleries—Goff's Rhythmic Abstractions," *Chicago Daily News*, Mar. 14, 1936, 4.
24. Eleanor Jewett, "Art Institute Is Vital Force in This Country," *Chicago Daily Tribune*, Aug. 2, 1936, F7; and "Art Exhibit of Photography Architectural Work and Color Composition Done by Clyde Brown and Bruce Goff," pamphlet, series XII, box 1, folder 6, BGA, AIC.
25. "'Accident' Technique Irks Fritzi," *Sunday Times Chicago*, Sept. 29, 1940; Eleanor Jewett, "Noted Portrait Display Opens New Art Season," *Chicago Daily Tribune*, Sept. 25, 1940, 23; and "Art Notes," *Chicago Daily Tribune*, Sept. 29, 1940, C4. For a complete checklist, see "Color Compositions by Bruce Goff's 'Friday Group,'" series V, box 1, folder 5a, BGA, AIC.
26. The other students who exhibited at Paul Theobald Gallery include Von Billings, Elizabeth Bowman, and L. Milton Hersh. Bartman's mother, Irma, became a client, commissioning Goff to design several projects (one built) for her in Louisville, Kentucky.
27. Hohenberg's work was included in exhibitions at the Solomon R. Guggenheim Foundation, New York, and the Art Institute of Chicago in the 1940s, and she received a Guggenheim Fellowship in 1943. She also taught at the School of the Art Institute of Chicago and opened the Gallery of Non-Objective Painting in Chicago in 1950. See C. J. Bulliet, "Marguerite Hohenberg," *Chicago Daily News*, June 17, 1939; Kathryn Loring, "Turns Artist at 55; Now to Open Gallery," *Chicago Daily Tribune*, Dec. 31, 1950; and Dorothea Kahn Jaffe, "Mrs. Hohenberg's Home as Modern as Own Paintings," *Christian Science Monitor*, Mar. 22, 1951.

FIG. 174 Bruce Goff viewing a painting by Kenneth Bartman, Louisville, Kentucky, 1953. Photograph by Charley Darneal. Published in *Louisville Courier-Journal*, Aug. 16, 1953. Bruce A. Goff Archive.

Oklahoma Art Center in Oklahoma City (opening May 16, 1948).[28] When Goff was invited to lecture on architecture at other schools, he would often send his architectural drawings and paintings in advance so they could be exhibited concurrently.

Goff also introduced the principles of abstraction that he formulated more than a decade earlier directly into his architectural pedagogy. He taught a basic design studio for first-year students, developing their drawing skills through exercises in line, plane, and point as individual elements and in combination—reminiscent of the mechanical drawing class Goff took in high school.[29] With students' foundation in formal elements established, Goff taught a fourth-year course grounded in principles of balance, ornament, rhythm, and scale, which culminated with design projects that straddled architecture and abstract drawing.[30] This student work did not need to be feasible: The lesson was in creativity and individual expression—that is, a pure and absolute art.

In some instances Goff gave his paintings to close friends and colleagues, which is instructive. In addition to the several he sent to Iannelli between 1927 and 1934, Goff gave German British architect Erich Mendelsohn a painting, *Untitled (Cosmos)* (fig. 175), in 1948, and wrote on the back, "For you—Eric [*sic*], in appreciation of the inspiration you have given your friend." In return Goff received *House of Friendship*, a black ink drawing that Mendelsohn made in 1917—one of the works that inspired Goff to create hypothetical studies in black ink in the 1920s (fig. 64).[31] Former students who later worked for Goff also received paintings as tokens of friendship. These people included architects Bob Faust, Herb Greene, and Tom Hart, who each maintained their own abstract painting practice following the model that they learned from Goff.

COMMISSIONS

Goff's architectural clients, perhaps not surprisingly, also proved interested in his paintings. Glen and Luetta Harder, for example, commissioned a painting for the dining room of their newly completed house. Others inverted this order, such as Al Struckus, who initially commissioned a painting from Goff and then hired him to design his house. Goff completed his largest work, *La Mer*, for Bruce and Su Plunkett in the late 1960s. This four-by-twelve-foot composition spans three square panels and features the sprayed, stenciled forms that Goff developed in other works and depicts one of his favorite pieces of music by Claude Debussy. Goff also painted an ambitious twenty-five-panel series, titled *Drunken Boat*, a rare, fully narrative work illustrating a poem by Arthur Rimbaud.[32] His friend and patron Joe Price engaged Goff to produce several works beginning in the 1950s, including the large *Untitled (Razorblade Mountain)* (fig. 176) and *Afternoon of a Faun* (c. 1973), which hung prominently over the central living space of Shin'enKan, Etsuko and Joe Price's home in Bartlesville, Oklahoma. He also challenged Goff to work in different media. For example, Price sourced two-panel screens from one of his many trips to Japan and asked Goff to paint a unified abstract composition across the surface. For the series *Ode to an Imaginary Ballet*, completed in the 1970s, Goff painted on lenticular plastic film over colored panels, adding another layer of dimension and distortion to the abstract composition, in effect enlivening some of the dancing, Art Nouveau-esque female figures depicted on four of the ten panels.

In these commissions for Bruce and Su Plunkett and Joe Price, Goff explored abstraction as a visual language

28. "Goff's Non-Objective Art Is Displayed at University"; "Art Center to Show Work of Bruce Goff," *Daily Oklahoman*, Apr. 22, 1948; and Sheets, "Art." After leaving OU, his paintings continued to feature in exhibitions, including at art museums, notably the Wichita Art Museum in 1960 and the Yellowstone Art Center in Billings, Montana, in May 1978. Charles Eldredge, director of the University of Kansas Museum of Art (now Spencer Museum of Art), planned a 1973 exhibition and catalogue focused on Goff's paintings. See series XII, box 3, folder 1, BGA, AIC.

29. Henderson, *Bruce Goff*, 101; and Luca Guido, "We Preach No Dogma: The Curriculum Under Bruce Goff," in *Renegades: Bruce Goff and the American School of Architecture*, ed. Luca Guido et al. (University of Oklahoma Press, 2020), 67–93.

30. Other topics included opacity, translucency, and transparency; modulation; theme, variation, and development; incident, terminal, and climax; orchestration of materials; and site relationships. Henderson, *Bruce Goff*, 105–27; and Guido, "We Preach No Dogma," 82–84.

31. The Mendelsohns especially cherished this work. Upon receiving it Erich responded, "Your 'Cosmos,' framed under glass, provides our living room with the scale we both love," and his wife Louise, after Erich's death, wrote, "I gave up our apartment and moved to a little room. The only picture I took along is the one you did and I love its infinite company." Erich Mendelsohn to Bruce Goff, July 19, 1948, series I, box 14, folder 26; and Louise Mendelsohn to Bruce Goff, Mar. 15, 1954, series I, box 14, folder 27, both BGA, AIC.

32. Arthur Rimbaud, *Sui dore sen* (Kyoto Shoin, 1988).

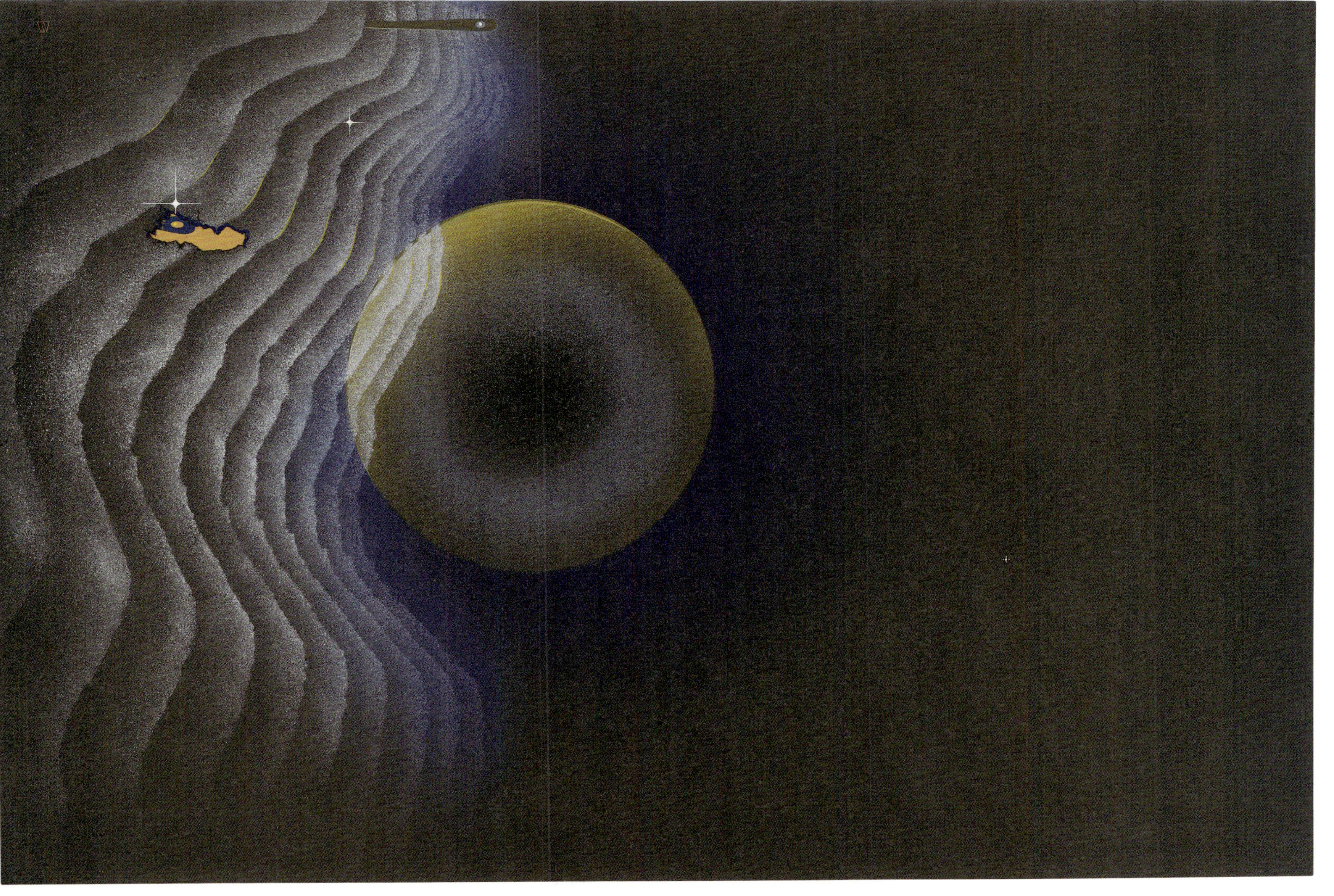

FIG. 175 Goff. *Untitled (Cosmos)*, 1948. Opaque watercolor with collage of cut, colored, and painted paper on black wove paper; 91.5 × 61 cm (36 × 24 in.). The Art Institute of Chicago, gift of Joseph Henry Wythe, 1997.457.2

FIG. 176 Goff. *Untitled (Razorblade Mountain)*, c. 1960. Acrylic on paper mounted on board; 152.4 × 152.4 cm (60 × 60 in.). Gift of Etsuko and Joe Price, Private collection, 2003.04.01.

OPPOSITE, FIG. 177 Goff. *Screen*, 1942. Piano roll, opaque watercolor, and enamel paint, with collage of cut-and-painted paper, gummed adhesive reinforcements, and colored and metallic foil stickers on painted hardboard attached to a wooden three-panel folding screen; open: 172.8 × 151.2 × 4.8 cm (68 × 59½ × 1⅞ in.); each panel: 173 × 50 × 4.8 cm (68 × 19½ × 1⅞ in.). The Art Institute of Chicago, gift of Sidney K. Robinson, 2022.240.

related to other creative mediums, such as music and poetry. Instead of working in his usual manner of free association, he employed abstraction to unite multiple arts. Perhaps the best example of Goff applying this ideal is the three-panel screen (fig. 177) that he created for Myron Bachman, a recording engineer in Chicago. The work is a tour de force, a synesthetic demonstration of the three primary arts that preoccupied Goff: architecture, painting, and music. Conceiving the piece as a record album—side A is the front and side B is the back—Goff laid commercial piano rolls atop three wooden panels and decorated them with elaborate patterns composed of paint and stickers, adding black enamel paint to unite the panels with a dramatic curving form. Upon receiving photos of the completed screen, San Jule admired its detail and execution, writing, "No daring sensitivity but yours could have correlated the cataract patterns of perforation in the music-roll with intricate accents of spot colors and with that great girder-like span which yokes the whole together. . . . It is truly a wonderful conception and flares from the fullness of your ever-changing and ever-growing genius."[33]

Initially designed for some minor interior alterations to an in-home recording studio, the screen was later placed to separate the entrance and waiting area after Goff's major interior and exterior alterations to Bachman's house in 1947. Music theorist Benjamin R. Levy has analyzed the screen in relation to Goff's understanding of modern music and organic architecture, but the key to fully understanding it is the ideal of abstraction Goff developed in his writings on modern art.[34]

As an example of a pure and absolute art, Goff's screen design illuminates how he considered discrete areas of the composition and the overall view. He embellished the piano roll's punch-cut holes with metallic and colored stickers, reinforcement rings, and various types of paint. These aestheticize the music, visually "playing" it as repeating patterns emphasize repeating notes or as new visual elements highlight new notes, tempos, and sound effects. Goff painted curving abstract forms to join these details in a dynamic fashion. The work is direct and intuitive, composed of found materials he responded to, to create something wholly original.

San Jule's deep understanding of Goff's creative goals and abilities extended to a canny appreciation for the architect's multivalient practice:

> And that quality of fantasy we both regard as the highest flight the mind can make is nowhere more sensitively expressed and vibrantly communicated than in the best of your paintings, and in music like *Outline*, and in architecture like the House on the Hill. Human as you are, with foibles galore, with blind spots as big as spiral nebulae, there is in you more of the crystal-clearness of perception of beauty distilled through the human imagination, and more creative electricity, than ever surged in any of those people we respect. For their awareness flowered in one expression only, and yours is manifold. In you is inexhaustible and timeless capacity for disclosing beauty and power of color and form, of materials and proportions, of timbre and sonority.[35]

The manifold nature of Goff's creative vision set him apart—his ability to think across the "color and form" of painting, the "materials and proportions" of architecture, and the "timbre and sonority" of music. And yet these elements and qualities in Goff's conception of an ideal abstraction did not apply to just one of these art forms: In his hands, eyes, and ears, they translated across all of them.

33. Richard San Jule to Bruce Goff, [Oct. 2–Nov. 28], 1942, series I, box 20, folder 17, BGA, AIC.
34. Benjamin R. Levy, "Material Connections: Bruce Goff, Music, and Modernism Across the Arts," *Music Theory Online* 23, no. 3 (Sept. 2021), mtosmt.org/issues/mto.21.27.3/mto.21.27.3.levy.php.
35. Richard San Jule to Bruce Goff, [Aug. 21–Sept. 23], 1942, series I, box 20, folder 16, BGA, AIC.

FIG. 178 Bruce Goff working on a composition (Art Institute of Chicago, 1990.574.335) in Bartlesville, Oklahoma, 1956. Photographer unknown. Bruce A. Goff Archive.

Strange Surfaces: Material Manipulation in Bruce Goff's Compositions

Kelly Keegan

Poured, wiped, dabbed, and sprayed paint—applied in a series of semi-controlled accidents—pairs with carefully articulated details.[1] Biomorphic forms appear beneath tinted patterns of frost; metal-foil star stickers are neatly arranged within a triangle on a Day-Glo red background; and diaphanous veils of color are punctuated by precise linear strokes. These are just a few descriptions of the array of arresting and unexpected visual qualities found in the painted works by architect Bruce Goff. In order to better understand these colors, patterns, and textures, this essay focuses on Goff's unconventional painting techniques on paper and paperboard as part of his broad-ranging exploration of material and form.

These findings are based on the thorough examination of twenty compositions and four architectural renderings, drawn from a pool of more than four hundred of his painted works in the Art Institute of Chicago's collection. Technical imaging, scientific analysis, and close looking led to new discoveries about Goff's materials and working processes, many documented for the first time.

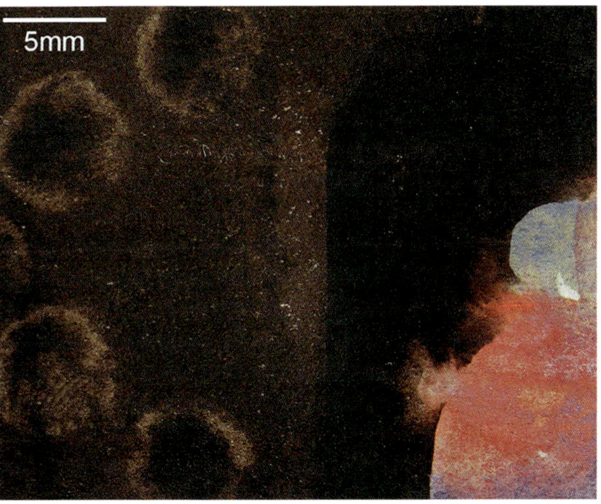

FIG. 180 Photomicrograph of the left side of *Untitled (Composition)* (fig. 179) showing Goff's fingerprints used as a textural element in the background and the settling of colored pigments in the paper texture.

ORIGINS OF PRACTICE

Goff was an apprentice-trained architect who maintained a prolific painting practice throughout his life. Encouraged as a child by his great-grandmother and his high school art teacher, he was also largely self-taught in the fine arts. His paintings, or "compositions" as he called them, are marked by their highly experimental and improvisational feel as well as their aesthetic breadth and technical variety. Despite their heterogeneity, close observation reveals a distinctive quality of mark making and a fusion of compositional elements that are evident from Goff's earliest explorations.

Goff's paintings from the early 1920s, primarily traditional watercolor on artist's paper, already show the artist pushing his medium and exploiting the nature of his chosen materials.[2] In a 1921 composition, the seventeen-year-old Goff painted an abstracted landscape in which gossamer, colored shapes contrast with an intense black-brown background (fig. 179). He worked without a graphite underdrawing, letting translucent watercolor drive a more immediate process.[3] For example, to produce the ombre effect in the willow tree–like forms, Goff applied highly thinned paint alongside drier areas, forming soft boundaries of resolubilized paint.

In addition to playing with the moisture content of his watercolors—applied straight from the tube or diluted—to produce different textures, Goff relied on a combination of chance and intentional manipulations. In some places, the paper support buckled in reaction to the added water, creating depressions where bright colors pooled, and in others the pigment settled unevenly, sinking into the paper texture for a dappled or spotty effect. Goff manipulated the more opaque, dark areas with his fingertips to echo these natural variations, forming small bubble-like circles where his fingerprints are still visible upon close examination (fig. 180). This example reveals Goff's close attention to the organic behavior of paint, which he amplified by using techniques such as excessive dilution and unconventional tools. Throughout the 1920s he continued to hone his skills and gain familiarity with new techniques of applying and working paint while also beginning to move away from representational painting to more seriously explore abstraction.[4]

NEW CITY, NEW AMBITIONS

A few years into the Depression, in 1934, Goff relocated to Chicago and began teaching at a local arts school, the Chicago Academy of Fine Arts. By July of 1935 he was appointed design director of the Vitrolite division of Libbey-Owens-Ford Glass Co., which produced the large colored-glass panels often used in Art Deco architecture.[5] Chicago offered Goff, perhaps for the first time, the opportunity to view modern art at local museums and art galleries and to access art supply and drafting stores with a wider array of materials than was available in Tulsa.

OPPOSITE, FIG. 179 Goff. *Untitled (Composition)*, 1921. Watercolor on cream wove paper; 19.5 × 14.9 cm (7 11/16 × 5 7/8 in.). The Art Institute of Chicago, gift of Shin'enKan, Inc., 1990.574.19.

1. Among the many colleagues and friends who aided my research, I would like to especially thank María Cristina Rivera Ramos, Ken Sutherland, Clara Granzotto, Allison Langley, and Mardy Sears in the department of Conservation and Science, as well as David Jones, Andy Penaluna, Pablo Garcia, Joseph Berlinghieri, Cynthia Schwarz, Eugene Tssui, Jay Clarke, Mary Weaver Chapin, and Britany Salsbury, for their expertise and contributions to this essay.

2. Paint media were characterized by visual assessment, stereomicroscopic examination and, selectively, solubility testing unless otherwise noted. Fourier transform infrared spectroscopic (FTIR) analysis of samples taken from *Glass Blocks and Vitrolite House, Isometric* (fig. 182), *Untitled (Composition)* (fig. 189), and *Untitled (Composition)* (fig. 187) indicated a polysaccharide gum-based binder, based on the presence of diagnostic features in the FTIR spectra including broad bands centered at 3378 and 1078 cm^{-1}, consistent with watercolor medium. FTIR analysis was performed by Ken Sutherland; for instrumental parameters, see Clara Granzotto and Ken Sutherland, "Black, Red and White: Characterization of Painting Materials on a Group of Bwa Masks from Burkina Faso," *Applied Sciences* 13 (2023): 12240.

3. From here onward Goff employed underdrawing selectively, usually when he made ruled lines and specific shapes.

4. Speaking in 1953 about this early moment in his career, Goff said, "I myself felt that when you put some paint on the paper it was beautiful in itself, that it didn't need to tell any story or represent anything." In Philip B. Welch, ed., *Goff on Goff: Conversations and Lectures* (University of Oklahoma Press, 1996), 26.

5. David G. De Long, *Bruce Goff: Toward Absolute Architecture* (Architectural History Foundation; MIT Press, 1988), 55–57.

FIG. 181 Goff. *Untitled (Composition)*, 1936. Opaque watercolor with graphite and collage of foil paper on cream wove paper; 45.8 × 61 cm (18 × 24 in.). The Art Institute of Chicago, gift of Shin'enKan, Inc., 1990.574.243.

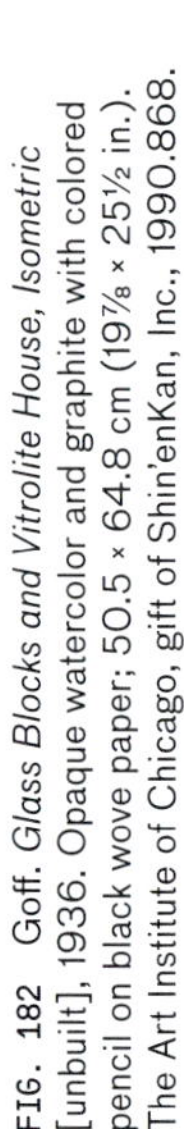

FIG. 182 Goff. *Glass Blocks and Vitrolite House, Isometric* [unbuilt], 1936. Opaque watercolor and graphite with colored pencil on black wove paper; 50.5 × 64.8 cm (19⅞ × 25½ in.). The Art Institute of Chicago, gift of Shin'enKan, Inc., 1990.868.

These new influences and opportunities contributed to a definitive shift in Goff's painted works, which increased in ambition, boldness, complexity, and scale throughout the 1930s.[6]

One 1936 composition illustrates a transitional moment in this development (fig. 181). The work features a stark black triangle that occupies most of the composition, floating on a deep-pink painted background covered with a fine spray of white paint. Visible in the foreground is a series of blue ombre stripes lightly ruled with graphite and then painted by hand, increasing in saturation from almost white to medium blue until being interrupted by an irregular stretch of bare cream paper. To the left of that, Goff drew a stylized torso in soft graphite on an opaque gray-blue field; it floats among sharp geometric angles and bold rivulets of red paint reminiscent of fresh blood. As a final touch, he adhered a rectangle of pink metal foil paper in the lower left quadrant and added his monogram in graphite.

This almost fully abstract work—one of Goff's earliest dated examples of collage—signals an interest in mixed media that he would also bring to his architectural projects. Importantly for this study, the composition includes another design element that would make frequent appearances in his painted works for the rest of his life: sprayed and spattered paint.

6. For more on Goff's time in Chicago, see Timothy Samuelson, "Bruce Goff in Chicago," in *The Architecture of Bruce Goff 1904–1982: Design for a Continuous Present*, ed. Pauline Saliga and Mary Woolever (Prestel; Art Institute of Chicago, 1995), 47–57.

SPRAY AND SPATTER

As Goff embraced opaque paints over translucent watercolors, he looked for new ways to manipulate them. Sprayed and splattered paint were among the techniques he used when trying to experiment with a great variety of effects and textures. In 1930s Chicago he would have had many options for spraying paint. One of the oldest and simplest tools is a mouth atomizer. This small handheld device (composed of two tubes joined at a right angles) channels breath to create a siphon effect on a liquid, drawing it up the tube and spraying outward.[7] Although it is relatively low-tech, the mouth atomizer requires a significant amount of air and excellent breath control, so it is best used in localized applications, as seen in several of Goff's works from this period (such as fig. 127).[8]

Another spraying technique is evident in *Glass Blocks and Vitrolite House, Isometric* (fig. 182), which Goff executed on black wove paper that resembles construction paper. The geometric, Art Deco–style house shows a variety of droplets, including fine and sparse spray and areas where the spray is layered and more thickly applied, resulting in characteristically three-dimensional droplets where they dried and stacked on top of one another. In experiments for this research, airbrushes and atomizers could not replicate this phenomenon or the extremely fine, sparse pattern seen in both works; the paint's drier appearance hinted at an application that required no air at all.

FIG. 183 Photomicrograph of a rectangular shrub on the right in Goff's *Glass Blocks and Vitrolite House, Isometric* (fig. 182) showing the dabbing technique of the top and right faces next to the crachis's layered paint droplets on the left.

In the nineteenth century, artist Henri de Toulouse-Lautrec popularized a method for creating a speckled atmospheric effect in his lithographs called *crachis*, derived from the French word for spit.[9] This technique involves running a stiff brush loaded with lithographic ink across a knife or screen. Outside of printmaking, the term could refer to any method of expelling paint from a stiff brush via contact with another object. Architect Eugene Tssui, who apprenticed with Goff from 1976 to 1982, recalled Goff executing this technique with an old toothbrush and a butter knife.[10] Flicking a stiff-bristle brush against one's finger or a dull knife produces the effects seen in both 1936 works, including the fine, sparse speckle; the dense, stacked droplets; and the perpendicular spray patterns. Moreover, crachis is relatively easy to control and works best when the paint consistency is thicker and drier, a useful quality for Goff's practice of masking and stenciling.

While his untitled 1936 composition features crachis in a single color, Goff's growing skill can be seen in *Vitrolite House*. Goff used this method with multiple colors to render a series of tall rectangular bushes over white paving stones and green grass. He used a blue-green crachis on the left faces of the shrubs and primarily dabbed paint for the other two faces, and by combining these techniques, he achieved remarkable volumetric effects (fig. 183). This work also highlights another emerging trend in Goff's work at this time: a move toward larger colored or otherwise pre-prepared supports, usually paper or paperboard.

It appears that Goff used crachis for this type of paint effect exclusively until 1937, when he made a number of architectural renderings for Vitrolite with an airbrush (such as fig. 78). A common tool for advertising and architectural renderings (it was originally patented in 1876 for retouching photographs), the airbrush was another spraying tool coming into wider use at this time.[11] By the 1920s avant-garde artists such as Man Ray and László Moholy-Nagy were using airbrushes to make paintings.[12] This approach allows for greater control than atomizers, and it can cover larger areas more easily than either atomizers or crachis; however, it is a pneumatic tool that requires training, maintenance, and a larger financial investment. Goff likely first encountered an airbrush

7. Receipts from later in Goff's life indicate that this tool was in his arsenal; however, there is no documentation from this early period. A receipt dated Dec. 21, 1971, from Dick Blick in Tyler, Texas, lists twelve atomizers. Buying in bulk suggests he used this instrument often. See series XV, box 16, folder 9, Bruce A. Goff Archive, Ryerson and Burnham Art and Architecture Archives, The Art Institute of Chicago (hereafter BGA, AIC).

8. The bulb atomizer, which produces a similar effect, was widely available for medical and perfume applications by the 1930s. It is unlikely Goff used this tool; he tended to paint flat on a table, and it is almost impossible to use this instrument pointed straight down. Still, it is interesting to consider given its ubiquity and Goff's tendency to choose materials and tools from his immediate environment.

9. Antony Griffiths, "The Prints of Toulouse-Lautrec," in Wolfgang Wittrock, *Toulouse-Lautrec, the Complete Prints* (P. Wilson for Sotheby's Publications, 1985), 36.

10. Eugene Tssui, interview with the author, Sept. 14, 2024. According to Tssui, Goff claimed he discovered this technique on his own early in life and continued to use it throughout his career.

11. For the history of airbrushes, see Mohamed Abdeldayem Ahmed Soltan, "An Investigation into the History of the Airbrush and the Impact of the Conservation Treatment of Airbrushed Canvas Paintings," unpublished doctoral thesis, University of Northumbria at Newcastle, 2015; and Andrew Penaluma, "A Critical Investigation into the Origins and Development of the Airbrush—1878–1906" (doctoral thesis, University of Wales, 2003).

12. Although Goff was a fan of Man Ray—he saved a copy of the artist's 1926 *Revolving Doors* print series, which is now in the collection of the Ryerson and Burnham Art and Architecture Archives—it is unclear if he would have been aware of Man Ray's early work with airbrush. For more on Man Ray's use of airbrush, see Francis M. Naumann and Gail Stavitsky, *Conversion to Modernism: The Early Work of Man Ray* (Rutgers University Press, 2003), 13–14.

FIG. 184 Goff working on *Joe Price Studio, Presentation Collage, Composition of Various Motifs and Design Elements* (fig. 186), Bartlesville, Oklahoma, 1956. Photographer unknown. Bruce A. Goff Archive.

when he began working for Libbey-Owens-Ford in 1936. The renderings for the 1937 Vitrolite work featured the kinds of reflective surfaces for which airbrushes were favored—providing him with the necessary experience in using and caring for the device and another opportunity to transfer techniques between his architectural and painting practices.[13]

Crachis and spraying techniques—all contactless modes of applying paint to a support—worked well with Goff's frequent use of stencils, which he cut from a variety of materials. Like Man Ray and the Surrealists, whom he admired, Goff also used found objects—bamboo window shades, doilies, safety razors, and toothpicks—as reverse or masking stencils to create unique or complex patterns.[14] The most common and adaptable stenciling material for Goff, however, appears to have been laminated paperboard, commonly used in advertising and in making three-dimensional models.[15]

A photograph taken during the filming of the documentary short *The Artistry of Bruce Goff*, even if somewhat staged, shows him using these boards as masking tools and reverse stencils in his compositions and select architectural renderings (fig. 184).[16] On a low table, Goff uses a fluorescent-green Day-Glo "Nat Mat" laminated

FIG. 185 Detail of *Joe Price Studio* (fig. 186) in specular light. When the work is exposed to this type of direct illumination, the only bright element is the glossy off-white spray paint; the rest of the work appears dark.

OPPOSITE, FIG. 186 Goff. *Joe Price Studio, Presentation Collage, Composition of Various Motifs and Design Elements*, 1956. Opaque watercolor, spray paint, graphite, and colored pencil on Day-Glo green laminated paperboard; 71.1 × 96.3 cm (28 × 37 15/16 in.). The Art Institute of Chicago, gift of Shin'enKan, Inc., 1990.895.24.

13. De Long, *Bruce Goff*, 55–57.

14. For examples of these see Goff's use of doilies (fig. 211), bamboo window shades (fig. 91), and toothpicks arranged in a flower-like pattern in *Untitled (Composition)* (fig. 187).

15. Laminated paperboard, later known as showcard, is composed of layers of brown paper topped with a lighter, higher-quality colored facing paper. Visual identification of this support board and its connection to showcard by Senior Conservation Technician Mardy Sears. Showcards were (and are) available in a wide range of standard sizes, including 28 by 44 inches, a size Goff frequently used. A 1977 receipt from Moody Marshall in Dallas, Texas, showing an order for nine "silver/gold backgrounds" likely refers to boards like this. See series XV, box 16, folder 9, BGA, AIC.

16. *The Artistry of Bruce Goff*, directed by Joe D. Price (Thorne Films, Inc., 1965), 14 min.

FIG. 187 Goff. *Untitled (Composition)*, c. 1955. Opaque watercolor and colored pencil on silver-toned laminated paperboard; 111.5 × 71.2 cm ($43\frac{15}{16}$ × $28\frac{1}{16}$ in.). The Art Institute of Chicago, gift of Mary Greene, 2022.1584.

paperboard as his painting support, held in place by thumbtacks. On a hexagonal side table to his left are a cache of brushes and a few small bowls of paint and water. While working on this architectural rendering for his client Joe Price's home addition, Goff covered the floor with newspapers—evidence of a messy paint application—and we can see a triangular paperboard masking stencil in the top left, which he used to create the black triangular form near the center. Looking at the finished work, *Joe Price Studio, Presentation Collage, Composition of Various Motifs and Design Elements* (figs. 185–86), it is clear that Goff used different methods to apply the black and off-white paints. The black has a more matte appearance typical of watercolors applied by airbrush, whereas the off-white demonstrates a sheen and spray pattern more often associated with aerosol spray paint (fig. 185).[17]

Aerosol spray paint, initially an aluminum-based radiator paint, was developed in the Chicago suburb of Sycamore in 1949 and soon became available in an array of colors.[18] Just seven years later, Goff began using spray paint in his works, pursuing his interest in new materials and experimentation. In some works, Goff used spray paint primarily to add a specific color or finish, as seen in the gold tone of a 1962 composition (fig. 190).[19] In others, like an atmospheric black-and-white untitled composition (fig. 91), he sprayed a fine mist of aerosol paint over unconventional masking stencils—in this case, bamboo window shades—to create a dynamic pattern in several areas of the composition.[20]

FIG. 188 Detail of *Untitled (Composition)* (fig. 187) showing the dandelion-like form created with an arrangement of toothpicks used as a reverse-stencil.

UNCONVENTIONAL TOOLS: AIR, WATER, AND AQUARIUM PAINT

By the mid-1950s Goff began experimenting with new techniques made possible by using larger supports, namely pouring and *soufflage*, or the blowing of paint, often associated with Surrealist artists.[21] As the size of his supports increased, Goff could pour large batches of paint directly onto the surface rather than apply it incrementally by brush. He took this technique to the extreme in a silver-toned composition (fig. 187), pouring white paint over the surface and then manipulating it with an exaggerated version of soufflage. Around the resulting field—a dramatic pattern of pale rivulets fanning out from a central point—Goff created a series of stenciled shapes resembling dandelion seedheads (fig. 188) using an unusual found tool: toothpicks, arranged like a pinwheel.

Goff often poured paint and tilted his support to create unregulated flows, but he also used different techniques to control the motion of the paint. For example, to create a striking composition in red, white, blue, and black (fig. 189), he controlled the flow, perhaps by brush-applying beads of water that led away from the poured paint, guiding the media along the path of least resistance. These dynamic gray and black drips lead away from rounded white shapes Goff created with soufflage—pouring a paint diluted with a surface tension-breaking agent, such as a liquid soap or alcohol, he then used air, potentially from an empty airbrush, to expand the paint into ovals. The eye-searing red is the fluorescent color of Day-Glo paperboard, which Goff began painting on in the mid-1950s. Developed during World War II and later trademarked as Day-Glo, daylight fluorescent pigments followed the invention of UV-fluorescing pigments in the 1930s.[22] Like his early adoption of spray paint, Goff began using Day-Glo papers and paperboards within a year of their launch, another testament to his enthusiasm for material innovations.

17. Analysis of a sample of the off-white spray paint using FTIR and pyrolysis gas chromatography mass spectrometry with thermally assisted hydrolysis and methylation (THM-Py-GCMS) indicated an alkyd binder, based on characteristic features in the FTIR spectra, and from the detection of dimethyl ortho-phthalate and methylated derivatives of pentaerythritol and fatty acids (including palmitic, stearic, and azelaic acids) by THM-Py-GCMS. Analyses were performed by Ken Sutherland; for instrumental parameters see Granzotto and Sutherland, "Black, Red and White." For more information on the chemical characterization of binders found in aerosol spray paints, see Giulia Germinario, Inez Dorothé van der Werf, and Luigia Sabbatini, "Chemical Characterisation of Spray Paints by a Multi-Analytical (Py/GC-MS, FTIR, μ-Raman) Approach," *Microchemical Journal* 124 (2016): 929–39.

18. Hillary Greenbaum and Dana Rubinstein, "The Origin of Spray Paint," *New York Times Magazine*, Nov. 4, 2011, nytimes.com/2011/11/06/magazine/who-made-spray-paint.html.

19. FTIR analysis of a sample of the gold-tone spray paint indicated a cellulose nitrate binder, based on the presence of characteristic features in the FTIR spectra including prominent bands at 1651 and 1278 cm^{-1}.

20. FTIR and Py-GCMS analysis of a sample of the black paint indicated a styrene-based binder, based on characteristic features in the FTIR spectra, and from the detection of series of styrene monomers, dimers and trimers by Py-GCMS. Visual assessment of the white paint suggested that it is also spray paint.

21. Mary Broadway and Katrina Rush, "Taxonomy of Techniques," in *Remedios Varo: Science Fictions*, ed. Caitlin Haskell and Tere Arcq (Art Institute of Chicago, 2023), 36.

22. Day-Glo pigments have some properties in visible light that help identify them, but UV-fluorescing pigments are only visible as such under ultraviolet illumination. Margaret Holben Ellis, Christopher W. McGlinchey, and Esther Chao, "Daylight Fluorescent Colors as Artistic

FIG. 189 Goff. *Untitled (Composition)*, 1956. Opaque watercolor, ink, crayon, and colored pencil, with metal foil pressure-sensitive stickers, on Day-Glo red laminated paperboard; 71.1 × 111.8 cm (28 × 44 in.). The Art Institute of Chicago, gift of Bob and Sherry Faust, 2022.241.

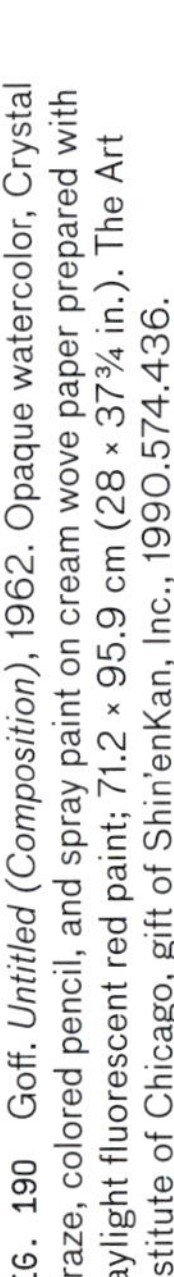

FIG. 190 Goff. *Untitled (Composition)*, 1962. Opaque watercolor, Crystal Craze, colored pencil, and spray paint on cream wove paper prepared with daylight fluorescent red paint; 71.2 × 95.9 cm (28 × 37¾ in.). The Art Institute of Chicago, gift of Shin'enKan, Inc., 1990.574.436.

Beyond all this, Goff frequently tried new materials not available in traditional art supply stores. One example is Crystal Craze, a solvent-borne resin available in various tints that dries in crystalline patterns and was intended for decorating glass aquariums.[23] First popular in the 1950s, Crystal Craze especially interested Goff because it could be applied to a work without disturbing previously applied watercolor paint. In fact, he created one composition (fig. 190) by repurposing an existing painting that he had finished and photographed sometime before (fig. 191).[24] Goff then proceeded to pour various thicknesses and tints of Crystal Craze over the original composition, achieving a wide variety of surface effects, including dramatic, radiating crystalline shapes as well as finer textures that resemble frost (fig. 192).[25] Clearly this resin material's inherent straight-edged geometry provided an intriguing contrast to the amorphous fluidity of his pouring techniques.

FINAL MOVEMENT

Bruce Goff developed a diverse array of paint handling techniques mostly from the early 1930s to the mid-1960s. Yet, remarkably, he continued to accumulate new materials and methods in his painting practice—such as lenticular plastic and liquid watercolors—until the end of his life.[26] As he traveled throughout the late 1970s and early 1980s giving lectures, one of Goff's favorite pastimes was visiting local art and hobby stores in search

Media," in *The Broad Spectrum: Studies in the Materials, Techniques, and Conservation of Color on Paper*, ed. Harriet K. Stratis and Britt Salvesen (Archetype, 2002).

23. Both Goff's former assistant Eugene Tssui and patron Tom Hart recalled his use of Crystal Craze. Tssui, interview; and Tom Hart, in conversation with curator Craig Lee, San Diego, Jan. 19, 2024. Also known as Cryst-L Craze, this product was originally manufactured by Plastics Fry Company in Los Angeles as early as 1951. See advertisement in *The Aquarium Magazine*, June 1951, in the collection of the Museum of Aquarium and Pet History.

24. There is limited documentation that attests to the prevalence of this practice; his former assistant Eugene Tssui recalled that Goff, toward the end of his career, sometimes reworked older compositions. Tssui, interview.

25. FTIR analysis of a sample of the resinous material indicated that it has a poly(ethylene/vinyl acetate) base, from the presence of characteristic bands in the spectra including those at 1738, 1464, 1372 and 1242 cm^{-1}. Once dry, Crystal Craze does not resolubilize when more is applied; this property allowed Goff to create islands of thicker and thinner resin patterns. The formation of crystalline patterns has been ascribed to the resin's inclusion of camphor, which has a characteristic odor of moth balls. For additional working properties, see Wallace Barry Turner, "The Chaplain's Media Manual" (PhD project, Claremont School of Theology, 1978), 23.

26. For his use of lenticular plastic, see figs. 228A–C. See also Goff's 1974 letter to Lewis Art Supply requesting two sets of Dr. Martin's Radiant Liquid Watercolor and a painted color chart, series I, box 13, folder 26, BGA, AIC.

FIG. 191 Goff's *Untitled (Composition)* (fig. 190), photographed before he applied Crystal Craze. This image suggests Goff inverted the orientation of the final work. Bruce A. Goff Archive.

of new media, which he would bring back to his studio in Tyler, Texas.[27] Like the unconventional materials he embraced in his architecture, each new medium offered a source of inspiration and new possibilities in his painted works, from Day-Glo paperboards and found-object stencils to Crystal Craze aquarium paint. Goff's compositions reflect a creative process unbounded by gravity and physics, constrained only by his imagination and chosen supports. His efforts to build layers and textures resulted in works that speak in contrasts: masking and revealing, playful and precise, hard and soft. Goff's expansive approach attests to his belief that "in any kind of art . . . everything does count, even the silence and the voids or the resultant forms and spaces. Everything is important; there is no background."[28]

FIG. 192 Detail of *Untitled (Composition)* (fig. 190) in specular light showing the varied scale of patterns achievable with Crystal Craze, including an area more thickly applied at the upper right.

27. According to Eugene Tssui, Goff often frequented art stores, record stores, and bookstores while traveling. Tssui, interview.
28. Bruce Goff, Feb. 7, 1954, quoted in Welch, *Goff on Goff*, 281.

FIG. 193 Elaine A. and William C. III Gryder House, Ocean Springs, Mississippi, 2018. Photograph by Elena Dorfman. Elena Dorfman/Redux © Elena Dorfman 2018.

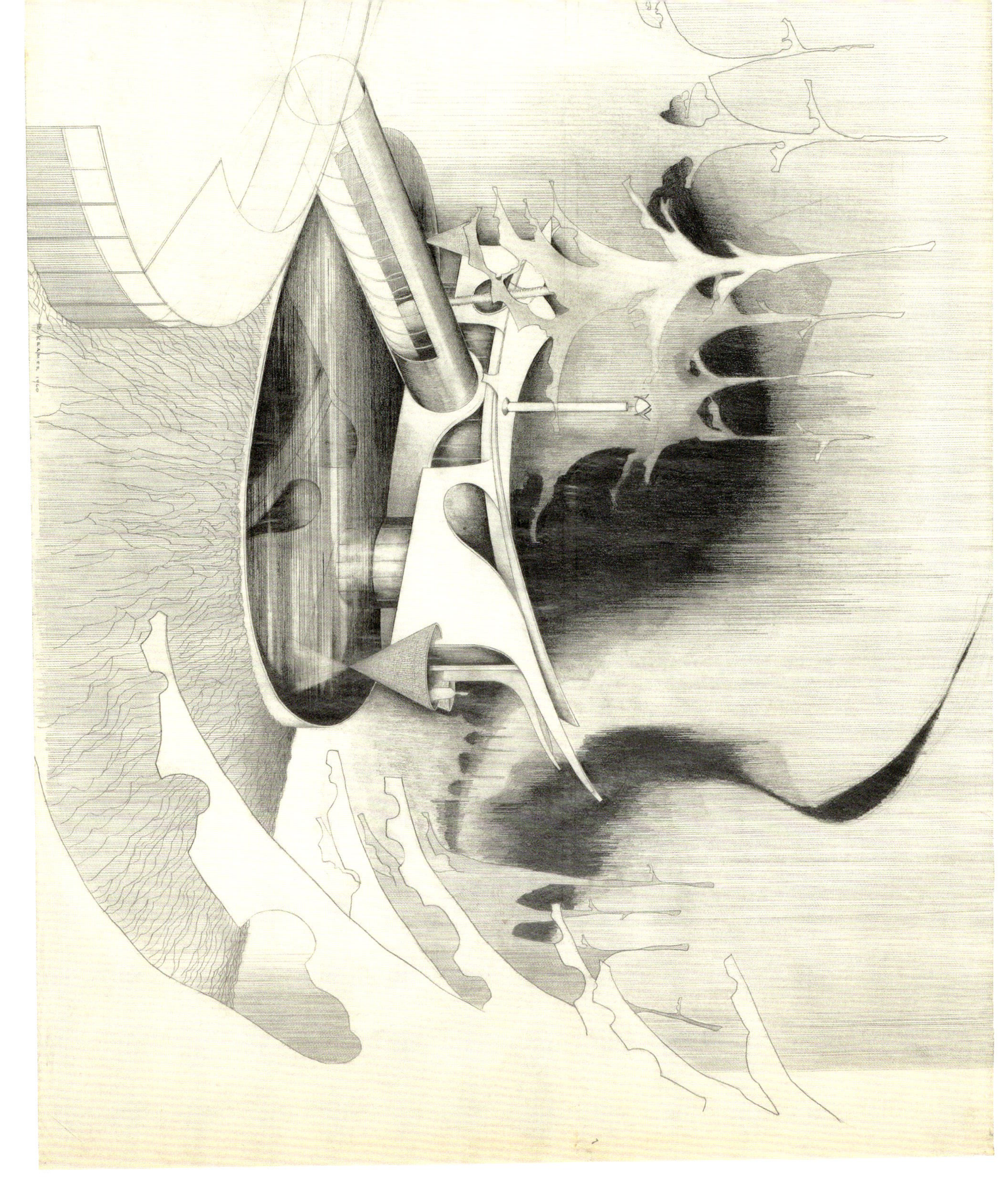

FIG. 194 Goff and Robert Kramer (American, born 1941). *Elaine A. and William C. III Gryder House, Ocean Springs, Mississippi, Perspective*, 1960. Graphite on tracing paper; 62.5 × 106.8 cm (24⁹⁄₁₆ × 42¹⁄₁₆ in.). The Art Institute of Chicago, gift of Shin'enKan, Inc., 1990.861.1.

FIG. 195 Goff. *Untitled (Composition)*, 1939. Opaque watercolor on blue wove paper; 99.4 × 73.7 cm (35 × 24⅛ in.). The Art Institute of Chicago, gift of Shin'enKan, Inc., 1990.574.348.

FROM TOP, FIG. 196 Cover of *Friends of Kebyar* 34.1, no. 88 (2019).
FIG. 197 Goff. *Charlotte and Emil Gutman House, Gulfport, Mississippi, Perspective*, c. 1958. Colored pencils on black wove paper; 78.8 × 54 cm (31 × 21¼ in.). The Art Institute of Chicago, gift of Shin'enKan, Inc., 1990.574.273.

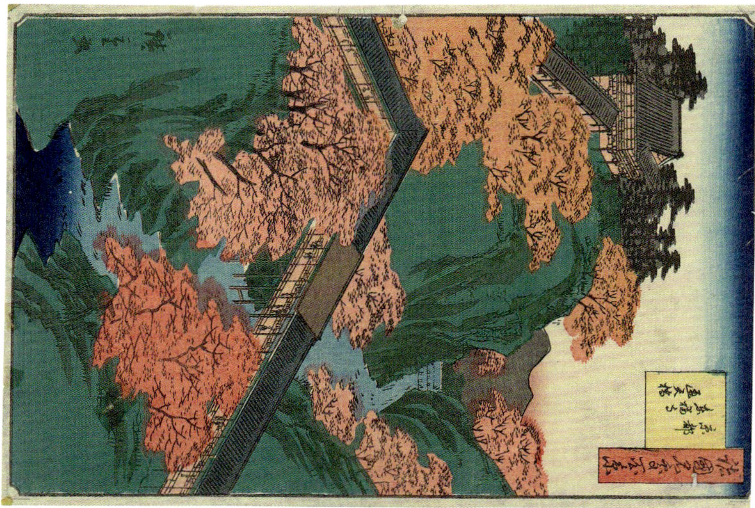

FROM LEFT, FIG. 198 Utagawa Hiroshige II (Shigenobu) (Japanese, 1826–1869). *Tsuten-kyo Bridge, Tofuku Temple, Kyoto* (*Kyoto Tofukuji Tsutenkyo bashi*), 1859. Color woodblock print; 35 × 24.2 cm (13¾ × 9½ in.). The Art Institute of Chicago, Bruce Goff Archive, gift of Shin'enKan, Inc., 1990.607.53. FIG. 199 Kawase Hasui (Japanese, 1883–1957). *Yuhi Waterfall at Shiobara* (*Shiobara Yuhi no taki*), 1920. Color woodblock print; 38.1 × 26.7 cm (15 × 10½ in.). The Art Institute of Chicago, Bruce Goff Archive, gift of Shin'enKan, Inc., 1990.607.772.

FIG. 200 Chiura Obata (American, born Japan, 1885–1975). *Silence, Last Twilight on an Unknown Lake, Johnson Peak*, 1930. Graphite and white colored pencil over watercolor monotype on cream Japanese paper; 28 × 39.4 cm (11 × 15½ in.). The Art Institute of Chicago, Bruce Goff Archive, gift of Shin'enKan, Inc., 1990.607.220.

FROM TOP, FIG. 201 Inagaki Toshijiro (Nenjiro) (Japanese, 1902–1963). *Red Fuji*, 1967. Color woodblock print; 30.5 × 44.5 cm (12 × 17½ in.). The Art Institute of Chicago, Bruce Goff Archive, gift of Shin'enKan, Inc., 1990.607.203. **FIG. 202** Kaoru Kawano (Japanese, 1916–1965). *Winter Mansion*, n.d. Color woodblock print; 28.6 × 42.6 cm (11¼ × 16¾ in.). The Art Institute of Chicago, Bruce Goff Archive, gift of Shin'enKan, Inc., 1990.607.237.

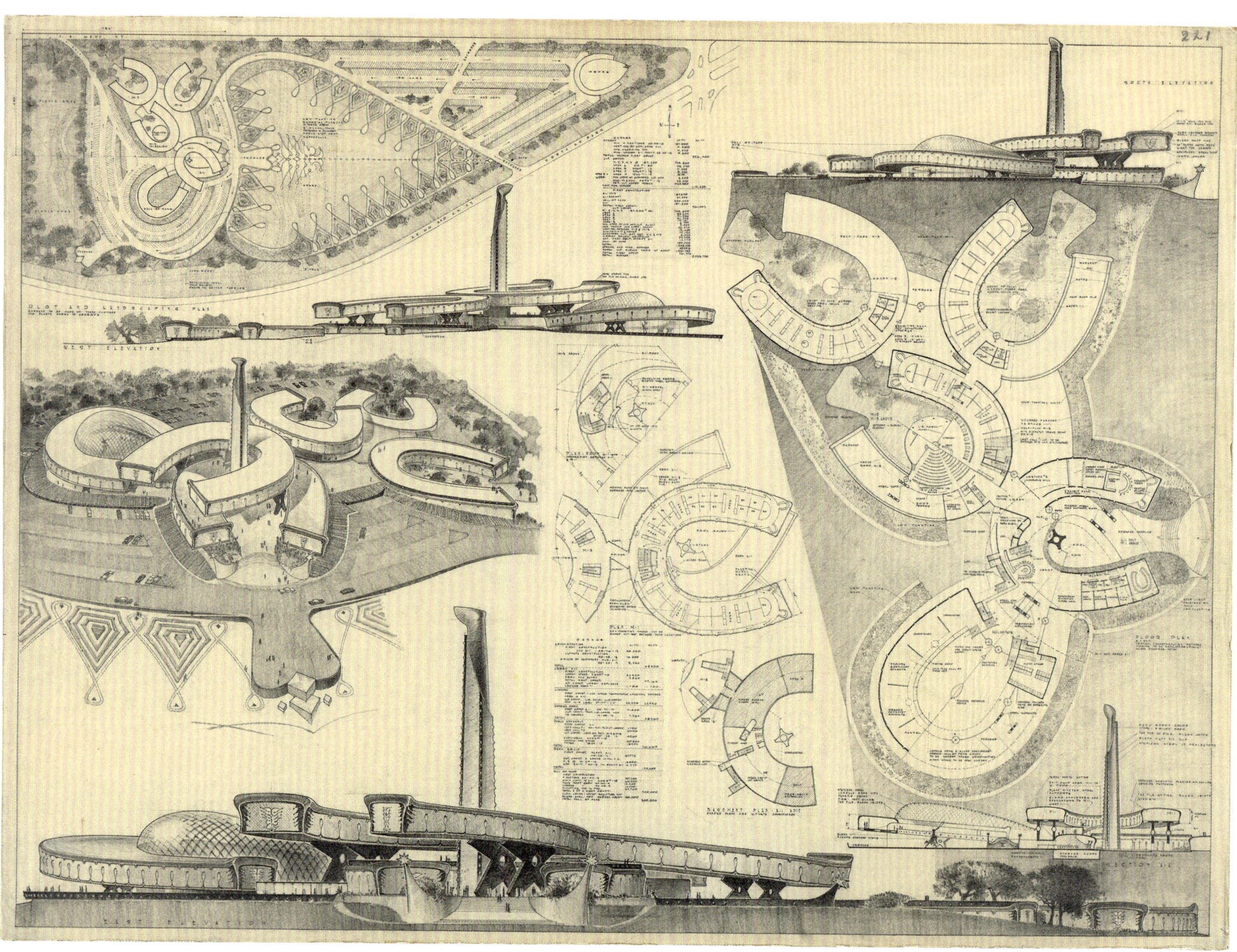

FIG. 203 Goff. *Cowboy Hall of Fame Competition, Oklahoma City* [unbuilt], 1956. Graphite on tracing paper; 76.5 × 101.7 cm (30⅛ × 40 1/16 in.). The Art Institute of Chicago, gift of Shin'enKan, Inc., 1990.823.1.

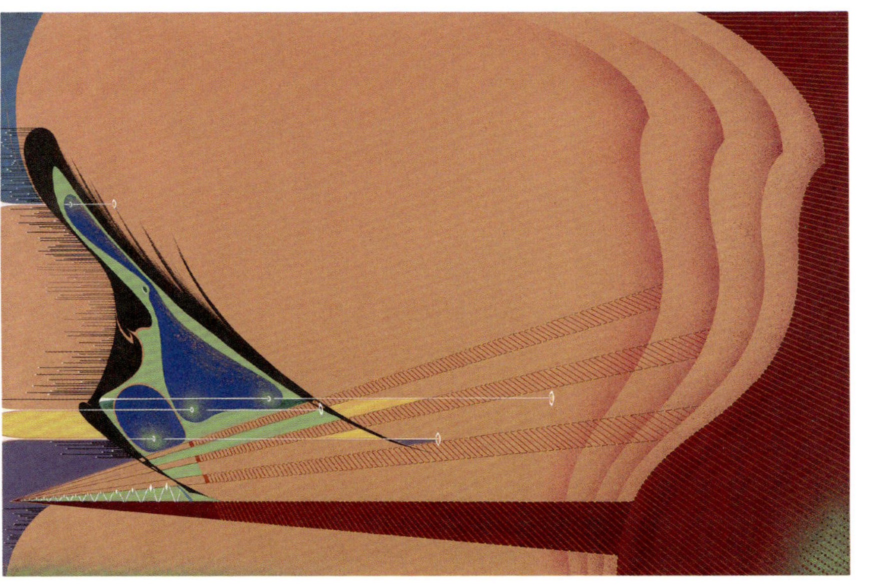

FROM TOP, FIG. 204 Goff. *Untitled (Composition)*, c. 1944. Opaque watercolor on red-orange wove paper; 91.5 × 61.3 cm (36 × 24⅛ in.). The Art Institute of Chicago, gift of Shin'enKan, Inc., 1990.574.391.
FIG. 205 Goff, Harris, and Richard Britz (American, 1941–2023). *Ski Lodge, Crested Butte, Colorado, Perspective*, 1965. Colored pencil and pastel, with ink, on tracing paper; 91 × 61 cm (35⅞ × 24¹⁄₁₆ in.). The Art Institute of Chicago, gift of Shin'enKan, Inc., 1990.1161.1.

FROM TOP, FIG. 206 Goff and Harris. *Phi Kappa Tau Fraternity House, Lawrence, Kansas, Perspective* [unbuilt], 1965. Diazo print on cream wove paper; 61 × 92 cm (24 1/16 × 36 1/4 in.). The Art Institute of Chicago, gift of Shin'enKan, Inc., 1990.1166.10. **FIG. 207** Goff. *Celestine Barby House, Tucson, Arizona, Design for Stenciled Beams*, 1974. Colored pencil and graphite on tracing paper; 18.2 × 70.8 cm (7 3/16 × 27 7/8 in.). The Art Institute of Chicago, gift of Shin'enKan, Inc., 1990.1239.30.

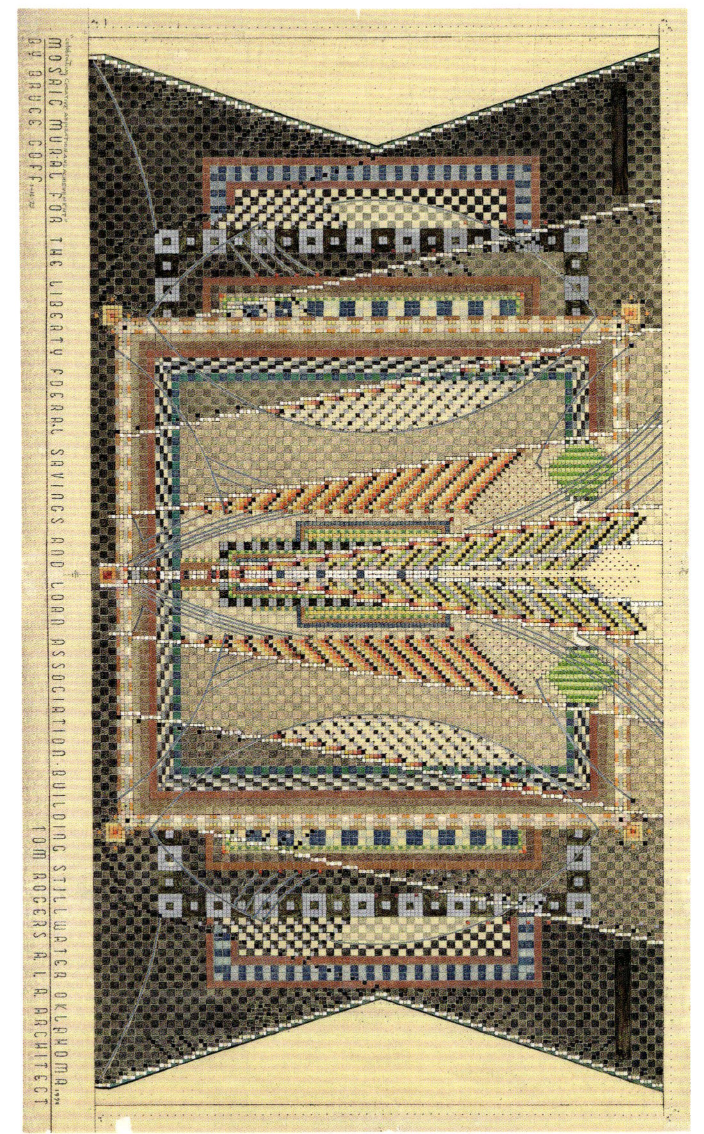

FIG. 208 Goff. *Mosaic Mural for Liberty Federal Savings and Loan Association, Stillwater, Oklahoma*, 1975. Graphite, colored pencil, and opaque and translucent watercolor over diazo print on tracing paper; 52.8 × 88.8 cm (20¹³⁄₁₆ × 35 in.). The Art Institute of Chicago, gift of Shin'enKan, Inc., 1990.870.2.

FIG. 209 Goff. *Untitled (Composition)*, n.d. Opaque watercolor on cream wove paper prepared with daylight fluorescent yellow ground; 111.8 × 69.9 cm (44 × 27½ in.). The Art Institute of Chicago, gift of Shin'enKan, Inc., 1990.574.352.

FROM TOP, FIG. 210 Goff. *Untitled (Composition)*, 1954. Opaque watercolor and graphite, with traces of colored pencil, on cream wove paper prepared with daylight fluorescent green ground; 109.9 × 71.2 cm (43¼ × 28 in.). The Art Institute of Chicago, gift of Shin'enKan, Inc., 1990.574.351. **FIG. 211** Goff. *Untitled (Composition)*, n.d. Spray paint, opaque watercolor, colored pencil, and charcoal on cream wove paper prepared with daylight fluorescent orange ground; 112 × 71.2 cm (44⅛ × 28$\frac{1}{16}$ in.). The Art Institute of Chicago, gift of Shin'enKan, Inc., 1990.574.357.

FROM TOP, FIG. 212 Glen and Luetta Harder House, Mountain Lake, Minnesota, 1980. Photograph by Julius Shulman. Julius Shulman photography archive. © J. Paul Getty Trust. Getty Research Institute, Los Angeles (2004.R.10). FIG. 213 Goff. *Untitled (Composition)*, 1952. Colored pencil, graphite, and opaque and translucent watercolor on cream wove paper prepared with daylight fluorescent peach ground; 70.2 × 109.3 cm ($27\frac{11}{16}$ × $43\frac{1}{16}$ in.). The Art Institute of Chicago, gift of Shin'enKan, Inc., 1990.574.385.

FIG. 214 Goff and Bart Prince (American, born 1947). *Glen and Luetta Harder House, Mountain Lake, Minnesota, Perspective*, 1970. Graphite on tracing paper; 45.6 × 61 cm (18 × 24 1/16 in.). The Art Institute of Chicago, gift of Shin'enKan, Inc., 1990.893.8.

FROM LEFT, FIG. 215 William Edward David Ryan (English, born 1936). Octons toy, designed 1973. Bruce A. Goff Archive. FIG. 216 Goff. Decorated architectural drawing tube, n.d. Bruce A. Goff Archive.

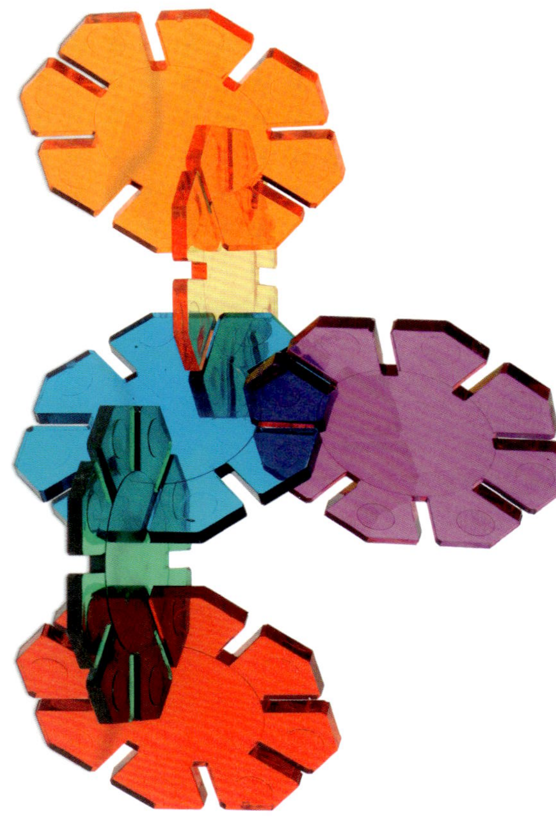

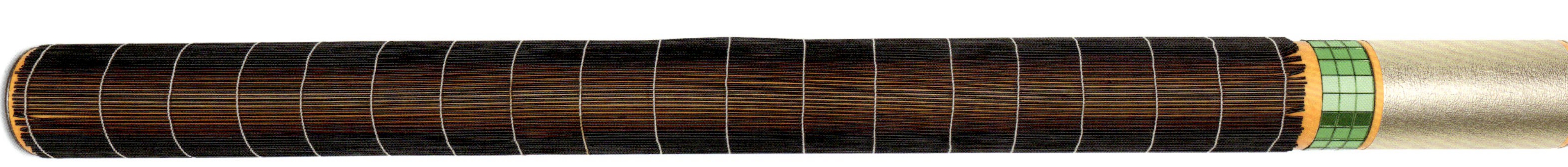

FROM TOP, FIG. 217 Disco ball ornament, n.d. Bruce A. Goff Archive.
FIG. 218 Adhesive mirror sampler, n.d. Bruce A. Goff Archive.

STUDIO FOR JOE PRICE

FIG. 219 Goff and James Parent (American, 1927–2008). *Joe Price Studio, First Design, Bartlesville, Oklahoma, Interior Perspective* [unbuilt], 1953. Graphite and colored pencil on tracing paper; 62 × 88.6 cm (24 7/16 × 34 15/16 in.). The Art Institute of Chicago, gift of Shin'enKan, Inc., 1990.859.2.

CLOCKWISE, FROM TOP LEFT, FIG. 220 Thai *hamsa* sculpture, late 18th century, installed in the garden of the Etsuko and Joe Price House, Bartlesville, Oklahoma. 20c Design, Dallas. FIG. 221 Goff. *Joe Price Studio, Bartlesville, Oklahoma Plan*, 1956. Opaque watercolor, colored pencil, crayon, and graphite with collage of cut, colored, and painted papers on Day-Glo green laminated paperboard; 96.3 × 71.1 cm (37 15/16 × 28 in.). The Art Institute of Chicago, gift of Shin'enKan, Inc., 1990.895.23. FIG. 222 Living room of Etsuko and Joe Price House, Bartlesville, Oklahoma, 1972. Photograph by Horst P. Horst. *Vogue*, Feb. 1, 1972. FIG. 223 Etsuko and Joe Price House, Bartlesville, Oklahoma, c. 1976. Photograph by Joe Price. Bruce A. Goff Archive.

FIG. 224 Goff. *Two-Panel Screen*, 1970. Two-panel Japanese screen; opaque watercolor and Crystal Craze on gold-tone paper; 152.4 × 190.5 × 2.6 cm (60 × 75 × 1 in.). Shin'enKan Inc.

FIG. 225 Goff. *Gate for Etsuko and Joe Price House, Bartlesville, Oklahoma*, 1976. Cast and welded metal; 235.6 × 84.5 × 4.5 cm (92¾ × 33¼ × 1¾ in.). 20c Design, Dallas.

FROM TOP, FIG. 226 Interior of Etsuko and Joe Price House, Bartlesville, Oklahoma, 1990. Photograph by Alan Barley. Bruce A. Goff Archive. **FIG. 227** Goff. Manufactured by Bluestem Foundry (American, 1951–1985). *Table and Stools for Etsuko and Joe Price House, Bartlesville, Oklahoma*, 1956. Cast aluminum, paint, glass, textile, and synthetic cushion; artist's proof; table: 69.9 × 190.5 cm (27½ × 75 in.); stools, each: 47 × 61 cm (18½ × 24 in.). Private collection, Chicago.

FIGS. 228A–C Goff. Three panels from *Ode to an Imaginary Ballet*, 1970–75. Lenticular, sandwich of clear textured plastic with applied paint, wavy metal sheet, and opaque plastic sheet; each: 141 × 61.6 × 2.6 cm (55½ × 24¼ × 1 in.). Private collection.

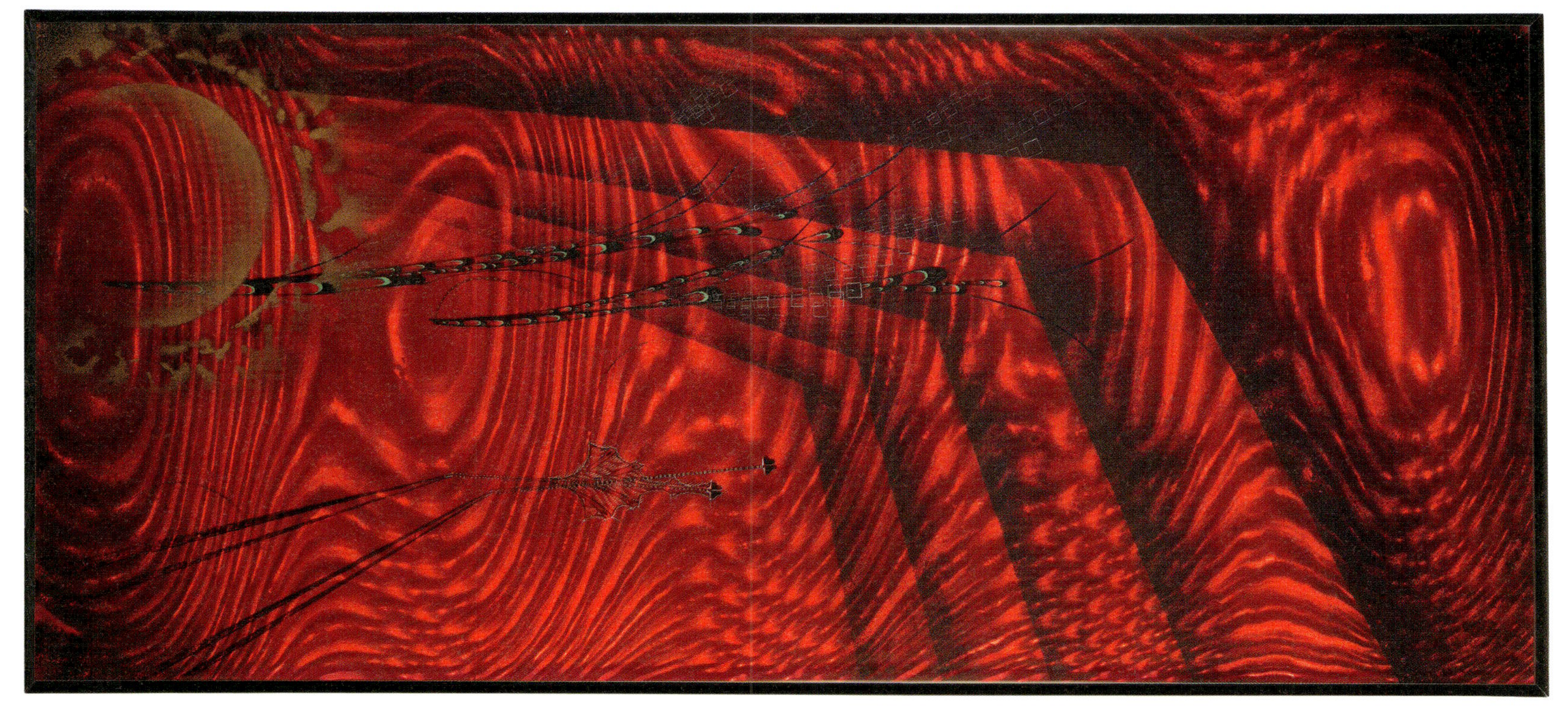

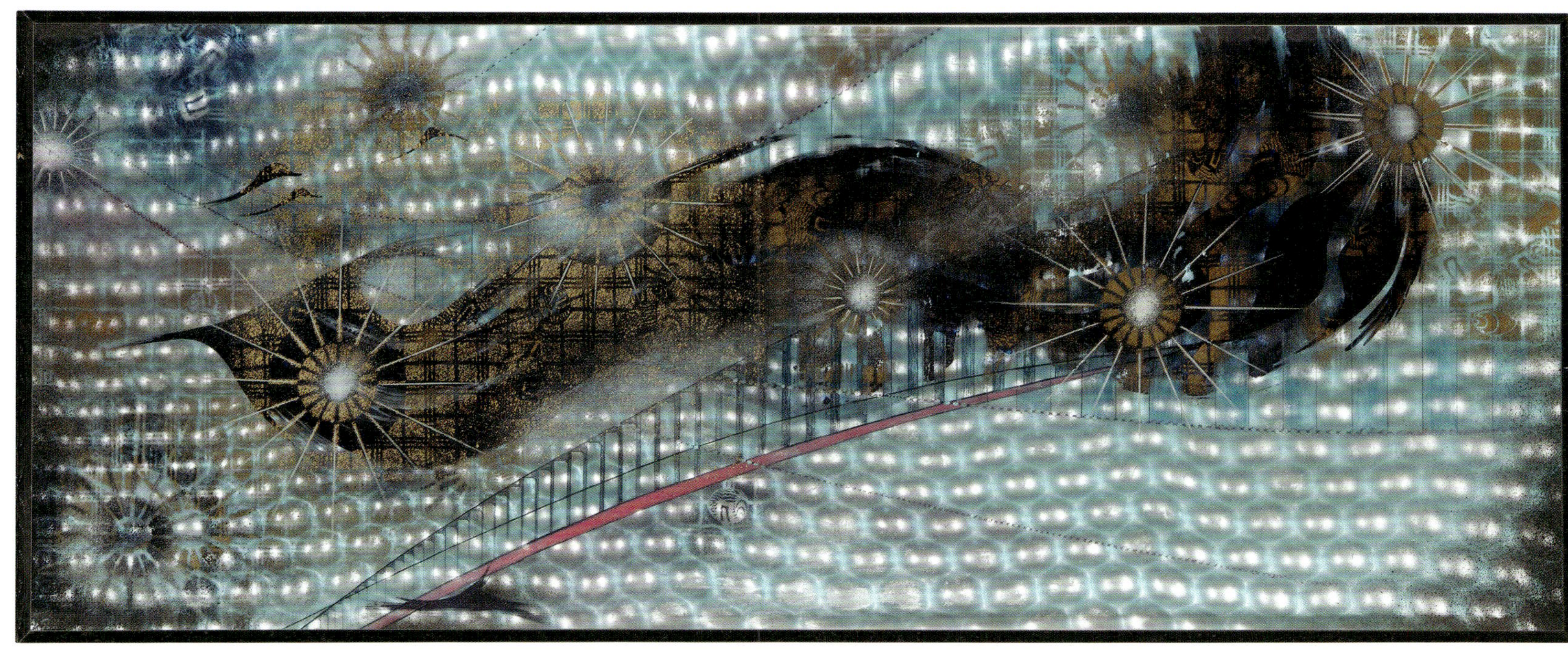

FROM TOP, FIG. 229 Sooner Park Playtower, Bartlesville, Oklahoma, 1965. Photograph by Robert Alan Bowlby. Robert Alan Bowlby architectural slides, WHC M2886, American School Archive, Special Research Collections, University of Oklahoma Libraries, Norman, Oklahoma. **FIG. 230** Goff. *Caddo Inn, Lake Village, Flint, Texas, West Elevation* [unbuilt], 1973. Colored pencil and graphite on cream wove paper; 66.2 × 93 cm (26⅛ × 36⅝ in.). The Art Institute of Chicago, gift of Shin'enKan, Inc., 1990.880.18.

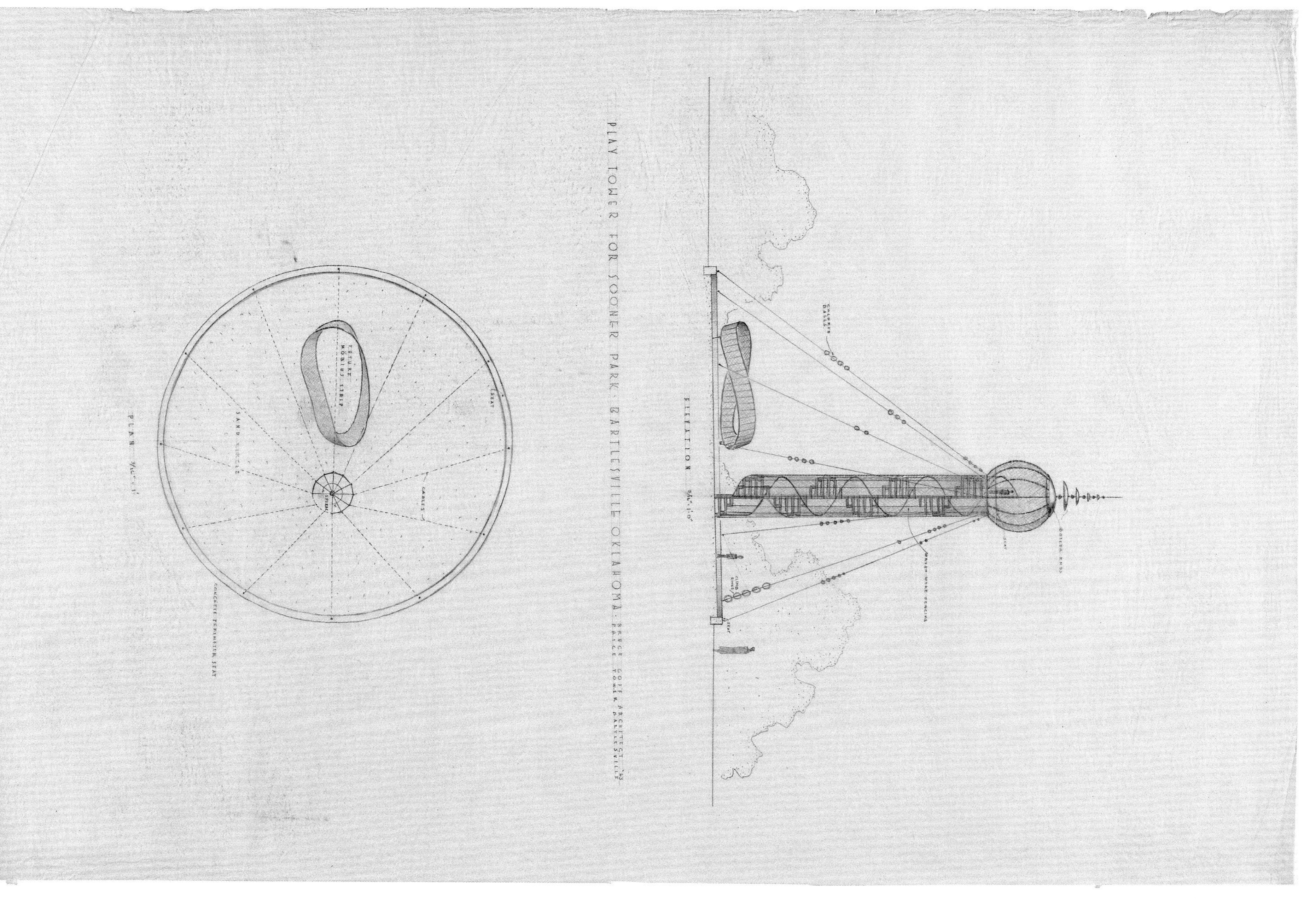

FIG. 231 Goff. *Playtower for Sooner Park, Bartlesville, Oklahoma, Elevation and Plan*, 1963. Graphite on tracing paper; 91.5 × 61 cm (36 1/16 × 24 1/16 in.). The Art Institute of Chicago, gift of Shin'enKan, Inc., 1990.1149.1.

FROM TOP, FIG. 232 Goff. *Untitled (Composition)*, 1970. Opaque watercolor, Crystal Craze, and colored pencil on yellow laminated paperboard in artist's frame; 81.3 × 122 cm (32 × 48 in.). Promised gift of Tom Hart and Chikako Terada-Hart. FIG. 233 Asian lion sculpture, n.d. Private collection.

CLOWISE, FROM TOP LEFT, FIG. 234 Japanese wind chime, n.d. Bruce A. Goff Archive. FIG. 235 Japanese glass and gilt vase, n.d. Bruce A. Goff Archive. FIG. 236 Asian textile with birds and animals, n.d. Private collection.

FIG. 237 Goff and Prince. *Pavilion for Japanese Art, Los Angeles County Museum of Art, Elevation*, 1980. Colored pencil on blueline print; 61 × 91.5 cm (24 × 36 in.). Collection of Bart Prince.

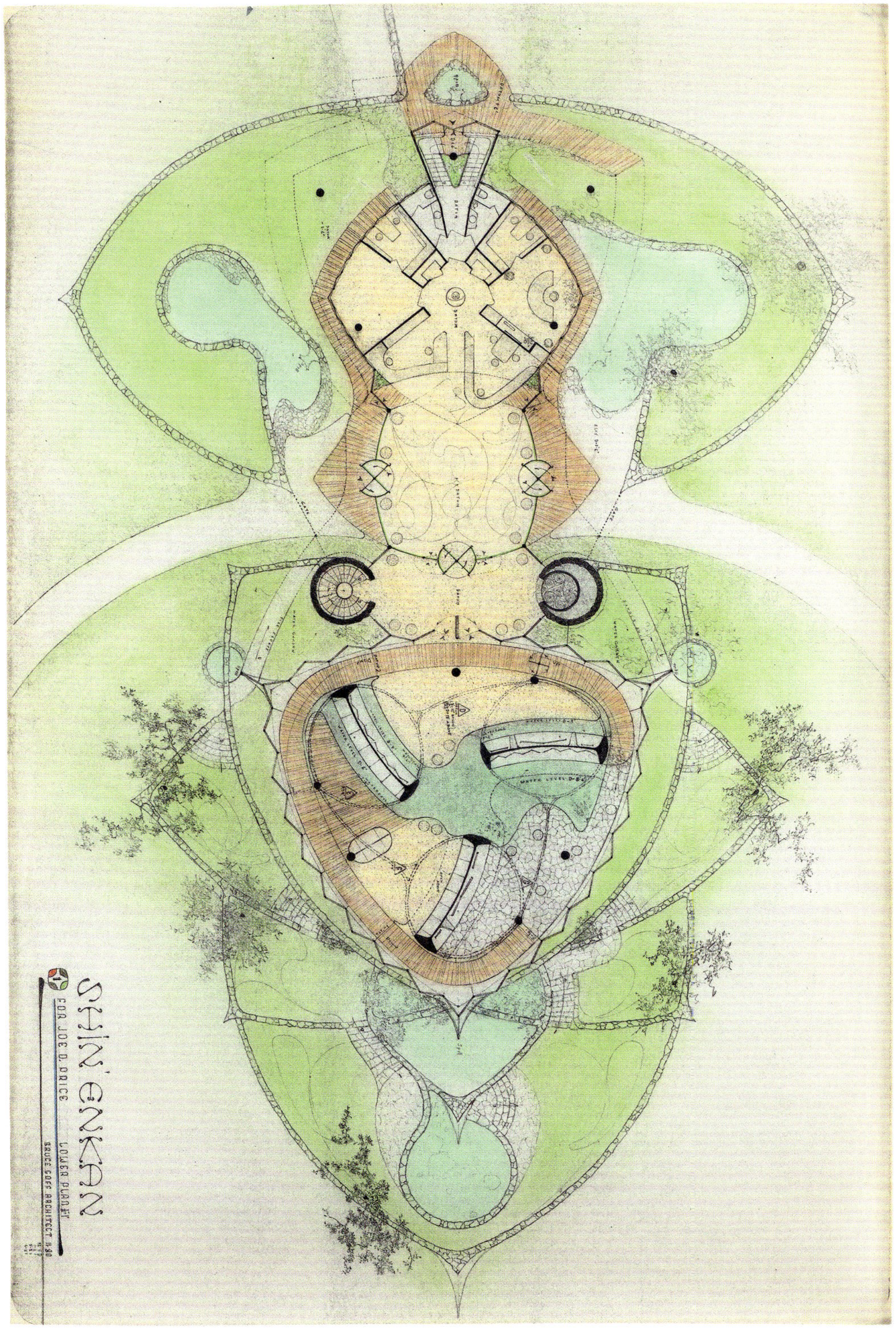

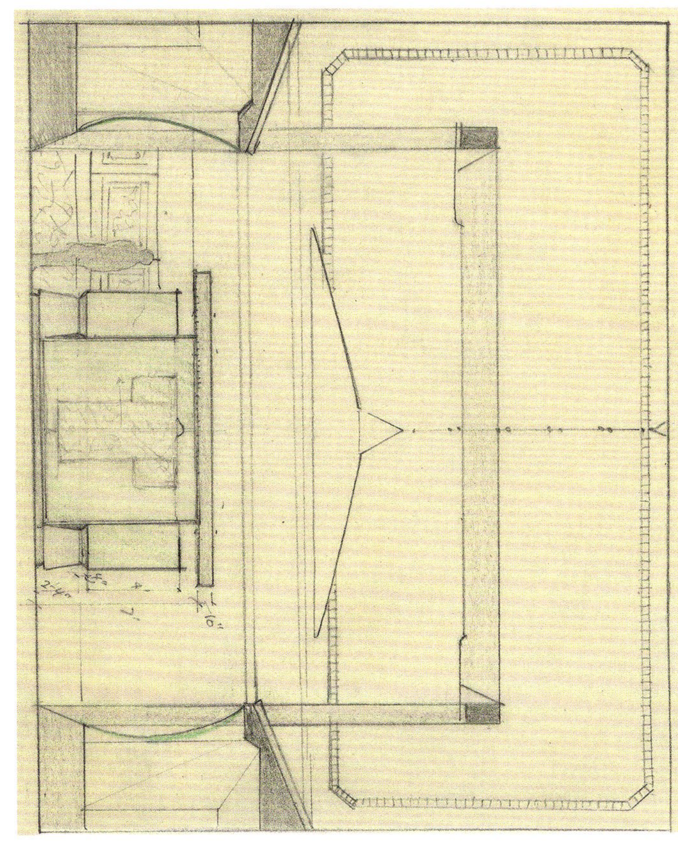

FROM TOP, FIG. 238 Goff. *Japanese Galleries for the Metropolitan Museum of Art, New York, Elevation* [unbuilt], c. 1977. Graphite, with colored pencil, on tracing paper; 16.6 × 17.8 cm (6½ × 7 in.). The Art Institute of Chicago, gift of Shin'enKan, Inc., RX18410/76.06.39. **FIG. 239** Goff and Prince. *Pavilion for Japanese Art, Los Angeles County Museum of Art, Lower Level Plan*, 1980. Colored pencil on blueline print; 61 × 91.5 cm (24 × 36 in.). Collection of Bart Prince.

FIG. 240 Goff and Prince. *Model for Pavilion for Japanese Art, Los Angeles County Museum of Art*, 1982–83. Mat board, Foamcore, Masonite, acrylic, plastic, wire, stone, and dried foliage; 208.3 × 196.2 cm (82$\frac{1}{16}$ × 77¼ in.). Los Angeles County Museum of Art.

FROM TOP, FIG. 241 Chris Hopkins (American, born 1953). *Pavilion for Japanese Art, Los Angeles County Museum of Art, Perspective Rendering*, c. 1980–84. Acrylic and gold leaf on illustration board; 42 × 68.6 cm (16½ × 27 in.). Los Angeles County Museum of Art.
FIG. 242 Pavilion for Japanese Art, Los Angeles County Museum of Art, 1988. Photograph by Wayne Thom. Wayne Thom Photography Collection, USC Libraries Special Collections.

FIG. 243 Southeast Asian *garuda* (eagle) figure, n.d. Private collection.

Asia as Method: Bruce Goff and the Plural Genealogies of Modern Architecture

Lawrence Chua

In 1960, some nine years before Bruce Goff made his first trip to Asia, the sinologist Takeuchi Yoshimi delivered two influential lectures in Tokyo on *Kindai nowa nanika* (Asia as method).[1] Although it is unlikely that either was familiar with the other's work, Goff and Yoshimi shared a complex understanding of modernism that departed from the ways it had been studied by scholars in the post–World War II era. Comparing the nineteenth-century projects of modernization in China and Japan, Yoshimi noted that although civil society, bourgeois literature, and even standardization could be claimed to have existed in Asia long before the first stirrings of European modernity in the fifteenth century, it was the production of a certain self-consciousness initiated by European colonial violence—and Asian resistance to that violence—that announced the arrival of modernity in Asia.[2] In short, it was only when Asia became an object for the West that it was considered to have entered modern times.[3] Yoshimi's observations were taken up more recently by literary scholar Chen Kuan-hsing, who argued for reorienting Asia as an object of scholarship by mobilizing the continent's diverse historical experiences and rich social practices in order to provide alternative horizons and perspectives, potentially advancing a different understanding of world history that does not center the emergence of the West as a distinct entity.[4]

In this essay I draw on both Yoshimi's original work and Chen's subsequent elaboration of "Asia as method" to better understand the ways Goff turned toward Asian arts and architecture to reframe the modern American landscape in which he worked. His understanding of modernism's plural roots, his efforts to untether architectural education from its institutional rigidity, his diverse collections of art and modern music, and his approach to organicism were shaped by a nuanced and profoundly contemporary understanding of Asian arts. Goff's unique approach to architectural modernism, I argue, shared much in common with Asian artists and intellectuals like Yoshimi who sought to reorient the history of modernism

FIG. 244 Mangkunegoro IV of Surakarta orchestra, from Java, performing in Arnhem in 1879. Gamelan music was first heard in Europe in 1879 when this orchestra performed in Arnhem and subsequently went on tour. Photographer unknown. Courtesy of Bronbeek Museum, Ministry of Defence, Netherlands.

1. Takeuchi Yoshimi, *What Is Modernity?: Writings of Takeuchi Yoshimi*, ed. Richard Calichman (Columbia University Press, 2005).
2. Ibid., 54; Christian de Pee's work on Song dynasty China is particularly enlightening regarding modernism before modernization. See Christian de Pee, *Urban Life and Intellectual Crisis in Middle-Period China, 800–1100* (Amsterdam University Press, 2022).
3. Naoki Sakai, "Modernity and Its Critique: The Problem of Universalism and Particularism," in *Translation and Subjectivity: On "Japan" and Cultural Nationalism* (University of Minnesota, 2008), 170.
4. Chen Kuan-hsing, *Asia as Method: Toward Deimperialization* (Duke University Press, 2010), 212.

away from its Eurocentric biases and attend instead to the diverse and complex global influences that shaped nineteenth- and twentieth-century expressions of modernism.

MODERNISM BEFORE MODERNITY

Among other things, using "Asia as method" means acknowledging the seeds of modernism that may have existed in Asia long before the conventionally accepted era of modernization in the West.[5] In turn, it also encourages reassessing the influence of modern and premodern Asian arts on the cultural responses to modernization produced by European and American avant-garde architects and artists like Goff. Early studies of Goff's work note that his search for new architectural ideas was rooted in the American heartland but did not end there.[6] They go on to cite his awareness of progressive architectural design in Europe. Others have noted the influence of modern European music on Goff's design. Few, however, have teased out the cultural practices of Asia, Oceania, and Africa that shaped the European and American cultural responses to modernization that inspired Goff.

Goff, however, was acutely aware of modernism's plural roots. Speaking of Asian music's seminal influence on Claude Debussy's work, Goff noted:

> He had the ability to find inspiration in all sorts of things—in nature or in cultures other than his own. For instance, at the Exposition of Paris ... Debussy was fascinated with the orchestras from these native islands, and particularly with the orchestra from Java.... He was probably the only musician in Europe who could understand such music at that time. He has written about it saying, "There have been [...] certain charming races who have learned to compose music as naturally as one learns to breathe. When we compare the sound of their percussion, and their delicate effects, with our music, we realize that ours is like the brash noise of a traveling circus band."[7]

Although Debussy's understanding of the contribution of "certain charming races" was conditioned by the pseudoscientific race theories that haunted European thought in the nineteenth and twentieth centuries, his comment speaks to the often-unacknowledged impact of Asian, African, and Oceanic culture on modernist culture (fig. 244). For example, it is possible to tease out the Southeast Asian musical structure in Debussy's "Pagodes," even though the instrumentation is entirely European.[8] Goff was aware that this appropriation of non-European structures and methods was not isolated to Debussy, or even to modern music. Reflecting on Igor Stravinsky's awestruck admiration of the complex rhythmic patterns of African drumming, Goff noted: "Stravinsky, who is no slouch in rhythm and was considered pretty wild when he composed *The Rite of Spring*, said, 'I felt like a schoolboy when I listened to these Africans.' I think the same can be said about our architecture when we see the great rhythmic patterns set up in Oriental buildings, and many others."[9]

Goff admitted that his own search for inspiration likewise took him far afield from the European sources that influenced his early career. Speaking of his discovery of Erich Mendelsohn's work, Goff discussed the ways it opened a door to other methods of design: "The design didn't have to follow the old classical work, which I had learned to detest in my youthful arrogance. I could see other ways of designing through Erich Mendelsohn's work—through the work in the Bauhaus, and Le Corbusier, as I grew into it—and particularly through Oriental architecture, thorough work in Japan, China, Siam, the south [*sic*] Sea Islands, Egypt, and all of the places that had done wonderful things—that there wasn't just one way to design."[10] In his "youthful arrogance," Goff detested an architecture rooted in a historicist narrative about Western civilization, whose apogee was modernism. Instead he came to understand that the alternative to the narrow path of European historicism required acknowledging the historicity of other cultures that had shaped modernism. One can see this mindset in the ways he transformed the curriculum at the University of Oklahoma (OU), which refuted the Eurocentrism of the Beaux-Arts as well as the ahistorical direction of the Bauhaus.

TEACHING ASIAN ARCHITECTURAL HISTORIES

Rather than approach Japan and Southeast Asia as a rich storehouse of dead precedents to raid for inspiration, Goff saw an alternative history of modernism in the ukiyo-e prints, landscape paintings, and diverse objets d'art that he encountered and collected. These cultural forms gave Goff a glimpse of the possibilities foreclosed

5. Yoshimi examined this in an earlier essay, "What Is Modernity? (The Case of China and Japan)," Calichman, *What Is Modernity?*.
6. David G. De Long, *The Architecture of Bruce Goff, Buildings and Projects, 1916–1974* (Garland, 1977), 33.
7. Philip B. Welch, ed., *Goff on Goff: Conversations and Lectures* (University of Oklahoma Press, 1996), 275.
8. Roy Howat, "Debussy and the Orient," in *Recovering the Orient: Artists, Scholars, Appropriation*, ed. Andrew Gerstle and Anthony Milner (Harwood Academic Publishers, 1994), 45–82.
9. Welch, *Goff on Goff*, 203.
10. Ibid., 22.

by the more doctrinaire approaches to modern architecture that had dominated the curricula at most American architecture schools in the early twentieth century.

As chair of a regional school of architecture in the United States just after World War II, Goff sought to move the school away from the *mission civilisatrice* of the Beaux-Arts on which OU had modeled its own early curricula.[11] He was equally dissatisfied with the amnesiac character of the transplanted Bauhaus curriculum, which had recently found favor at schools like Harvard and the Illinois Institute of Technology. Goff understood the importance of history in an architect's training and encouraged students to find inspiration in the real histories of the so-called non-West, rather than the imagined classical past of European empires celebrated by the Beaux-Arts. Although Goff appointed Elizabeth Mock to teach history and serve as the architecture school's librarian, he took it upon himself to teach an alternative history of modernism focused on non-European architecture.[12]

Goff was perhaps one of the first architectural educators in the United States and Europe to elevate case studies from outside the Western canon to a position equivalent to European architecture in the curriculum of an architecture school. It would be an exaggeration, however, to assign Goff a heroic role in "decolonizing" architectural education. Rather, Goff saw the rich history of Asian arts as a source of potential methods and creative approaches. Comparing realist, Surrealist, and "Oriental" approaches to painting a flower, Goff explained that the latter prioritized contemplation and meditation on the character of the poppy, what makes it different from other flowers and from other poppies, and on the architecture of the poppy. "You would try to understand it to the point where you could, from memory, draw the essential things about the poppy, not as your interpretation of it, but of the real essence of the thing itself. This is one of the big differences between Oriental and Occidental art in that approach where the artist subordinates himself to nature or to his idea, rather than using it as a means of expression, as we do."[13] Goff sought to expose his students to these approaches in several ways. He brought back Honolulu-born OU alumnus Shizuo Oka from Japan, where he had gone to continue his education and became a master carpenter in the 1950s.[14] Goff also displayed Japanese prints prominently at the school and invited Japanese print dealers to visit. As a result, many of his students started their own collections of Japanese art.

FIG. 245 Ito Jakuchū (Japanese, 1716–1800). *Eagle*, 1800. Hanging scroll: ink on silk; 102.3 × 40.2 cm (40 5/16 × 15 13/16 in.). Etsuko and Joe Price Collection, Los Angeles County Museum of Art.

11. Luca Guido et al., eds., *Renegades: Bruce Goff and the American School of Architecture* (University of Oklahoma Press, 2020), 6.

12. Luca Guido, "We Preach No Dogma: The Curriculum Under Bruce Goff," in Guido et al., *Renegades*, 72. The architect Jim Gresham, a 1953 graduate of OU, noted that Goff "taught courses in pre-Columbian and oriental history (at the time no other school could match this specialty) and preferred leaving western civilization to others." Jim Gresham, "Lessons Learned," *Friends of Kebyar* 6, no. 4 (Oct./Nov. 1988): 6.

13. Welch, *Goff on Goff*, 160–61.

14. An overlooked figure in the history of American architecture, Oka contributed much to the architecture of post–World War II Hawai'i. Arn Henderson, *Bruce Goff: Architecture of Discipline in Freedom* (University of Oklahoma Press, 2017), 91; and "Minutes of a Regular Meeting, Board of Regents, University of Oklahoma, Thursday, September 8, 1955, 10 am," hdl.handle.net/11244/327870.

As an educator, Goff treated Asian, African, and pre-Columbian cultures as an integral part of modern history rather than a pattern book of motifs. Introducing his students to cultures outside of the Western canon was part of Goff's overall pedagogical ambition to shake them out of their reliance on what had become stereotypical models in the mid-twentieth century. Under Goff's direction, history courses at OU were ordered chronologically, beginning with ancient architecture (to this day, predominantly the architecture of Asia and Africa), medieval architecture in the sophomore year, and ending with Renaissance and American architecture in the third year. However, Goff took it upon himself to teach ancient cultures and contemporary American architecture, reflecting his interest in tying these two otherwise distinct periods together.[15]

SHIN'ENKAN

The design lessons Goff drew from Asian art and architectural history added complexity to the way he understood the relationship between the built and natural environments. We can see his fondness for painting of the Edo period—in particular the mid-eighteenth-century Kyoto painter Itō Jakuchū—and the subordination of an artist's vision to nature in his design for the home and studio of Etsuko and Joe Price. The Price collection of Japanese art contained many notable examples of Jakuchū's work, and it is likely that Joe Price introduced Goff to these paintings.[16] Jakuchū is considered a maverick figure in the history of Japanese painting, and it is perhaps this reputation that resonated with Goff's independent approach to modern architectural design.

The name of the home Goff designed, and ultimately the name of Price's collection of Japanese art, references the two-story studio Jakuchū built on the west bank of the Kamo River: Shin'enkan (心遠館 or Villa of the Detached Heart).[17] Jakuchū in turn borrowed it from a poem by the fifth-century Chinese poet Tao Qian (陶潛 né Tao Yuanming 陶淵明), author of the classical utopian fable *Peach Blossom Spring* (桃花源記). Active in the mid-Edo period, Jakuchū worked in a diverse range of styles, much like Goff. Jakuchū's early work demonstrates a mastery of idioms and techniques derived from Chinese painting, and his later work exhibits a uniquely modern approach derived from a close study of nature and its forms. An example of this period Goff admired is Jakuchū's *Eagle* (fig. 245), an ink painting on silk the artist made in the last year of his life.[18]

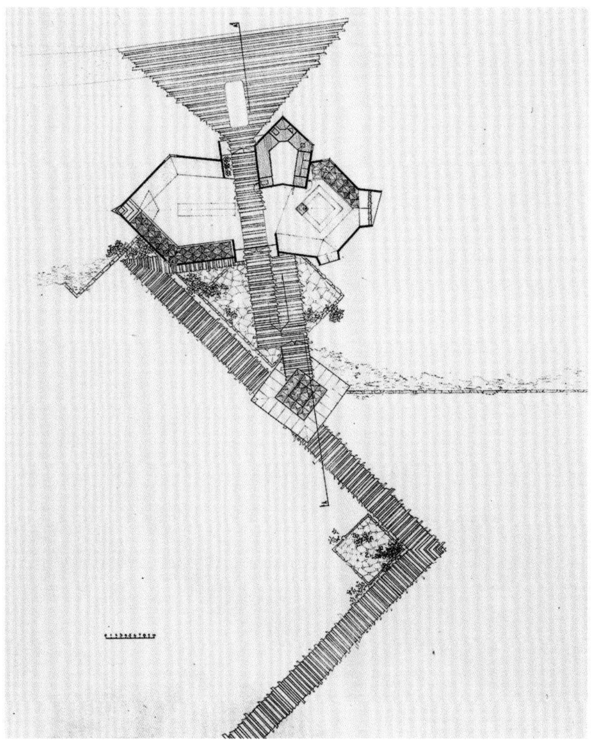

FIG. 246 Plan for Joe Price Studio based on 1953 drawing by James Parent, n.d. Photograph by Griggs Studio. Bruce A. Goff Archive.

In this painting an eagle perches confidently on a snow-covered branch, which forms a hard line mirrored by the eagle's profile. The rigidness of the two forms is juxtaposed against the curving gusts of snow in the lower left and the white stone backdrop behind the branch. In his restrained use of empty space, Jakuchū established a dramatic relationship between the landscape and the creatures that inhabit it. One can see the ways Goff brought this sense of composition to the bachelor pad and studio that he designed for Price on his family's ranch, Star View Farm. Although the original 1953 plan for the Price studio (fig. 246) was abandoned in favor of Goff's more geometrically regular 1956 design, the initial design demonstrates a strong affinity for the composition of *Eagle* in its integration of dissonant and angular fragmented forms.[19]

Goff's second design of the Joe Price studio featured a modified swastika plan, or a triangle with projecting corners. It retains Goff's affinity for Jakuchū's sense of composition, particularly in the dramatic interior

15. Guido, "We Preach No Dogma," 72.
16. Price began collecting Japanese art in earnest after a 1953 visit to an antique shop in New York with Wright. See De Long, *Bruce Goff*, 124; and Tokyo National Museum, National Museum of Modern Art, Kyoto, Kyushu National Museum, and Aichi Prefectural Museum of Art, *The Price Collection: Jakuchu and the Age of Imagination* (Nihon Keizai Shimbun, 2006).
17. Although the Price studio and home was built in 1958, the name Shin'enKan was chosen for the museum in 1970. Joe Price to Bruce Goff, Oct. 26, 1970, series I, box 18, folder 20, 1990.1, Bruce A. Goff Archive, Ryerson and Burnham Art and Architecture Archives, The Art Institute of Chicago (hereafter BGA, AIC).
18. I am grateful to Eugene Tssui for his recollection of Goff's enthusiasm for *Eagle* in a phone conversation on August 12, 2024.
19. Henderson, *Bruce Goff*, 180.

FIG. 247 Thai *hamsa* (mythical bird) sculpture at Shin'enKan, 1960. Photograph by Joe Price. Bruce A. Goff Archive.

conversation pit. Here Goff used unconventional building materials, such as cellophane and goose feathers, to emulate the presence of rain and foliage without including actual water or trees. On the exterior, the rigid gold-colored finials or "horns" extend from the outer corners of the roof, integrating the sky into the building's profile, just as the sharp line of Jakuchū's branch brings the eagle into the snowy landscape.

On the lower terrace of Price's studio, a large pier of coal with an irregular opening framed a Thai *hamsa* sculpture made of bronze (fig. 247).[20] This mythical migratory bird proliferates in South and Southeast Asian literature and imagery and is associated with liberation from the cycle of birth, death, and reincarnation.[21] Traditionally used as a finial for ceremonial standards, the *hamsa* was associated with the sun. In mid-twentieth-century Thailand, its form was appropriated for streetlights in cities like Bangkok and Lopburi, linking premodern belief systems with modern urban infrastructure. In descriptions of the Price studio, the hamsa has been identified as a "phoenix," suggesting perhaps the personal—albeit inaccurate—meaning Goff attributed to the image.[22] Nonetheless, its prominent placement can be read as Goff's formal nod to Jakuchū's *Eagle* and as a symbolic statement about both the reincarnation of Goff's original design and the persistence of the architect after his entrapment and ensuing resignation as head of the School of Architecture at OU.[23] It also spoke to the multiple lives of the Price studio and its transformations.

20. Ronald Menish, Assistant Director of Oriental Arts, Gumps, to Bruce Goff, Nov. 24, 1956, series II, box 8, folder 19, BGA, AIC.

21. Donald K. Swearer, *Becoming the Buddha: The Ritual of Image Consecration in Thailand* (Princeton University Press, 2004), 56–58.

22. Roseanne McKee, "Shin'enKan Retrospective—Part III," *Examiner-Enterprise*, Sept. 15, 2019, examiner-enterprise.com/story/lifestyle/columns/2019/09/15/shin-8217-enkan-retrospective-8212/2786802007/.

23. For more on this event see the introduction to this volume and Carol Mason, "Bruce Goff: How to Stop Enjoying and Learn to Fear Queer Art," in *Oklahomo: Lessons in Unqueering America* (State University of New York Press, 2015), 111–37.

The Price studio was completed in 1958, and major additions were made in 1966–69 and 1974–76 to accommodate Price's changing lifestyle."[24] The studio's first iteration as a bachelor pad was described by Ada Louise Huxtable as "a Playboy dream."[25] The second phase of the studio's life was ushered in when Price married Etsuko Yoshimochi (pictured in fig. 248), his erstwhile Japanese translator, who also became Goff's client.[26] Although it is not clear whether he was also speaking of his wife, Price described this design as having "a quiet elegance," and Yoshimochi's needs certainly guided many aspects of the 1966 renovation.[27] Goff's third intervention, a tower, was added to accommodate bedrooms for the couple's children in the 1970s.

The additions in the 1960s and 1970s not only organically integrated Price's family into the original design but also included a museum for his art collection, the primary element of the 1966 expansion.[28] At the center of the 1966 museum addition, Goff installed a hexagonal koi pond. The bottom of the pond extended into the level below it, acting as a skylight over a mosaic-covered Japanese bath, an important feature of Japanese domestic life and an example of the accommodations made to welcome Yoshimochi to her new home. Shin'enKan can thus be understood as more than a simple architectural commission; it was the culmination of a long and rich relationship between Goff and Joe Price that was rooted in Price's patronage of Goff, but that also celebrated their many shared interests including Japanese art, travel, and a life of culture.[29]

FIG. 248 Etsuko Price in front of sliding doors and Japanese folding screens by Hoitsu, Etsuko and Joe Price House, Bartlesville, Oklahoma, 1972. Photograph by Horst P. Horst. Published in *Vogue*, Feb. 1, 1972.

In addition, Goff's use of cullet or recycled waste glass to create a Japanese dry garden at Shin'enKan suggested the interrelationship between the man-made and the natural and reflected his distinctive approach to architectural organicism, the style that dominated architectural modernism in the United States and Europe during the nineteenth and early twentieth centuries. Goff's approach drew on the conventions of Chinese and, later, Japanese landscape painters who depicted the human world integrated within the natural order. Even as late as the nineteenth and twentieth centuries, Japanese landscape painting continued to treat the human figure and the built environment as another element in the composition of nature.

ORGANICISM

As an architect whose prolific body of work spanned the transition from the regional modernism of the early twentieth century to a more international and industrial idiom, Goff's work is often discussed as part of the lineage of organicism.[30] Goff shared many ideas in common with the leading proponents of this movement, namely Frank Lloyd Wright and Louis Sullivan. Sullivan and Wright were deeply influenced by Darwinian understandings of human evolution in which the architectural styles of the past were unfit to survive and were replaced by a new, modern style.[31] However, Goff's conception of organic architecture drew on Asian representations of the relationships between man and nature to refine his understanding of modern architecture's organic roots.

Analyzing the racialized origins of organic architecture, Charles L. Davis II pointed out the potential role that Western civilizational frameworks, and especially white nativist discourses, had in shaping these design movements. Davis argued that scientific conceptions of racial character played an influential role in this paradigm because race was perceived as a defining characteristic of organic life.[32] Examining the racial politics of Wright's work, for example, Davis observed a contradiction: although Wright maintained a persistent interest in Japanese art, he also disavowed any influence beyond his own "autonomous genius."[33] Thus, Wright could

24. For more on Price's working relationship with Goff, see Joe D. Price, "A Personal Recollection of Bruce Goff," in *The Architecture of Bruce Goff, 1904–1982: Design for a Continuous Present*, ed. Pauline Saliga and Mary Woolever (Prestel; Art Institute of Chicago, 1995), 61–62.
25. Ada Louise Huxtable, *On Architecture: Collected Reflections on a Century of Change* (Bloomsbury, 2010), 300.
26. In a local newspaper interview, Yoshimochi identified herself as a former dental assistant. "New Citizen Pleased: Etsuko to Take Part in US Rites," *Tulsa World*, Mar. 25, 1972, series I, box 18, folder 20, BGA, AIC.
27. Price, "A Personal Recollection of Bruce Goff," 61.
28. Henderson, *Bruce Goff*, 186–87.
29. See, for example, the voluminous correspondence between Goff and Price in series I, box 18, folders 17–26, BGA, AIC. Many of these letters from Price describe his travel and art purchases in Asia.
30. Guido, "We Preach No Dogma," 75–78; Henderson, *Bruce Goff*, 12–17 and 52–56; and David G. De Long, *Bruce Goff: Toward Absolute Architecture* (Architectural History Foundation; MIT Press, 1988), 303.
31. Louis H. Sullivan, *The Autobiography of an Idea* (Press of the American Institute of Architects, 1924), 249–50.
32. Charles L. Davis II, *Building Character: The Racial Politics of Modern Architectural Style* (University of Pittsburgh Press, 2019), 5–6 and 13.
33. Ibid., 219.

FIG. 249 Kawase Hasui (Japanese, 1883–1957). *Kanaya-cho, Nagasaki*, from the series *Selection of Scenes of Japan* (*Nihon fukei senshu, Nagasaki Kanaya-cho*), 1923. Color woodblock print; paper: 30.6 × 22.8 cm (12 1/16 × 9 in.); block: 28.4 × 20.7 cm (11 3/16 × 8 3/16 in.). The Art Institute of Chicago, Bruce Goff Archive gift of Shin'enKan, Inc., 1990.607.397.

draw on Japanese art and architecture while simultaneously denying their influence on his work because he subscribed to the prevailing notion that these influences belonged to a distant tradition outside of the modern time in which he operated.

Goff, on the other hand, was candid about the influence of Japanese art and architecture on his practice. As an early disciple of Wright, he interpreted his mentor's conceptualization of organic architecture as the assimilation of nature's "essence" into architectural composition. A harmoniously organized building, Goff believed, corresponded to the organic principles of the natural world.[34] He considered the inorganic or synthetic to rely on externally received ideas, whereas the organic began with a creative impulse that grew outward. Unlike Wright, Goff advocated for integrating the two, and he was critical of Sullivan's search for a rule "so broad as to admit no exception."[35] Like Wright, Goff drew on Asian art and spatial practices in his own work, but Goff's engagement with Japanese arts was dynamic and continued into the present.

FIG. 250 Goff and Golden. *Joe Price Studio, Bartlesville, Oklahoma, Perspective*, 1956. Graphite and colored pencil with opaque watercolor on cream wove paper; 61.6 × 106.3 cm (24 5/16 × 41 7/8 in.). The Art Institute of Chicago, gift of Shin'enKan, Inc., 1990.895.15.

34. Henderson, *Bruce Goff*, 53.
35. Sullivan, *Autobiography of an Idea*, 221; and Henderson, *Bruce Goff*, 106–7.

FIG. 251 Tanaka Ryohei (Japanese, 1933–2019). *Grasses on the Roof*, 1981. Etching; 17.7 × 55.3 cm ($6\frac{15}{16}$ × $21\frac{3}{4}$ in.). The Art Institute of Chicago, Bruce Goff Archive, gift of Shin'enkan, Inc., 1990.607.821.

This can be seen in Goff's ever-expanding collection of contemporary music from Asia as well as his own collection of primarily twentieth-century images. For example, a 1923 color woodblock print of Kanaya-cho, Nagasaki (fig. 249), by the artist Kawase Hasui depicts Japan already modernized. Electricity poles, streetlights, and bicycles are integrated into a street view that might otherwise have been painted in the eighteenth century, with gabled roofs, stone walls, and timber houses. Recognized as a "Living National Treasure" by the Japanese government, Hasui was a key protagonist in the *shin-hanga*, or "new prints," movement of the twentieth century.

Goff collected several images by Hasui, including one of a *minka*, a Japanese vernacular dwelling, in autumn and one of an *onsen* in an Iwate prefecture. Both images from the 1940s reflect a preoccupation of Goff's with thatched *gassho*-style roofs.[36] One can see the ways Goff sought to bring this interest into his design of the Price studio's rooflines (fig. 250). One can also see the ways Goff inserted his own work within both the history of modern architecture and the longer history of Japanese art and architecture by considering a series of images in his collection of Japanese painting and their relationship to his design of the Price studio. Goff's fascination with the roof as a living, organic element of Japanese architecture is further reflected in Tanaka Ryohei's *Grasses on the Roof* (fig. 251), a 1981 etching Goff acquired toward the end of his life as he was working on the design for Price's own collection, which would eventually be housed in a new wing of the Los Angeles County Museum of Art.

The Pavilion for Japanese Art at the Los Angeles County Museum of Art was Goff's last project. He worked on the design between 1978 and 1982, the year of his death, and it was posthumously completed by architect Bart Prince, a protégé of Goff's, between 1982 and 1988 at a cost of US $12.7 million. Described as an "original rethinking of museum design," the museum plan—in many ways a continuation of his unrealized proposal for the Japanese gallery at the Metropolitan Museum of Art—was attentive to the ways Japanese art had originally been conceived to interact with architecture.[37] In the first iteration of the project, scrolls and paintings hung in elevated multistory alcoves or *tokonoma* which were placed within a curvilinear volume with translucent walls (fig. 252). Goff drew on the tokonoma as a module that consistently structured the different iterations of the design.[38]

In a c. 1977 drawing of the pavilion's upper levels, three gently curved, double-story tokonoma form a modified swastika within a "tricular," or curved triangle, volume (fig. 238). As in his studio for Price, the swastika served as the plan's anchor. Three columns rise above the roof, connected by curved beams that resemble either the *maedate* of samurai helmets or the *chigi*, or forked roof finials, of Shinto temples (fig. 237). Suspension cables run from these to support the roof. Pleated translucent Kalwall panels on the building's facade recall *shoji* screens, diffusing the natural light which illuminates the interior exhibition spaces, recreating the original conditions under which the artwork would have been viewed. There is a thoughtful interplay between the industrially manufactured elements of the building and its natural features (such as the water garden on the lower level) that speaks to Goff's sophisticated take on organicism. Goff's attention to the principles of not only making but viewing speaks to his grasp of the ways Japanese painters understood their place, and the place of the modern, in an ever-changing environment as part of, rather than distinct from, the organic rhythms of the natural world.

KEBYAR

Like Wright sixty-four years earlier, Goff visited Asia, rather than Europe, on his first international excursion. At the invitation of Joe Price, he traveled throughout Japan before embarking on an intensive itinerary in Thailand, Bali (fig. 253), and Singapore.[39] Whereas

36. Goff also used orange AstroTurf for the Glen and Luetta Harder House (1970–72), demonstrating a material likeness to the gassho style roofs.
37. Christopher Mead, "Shin'enKan, A Collaboration in L.A.," *Cite* 29 (Fall 1992/Winter 1993): 37.
38. De Long, *Bruce Goff*, 290.
39. Ibid., 248–49.

FIG. 252 Interior of the Los Angeles County Museum of Art's Pavilion for Japanese Art, 1988. Photograph by Wayne Thom. Wayne Thom Photography Collection. Special Collections, USC Libraries, University of Southern California.

FIG. 253 Goff in Bali, Indonesia, 1969. Photographer unknown. Bruce A. Goff Archive.

Wright's and many other modern architects' interests were exclusively in Japan, Goff's were much broader in scope.

Goff also understood that art being made in Asia was contemporary to his own. In 1941 Goff purchased a 7.89-acre plot outside of Louisville, Kentucky, intending to build a home and studio there. He wanted to name it *kebyar*, a Balinese word that means "to flare up" or "to burst open" like a flower.[40] Given Goff's eclectic knowledge of world music, it seems likely he would have also known about the gamelan gong kebyar, a twentieth-century genre of Balinese gamelan so named because of its explosive changes in tempo.

The birth of the kebyar gamelan and its accompanying dance has been traced to the northern part of Bali around the 1920s.[41] The new genre spread like wildfire, and today it is the most popular form of orchestral music in Bali. Across the globe at almost the same time, Stravinsky debuted "The Rite of Spring" in Paris, a watershed event in the history of modern music. Stravinsky's and Debussy's appreciation for African and Asian music is well documented, but theirs was an affinity for sounds they considered "traditional" and part of an unchanging past. Asian artists were simultaneously engaged in a transformation of their own classical arts as they wrestled with the experiences of inhabiting a new global order conditioned by European colonialism and the world capitalist economy. Reflecting on the "fundamental DNA" that composers such as Stravinsky shared with kebyar artists, Wayne Vitale wrote, "It was as if those first Balinese kebyar artists, dizzy with the pandemic fever of experimentation and change, lit a fuse under their traditional forms only to reassemble the pieces in new ways, and they did so in unwitting synchrony with another artistic explosion half a world away."[42]

Goff understood this "unwitting synchrony" and its importance to his own genealogy of ideas and influences: "Of course, when we consider that we are descended from our mothers and fathers, and they from their mothers and fathers, it doesn't take many generations to get a very complex background. . . . Naturally, the physical characteristics are quite obvious many times. . . . The more obscure things, such as feelings and talents, are much more mysterious, more personal with each of us. Still they have come to us from all of this background."[43] He further grasped that Asian arts were a dynamic expression of his global inheritance as a modern architect as well as what it meant to inhabit modern times. Examining Goff's pedagogical approach, design philosophy, and collecting practices using Asia as method illuminates this acknowledgment of modern architecture's many birthdates and birthplaces, a flowering of creativity that blossomed in diverse locations simultaneously.

40. Bruce Goff to Irma Bartman, Sept. 30, 1941, in De Long, *Bruce Goff*, 69.
41. Gamelan has a much longer, multicentury history, but scholars date the birth of kebyar within the history of the Dutch colonial incursion into Bali in the early twentieth century and the violent dismantling of the island's kingdoms.
42. Wayne Vitale, "Distant Explosions: Kebyar and the Rite of Spring," asia-archive.si.edu/essays/article-vitale/.
43. Welch, *Goff on Goff*, 157.

FIG. 254 Mosaic door looking into the living room of the Joe Price Studio, Bartlesville, Oklahoma, c. 1960. Photograph by Joe Price. Bruce A. Goff Archive.

Electronic Enclosure: Bruce Goff and the Postwar Bachelor Pad

Paula Lupkin

Joe Price had just three requirements when he first commissioned a home in Bartlesville, Oklahoma, from Bruce Goff in 1954: "It would be inward looking . . . a place of relaxation for him and his friends, and"—perhaps most importantly—"it was to be a bachelor pad and not a family home."[1] "You leave your shoes at the door," he instructed, "Come in and flop on the floor, lean back, mix a drink, turn on the music. Just relax."[2] This unusual design prompt inspired Goff to create an enclosure and retreat from the social mores that defined most domestic interiors of the day. Addressing larger conversations about technology and new lifestyles, this essay situates the Joe Price Studio as a radical reshaping of the domestic realm in the postwar United States.

By the late 1950s Goff had earned a reputation for designing highly individualistic, custom homes for clients who embraced his rejection of normative domestic design.[3] He understood the importance of carving out a personal and community space in rural Oklahoma that would offer that cultural immersion, fantasy, and privacy that would shape his client's home life for decades to come.[4] The result was a sybaritic and experimental bachelor pad that was attuned to the hypermasculine ideals promoted in Hugh Hefner's new *Playboy* magazine, first published in 1953. This private, comfortable world on the Oklahoma prairie, outside of Bartlesville, was organized not around traditional family life but around shared experiences of music, art, and televised football games with like-minded people. This commission enabled Goff and Price to creatively engage with complex issues of the postwar domestic interior, including gender and sexual identity, the increasing informality of lifestyles (especially among young adults), and the impact of television and high-fidelity (hi-fi) sound systems on the concept and design of the home.

FIG. 255 Living room of Joe Price Studio, 1960. Photograph by Joe Price. Bruce A. Goff Archive.

THE CLIENT AND THE COMMISSION

Designed and built between 1956 and 1958 for his wealthy client, the Price studio was one of Goff's most elaborate and individualistic commissions, an opportunity to realize a Gesamtkunstwerk with a generous budget. Before the project, Goff had worked for Ruth and Sam Ford and Eugene and Nancy Bavinger, clients who wished to lead unconventional lives in experimental spaces. Their homes and studios emphatically rejected the compartmentalized, gendered, and traditional plans of the mass-produced "ranchburger," as Goff described it.[5] The design for Price's studio pushed the alternative living concept further: It embraced and supported the sexually active lifestyle of a single male whose identity was, in part, formed by the consumption of advanced entertainment technologies. Like the innovative penthouse apartment *Playboy* featured in two 1956 issues, the Price studio was designed for a single man who wanted to entertain guests at home.[6]

Joe Price, born in 1929, was heir to H. C. Price, the founder of an extraordinarily successful oil-field services company. While attending the University of Oklahoma, he met Goff and became an architectural enthusiast. When his father planned to build a corporate headquarters in Bartlesville, Joe was instrumental in securing Frank Lloyd Wright to design the iconic 1953 Price Tower—a testament to his early understanding of architecture and design's power to shape and express an identity, whether corporate or personal. Just a year later, with extensive financial resources at his command, he hired Goff to create an elaborate studio or bachelor pad comprising a multipurpose living room (fig. 255), a small bedroom, one bathroom, and a kitchenette. He knew

1. Mary Winn Dills, former curator and caretaker of the Price house, quoted in "Remembering the Layout of Shin'enKan," *Examiner-Enterprise*, Sept. 1, 2019, examiner-enterprise.com/story/entertainment/arts/2019/09/01/remembering-layout-shin-8217-enkan/4225548007/.
2. Elizabeth Venant, "Welcome to L.A., Mr. Price: An Oklahoma Millionaire Follows His Japanese Art Collection West—and Southern California Gets a Major New Art Patron," *Los Angeles Times*, July 5, 1986, 14.
3. He was well known nationally for his unusual, even shocking, Ford and Bavinger residences, which had been published in *Life* magazine in 1948 and 1955. See "Consternation and Bewilderment in Oklahoma" *Life*, June 28, 1948, 71–74; and "Space and Saucer House: Oklahoma Family Lives in Suspension in a Unique New Structure," *Life*, Sept. 19, 1955, 155–56. Conformity and standardization, particularly in housing, formed part of Goff's critiques of architecture in the 1950s and 1960s. See Bruce Goff, "The Continuous Present in Architecture," in *Goff on Goff: Conversations and Lectures*, ed. Philip B. Welch (University of Oklahoma Press, 1996), 191–225.
4. Price later reflected on his requests for freedom and cultural immersion in Joe D. Price, "Bruce Goff," in *Architecture*, ed. Takenobu Mohri (Kenchiku Planning Center, 1970), 210.
5. Multiple sources attribute the term *ranchburger* to Goff. One suggests he first used it at a Kansas City conference of home builders and developers in 1952. Goff spoke of it in a lecture given to the Wisconsin chapter of the American Institute of Architecture in 1956, published as "Advancing Architecture," in Welch, *Goff on Goff*, 321. For more on the gendered mass-manufactured home, see Rebecca Devers, "Miracle Kitchens and Bachelor Pads: The Competing Narratives of Modern Space," in *InHabit: People, Places, and Possessions*, ed. Anthony Buxton, Linda Hulin, and Jane Andersen (Peter Lang; International Academic Publishers, 2017), 153–72.
6. "Playboy Penthouse," *Playboy*, Sept. 1956, 53–57 and 195–96, and *Playboy*, Oct. 1956, 65–70.

Goff to be a creative nonconformist and outsider in a morally conservative community, and he trusted him to create a space that would support and express his emerging identity as a swinging bachelor without drawing unwanted attention in his small community.

When the studio was completed in 1957, the exterior offered little to indicate the innovative living concept and luxurious materials inside. The low-slung rooflines hung over walls with just a few diamond-shaped wall openings, like angular portholes. These restricted views of the interior and offered substantial privacy, one of Price's priorities. Inside, the compact home revolved around a large, double-height multipurpose room rising more than thirty feet high. The great room's skylight, partially covered by goose feathers, provided filtered light, further distancing Price from the bright Oklahoma sun.

Though not small, the home functioned more like a studio than a conventional house because the spaces for entertainment and relaxation covered the greatest footprint. Three doors were positioned at the points of the triangular great room, and at these corners Goff placed small storage closets, Price's bedroom, and a small kitchenette (equipped, most likely, to provide a space for catering staff). The home's generous budget allowed Goff to imbue the project with a sense of luxury, and he did, using anodized gold trim, intricate stained-glass windows, expensive zebra wood built-ins, custom decorated glass partitions, and plush white carpet, as well as a glass-cullet garden (for the bachelor who did not want to water his plants). At the center of the living room, Goff incorporated a seating concept he had used before: the conversation pit (fig. 256), or as Price later called it, the "passion pit."[7]

FIG. 256 Goff. *Joe Price Studio, Bartlesville, Oklahoma, Interior Perspective*, 1956. Graphite and colored pencil on diazo print on paper; 67 × 96 cm ($26\frac{7}{16}$ × $37\frac{13}{16}$ in.). The Art Institute of Chicago, gift of Shin'enKan, Inc., 1990.895.16.

7. Joe Price to Bruce Goff, Nov. 25, 1958, series II, box 8, folder 22, Bruce A. Goff Archive, Ryerson and Burnham Archives, The Art Institute of Chicago (hereafter BGA, AIC).

PLAYBOY AND THE BACHELOR PAD

Price's term bears a striking resemblance to the language of another cultural maverick, Hugh Hefner. Since *Playboy*'s first issue in 1953, Hefner and his publishing team put forth an alternative, nonconformist model for modern urban bachelorhood. In the postwar United States, suburbia was well-promoted through advertisements, exhibitions, model homes, and television, but the concept of an apartment for unmarried men required a reinvention. The model for rooms in men's clubs, hotels, and artists' studios dated back to the nineteenth century, and they were associated with exotic, orientalist furnishings: bolsters, carpets, divans, screens, and perhaps a caged parrot.[8]

Playboy advertisements, articles, and photograph spreads offered men a white, masculine, middle-class alternative to the single-family suburban homes being published in *Life*, *Better Homes and Gardens*, and other shelter and ladies' magazines.[9] Both domestic approaches served as guides for constructing class and sexual identity in the postwar period. Consumption—particularly of new technology like hi-fi phonograph systems and television sets—was integral to creating an American middle-class identity and showcasing newly possible lifestyles.

In 1956, just as Goff and Price were discussing the final details of his realized design for the Bartlesville studio, *Playboy* reinvented the concept of the bachelor pad in articles and in an idealized design.[10] In the July issue, Shepard Mead contributed "The Dream Home and How to Avoid It," a humorous piece candidly claiming that the home was a woman's domain where men could not be themselves.[11] The magazine pushed back against a normative postwar idea of domesticity and urged men to enjoy themselves as they wished—to drink, dress finely, seduce women, openly explore their sexuality, and cultivate artistic sophistication.

Months later Hefner published a sophisticated, luxurious penthouse designed by Chrysalis Group architects (fig. 257). It featured the latest electronics, an open plan, and an adjustable sofa that could easily be turned from the fireplace and stone hearth to face the entertainment wall, a built-in television and sound entertainment system.[12] Described as "tasteful and gracious," this apartment was a man's domain arranged around his needs and interests, including built-in color television, speakers, and a hi-fi sound system.

A big breakthrough in technology, high-fidelity sound was mass-marketed in the mid-1950s alongside televisions.[13] Automatic changers enabled playing mood music for hours on end, allowing for uninterrupted relaxation or seduction. Built around high-quality sound reproduction, these systems became an essential part of the bachelor pad and a frequent subject of *Playboy* advertisements and articles.

The sofa featured in the *Playboy* spread is the Borsani D70, an innovative, adjustable sofa from Italy that would let the man of the house (and his guest) flip from cozy relaxation to watching a football game at the touch of a button. It could even be flattened to use as a bed. Multipurpose functionality was also built into the dining room, which could accommodate a large party just as easily as a meal for two. Playboy's bachelor pad was furnished with the latest midcentury furniture: Noguchi rocking stools, a Saarinen Womb Chair and Sofa upholstered in blue and red, and dark wood-paneled cabinetry from Herman Miller and Knoll. The article included the prices and manufacturers of these items so that readers could reproduce the design. As the article suggests, the penthouse explicitly rejected the nuclear family household; it was a place for a man to entertain, relax, and seduce.

It seems plausible, even probable, that Price was familiar with this design, perhaps through a subscription. The September 1956 design issue was, according to Hefner, the most popular in the magazine's history, and it received a high volume of letters to the editor.[14] Although no archival documentation confirms that the Playboy penthouse served as a model for Goff and Price, the timeline suggests a connection—as do elements of the unrealized 1953 design, which included a mahogany bar and stereo cabinet, built-in seating, and a white carpeted conversation pit, the very elements of a bachelor pad in the making.[15]

FIG. 257 Design for living room for the Playboy penthouse, designed by Chrysalis Group Architects. Illustrated by Robert Branham. Published in *Playboy*, Sept. 1956, 57.

8. See Horace Townsend, "A Scheme of Decoration for a Bachelor's Room: With Illustrations by G. M. Elmore," *The Studio*, vol. 16 (1899): 243–49.
9. See the already extensive research on *Playboy*, including Beatriz Colomina and Pep Aviles, "Radical Interiority: Playboy Architecture 1953–1979," Elmhurst Art Museum, May–Aug. 2016; Jessica Ellen Sewell, "Power, Sex, and Furniture: Masculinity and the Bachelor Pad in 1950s–60s America," *Occasional Paper* 43, Institute for Advanced Study (Dec. 2011); and Paul Preciado, *Pornotopia: An Essay on Playboy's Architecture and Biopolitics* (Zone Books, 2019). See also Ruth M. Allison, "Radios in Disguise," *Better Homes and Gardens*, Feb. 1939, 28; and "Crosley Automatic Television," advertisement in *Better Homes and Gardens*, Mar. 1952, 224.
10. See Bill Osgerby, "The Bachelor Pad as Cultural Icon: Masculinity, Consumption and Interior Design in American Men's Magazines, 1930–65," *Journal of Design History* 18 (2005): 99–113; and "Playboy's Penthouse Apartment," *Playboy*, Oct. 1956, 65–66.
11. Shepard Mead, "The Dream Home and How to Avoid It," *Playboy*, July 1956, 53–54.
12. Ten years later the term *entertainment wall* was codified in "Playboy's Electronic Entertainment Wall," *Playboy*, Oct. 1964, 122–25; and "Entertainment Wall in the Playboy Mansion," *Playboy*, Jan. 1966, 109.
13. Dianne Harris, "A Tiny Orchestra in the Living Room: Hi-Fidelity Stereo and the Postwar House," in *Making Suburbia: New Histories in Everyday America*, ed. John Archer and Katherine Solomonson (University of Minnesota Press, 2015); and Lynn Spigel, *Welcome to the Dreamhouse: Popular Media and Postwar Suburbs* (Duke University Press, 2001), 33, 45, and 48.

FIG. 258 Conversation pit in the Irwin and Xenia Miller House, Columbus, Indiana, 1957. Photograph by Ezra Stoller Esto.

THE CONVERSATION PIT

Goff's interior departs from *Playboy*'s in its furnishings. In place of the midcentury corporate aesthetic, he favored carpeted walls and floors and, importantly, a conversation pit. Hexagonal in shape, it stepped down four levels and was surrounded by three white carpeted walls that leaned away from the center, providing space to sit or lounge. The tufted walls could be used to display artworks, and presentation drawings for the project show piles of pillows arranged near the television, cascading down the steps of the conversation pit below (fig. 256).

As early as the 1920s, Goff was instrumental in developing the conversation pit as an informal, sunken, built-in seating arrangement meant to foster social interaction and relaxation. Its origins can be traced back to the inglenook: cozy, intimate spaces for family togetherness favored by Arts and Crafts designers at the turn of the twentieth century.[16] Goff would have been familiar with the inglenook in Wright's 1889 home and studio, which included two parallel benches on either side of the fireplace. In 1923 Goff designed a studio for artist Adah Robinson with a stepped, sunken bench. The semicircle curved around an expressively designed hearth embellished with dynamic abstract flames that provided fireside seating for a small group.

After 1945 the conversation pit emerged as an avant-garde interior element in the progressive, even radical, rethinking of the American home. Goff and other designers undertook projects that sought to reconcile the geometries of modern interiors with the emerging concept of cozy informality.[17] Hailed as an innovative midcentury domestic design, the Eames House (1949) in Los Angeles, by industrial designers Charles and Ray Eames, includes a carpeted, low-ceilinged conversation nook strewn with rugs and cushions. Eero Saarinen and Alexander Girard furnished the influential open plan of the 1953 Irwin and Xenia Miller House (fig. 258) in Columbus, Indiana, with a colorful and comfortable square conversation "center." Paul Rudolph included sunken living rooms in several of his Florida commissions.[18] All three projects dispensed with room "boxes," challenged the necessity of traditional furniture, and scooped out and sculpted multilevel spaces for lounging and casual interactions.[19]

Goff's postwar conversation pits went further than any other in the restructuring of the family home. Circular

14. Hefner made that claim in *Playboy*, Apr. 1959, 3, quoted in Carrie Pitzulo, *Bachelors and Bunnies: The Sexual Politics of Playboy* (University of Chicago Press, 2011), 84. Goff also had a connection. The architect of the *Playboy* mansions in Chicago and Los Angeles, Ron Dirsmith, trained under Ambrose Richardson at the University of Illinois, Urbana-Champaign, in the 1970s. Richardson knew Goff from his student days at the School of the Art Institute of Chicago and followed his career. Ambrose Richardson, interviewed by Betty J. Blum, Chicago Architects Oral History Project, Art Institute of Chicago, 1990 and 2005.

15. David G. De Long, *Bruce Goff: Toward Absolute Architecture* (Architectural History Foundation; MIT Press, 1988), 124–28.

16. Richard Guy Wilson, "American Arts and Crafts Architecture: Radical Though Dedicated to the Cause Conservative," in *Arts and Crafts Movement*, ed. Elizabeth Cumming and Wendy Kaplan (Thames and Hudson, 1991), 124–25.

17. See James M. Jacobs, "Casual Living," in *Detached America: Building Houses in Postwar Suburbia* (University of Virginia Press, 2015).

18. "A New Kind of Conversation Center," *House and Garden*, Feb. 1959, 67–68. A couple of Rudolph's Florida commissions with sunken conversation areas are the Umbrella House (1953) in Lido Shores and the Cohen House (1955) in Sarasota. In 1957 Goff described the open flow in the Eugene and Nancy Bavinger House in similar terms, quoted in Ben Allan Park, "The Architecture of Bruce Goff," *Architectural Design*, May 1957, 151–74.

19. "Milam Residence," Archives of the Paul Rudolph Institute for Modern Architecture, paulrudolph.institute /195903-milam-residence.

sunken-bench seating around a central fireplace dominates Goff's design for the Ruth and Sam Ford House (1948). The Grace Lee and John Frank House (1955–56) features a rectangular and shag-carpeted sunken living room with built-in seating and a massive ceramic-tiled fireplace. The conversation pit, no longer anchored in the floor, was reimagined in the Eugene and Nancy Bavinger House (1950–55) as carpeted flying-saucer pods for sitting and sleeping. They hung from the ceiling in a spiraling composition, stunning their Oklahoman neighbors who lived in traditional Victorian farmhouses, ranches, and foursquares.

Price's conversation pit centered on a cabinet with a mosaic designed by Goff and fabricated by glass artist Emil Frei, which dynamically reinforced the room and house's triangular modular design. With a flick of a switch located on the television cabinet, the mosaic would rise from its flush position on the floor to form a hexagonal tabletop. In many ways the heart of the design, this high-tech table enclosed two of the most important elements of the bachelor pad: a bar and a hi-fi sound system. The setup challenged conventional domestic arrangements by centering new entertainment technologies that were transforming interior design and family life across the country.[20]

TELEVISION AND INTERIOR DESIGN

As early as 1942, *Better Homes and Gardens* published "Television Is Coming to the Home," forecasting the adaptation of wartime electronics technology to postwar domestic life.[21] It featured a two-page illustration focusing on the interconnection between the tube of a camera, an antenna, and a glowing picture in the living room—linking a live football game to a family gathered to watch at home.[22] In 1950 just 9 percent of US households owned a television; by 1960 the number rose to 90 percent: it had become a standard element of the American home.[23] Most people were prepared for this shift thanks to popular magazines, which put out dozens of articles about the new phenomenon and what it all meant. Bartlesville, Oklahoma, received transmission by 1954, and Goff himself was drafted to design a studio for the country's first cable television company in Bartlesville, Oklahoma: Telemovie (fig. 259).[24]

This early project aside, Goff was not the first architect to include television in the postwar home. In 1945 Marcel Breuer integrated built-in entertainment cabinetry for television and stereo in his Geller House. Then for the Museum of Modern Art, New York, exhibition *The House in the Museum Garden* (1949), Breuer took on the role of industrial designer, providing a custom-built cabinet for the television and a combined coffee table, radio, and control console. For those financially unable to build their television into a wall or add a family room to their home, designers such as Pierre Koenig, Raymond Loewy, and George Nelson offered midcentury entertainment consoles for radio, stereo, and television as early as 1947. Merchant builders, including Joseph Levitt, made it possible for thousands to own a television set, which was mass-marketed to the public beginning in 1950.[25]

The television's arrival in the postwar home spawned a fundamental transformation, in terms of both floor plan and social dynamics. From the late 1940s through the 1950s, this challenge was discussed in the pages of popular shelter magazines such as *House and Garden*, merchant builder periodicals such as *House and Home*, and professional journals including *Architectural Record* and *Interiors* (formerly *Interiors and Industrial Design*).[26] *Playboy* also weighed in with its own critique, "The magic box changed our society and has a greater influence on our nation than the atomic bomb."[27] Less apocalyptic observers suggested that television was a menace to children, whose eyesight, intelligence, and social skills would be affected. Others described it as a "brutal conversational stopper" for adults.[28] Moralistic commentators were concerned about the disruption of marital harmony, but *Playboy* felt it kept households intact, dryly observing, "It was the best invention—since the discovery of sex—'to keep the old man home at night.'"[29]

Homeowners, interior designers, and architects all felt the challenge of placement and visibility. Television, particularly the small-screened models of the late 1940s and early 1950s, required close viewing. This raised questions about placement for a large group, seating arrangements, and issues of social and moral propriety. Early on, the enclosure that housed picture tubes was the responsibility of the consumer. In interior design circles, questions about this abounded, but the general consensus was that the television screen, when not being used, should be concealed in period furniture that suited the living room décor. Designers generally considered the television an interruption to carefully balanced rooms, and architects frowned on it as déclassé and resisted including it in their domestic buildings. The September 1948 *Architectural Forum* half-jokingly

20. On the concept of anti-urban design, see Scott Herring quoted in Nolan Vallier, "Sacred Sounds and Natural Grounds: Designing Acoustic Communities with the Prairie Style and Organic Architectural Spaces" (PhD diss., University of Illinois Urbana-Champaign, 2021), 15. See also Harris, "A Tiny Orchestra"; and Spigel, *Welcome to the Dreamhouse*, 33, 45, and 48.

21. Exciting postwar plans for new technology are chronicled in Andrew M. Shanken, *194X: Architecture, Planning, and Consumer Culture on the Home Front* (University of Minnesota Press, 2009).

22. Darrell Huff, "Television Comes to the Home," *Better Homes and Gardens*, Nov. 1942, 18–19. The first television station in the United States opened in 1929 in Schenectady, New York, but did not gain popularity due to its primitive technology and lack of broadcasting stations.

23. SFO Museum, *Television: TV in the Antenna Age*, exhibition on view July 2011–Jan. 2012, sfomuseum.org /exhibitions/television-tv-antenna-age.

24. De Long, *Bruce Goff*, 160–61. The network lasted only one year but received national coverage, highlighting the modernity of Bartlesville. "Television: A Little Premature," *Time*, June 2, 1958, time.com /archive/6828986/television-a-little-premature/.

25. "New Levitt Houses Break All Records," *House and Home*, Feb. 1952, 103.

26. "Make Room for Television in Your Life," *House and Garden*, Nov. 1948, 219–21; and "Television," special issue, *Interiors* 110 (July 1951): 61–112.

27. "The Magic Box," *Playboy*, Mar. 1954, 22–23.

28. Karl Holzinger Jr., of Edward Stone's office, quoted in "Television," 80.

29. "Playboy's Penthouse Apartment," *Playboy*, Oct. 1956, 65–66.

FIG. 259 Goff, *Telemovie Building, Bartlesville, Oklahoma, Presentation Drawing* [unbuilt], 1957. Graphite on tracing paper; 119 × 92 cm (46⅞ × 36¼ in.). The Art Institute of Chicago, gift of Shin'enKan, Inc., 1990.838.2.

weighed in with the article "Television: Its Hypnotic Screen Will Change Our Approach to Designing Living Rooms and Making Love."[30]

FROM HEARTH AND PIANO TO HI-FI

Through its embrace of modern technology, the Price studio challenged the centrality of two traditional symbols of the home: the fireplace and the grand piano. As a composer and Claude Debussy aficionado, Goff took a strong interest in music, sound, and advances in music technology.[31] As such, he explored acoustical strategies long before working on Price's home. He produced player piano rolls, used cork for soundproofing, and accrued knowledge about the resonance of building and furnishing materials.[32]

Like his mentor Frank Lloyd Wright, Goff considered the grand piano a central element of his domestic commissions, particularly in his early career. His 1932 *Hypothetical Study for a House*, for example, is almost entirely unfurnished apart from a distinctive grand piano, which occupies pride of place by taking up nearly the entire triangular room. The design for the Frank and Ruth Cole House, completed in 1939, included a piano and integrated speaker. Early postwar house designs for music-loving clients such as the Cheetams, Gutmans, Innis family, and Murdochs, as well as James San Jule, also included a piano as a major freestanding piece of furniture or sculpture. Best known, perhaps, is the red-orange painted piano in the Ford house. Placed amid artworks in the gallery, the piano picked up the brightly hued ribs of the building's structural supports. It served not only as an instrument but also as a sensuously curved objet d'art.

Price did not care much about pianos or the symbolism of the primeval hearth. The house's eventual fireplace was small and tucked in a corner, and a piano was added only after he married and had children. His studio was an altogether different kind of installation where technology—represented by the bar and television—came front and center. Meeting the needs of his client, Goff shifted from his totems to electronics, relinquishing his symbolic anchors and devising new ones.

One key component was high-fidelity audio equipment, which transformed the sonic landscape of the American living room.[33] Major manufacturers began to advertise their components to male, middle-class consumers using female models, sometimes featuring wives but more often adventurous temptresses.[34] In 1951 the Admiral Television Company promoted an all-in-one cabinet, the Tele-bar, in proximity to attractive women (fig. 260).[35] Whether for family men or bachelors, hi-fi systems housed in credenzas and cabinetry served as a symbols of masculine consumption and identity.[36] Goff customized his Price studio design for this mass-market phenomenon, expanding it from a piece of furniture to an electronic layout embedded in the design and infrastructure of the studio.

FIG. 260 Advertisement for the Admiral Tele-Bar. *Cosmopolitan*, June 1951. Courtesy of the Hagley Museum and Library.

The Price studio interior itself was a chamber for music and television, tying the design closely to the requirements of the technology. To achieve this comprehensive centrality of sound, Goff asked for help selecting and installing the best technology. Price gave Goff the name of an electronics engineer in Tulsa, J. R. Higgins, who set up the system with high-end components.[37] Working from late 1957 to early 1958 with Higgins, Goff tried to maximize the sonic experience: He set out the triangular plan and dimensions of the room, and Higgins advised on placement and equipment, providing measurements for the openings in the cabinetry.

Permeable fabric concealed two "horns" projecting in different directions to maximize the triangular sonic field

30. "Television: Its Hypnotic Screen Will Change Our Approach to Designing Living Rooms and Making Love," *Architectural Forum*, Sept. 1948, 118–20.
31. Bruce Goff, "Music and Architecture," and Philip B. Welch, "Goff on Debussy," in Welch, *Goff on Goff*, 227–54 and 271–82.
32. Vallier, "Sacred Sounds," 188.
33. Dianne Harris, "Built-Ins and Closets: Status, Storage, and Display," in *Little White Houses: How the Postwar Home Constructed Race in America* (University of Minnesota Press, 2013), 185–227.
34. John M. Conley, "The Complete Fideletarian," *Playboy*, Oct. 1957, 31–33.
35. The record player in Goff's studio included an automatic record changer, made custom by a local company in Dewey, Oklahoma. See Bruce Goff to Haskell Culwell Construction Co. (cc Joe Price), Feb. 28, 1957, series II, box 8, folder 20, BGA, AIC.
36. Harris, "Built-Ins and Closets," 185–227.
37. On J. R. Higgins, see Goff to Haskell Culwell Construction Co. (see n. 35). J. R. Higgins, bid for audio and tv components, Apr. 10, 1958, series II, box 8, folder 24, BGA, AIC.

in the conversation pit. Goff specified laying white nylon Schumacher carpeting over foam-rubber padding on the floor and in the conversation pit to allow for comfortable reclining.[38] The plush carpeting over foam rubber would also affect the acoustics of the space, absorbing high frequency sound in the open-plan space.

THE ANTENNA AND "TV SCULPTURE"

Goff's design for Price was perhaps the first built project to realize the *Playboy* bachelor pad ideal in the countryside, rather than an urban center. Anchored in the open prairie, there was little on the exterior that indicated the innovative living concept, but one feature offered a clue to the interior. Extending upward from the ground above the roofline, it reaches for the sky: a sculpted brass pole and television antenna (fig. 261).[39]

Goff must have been intrigued by the diversity of antenna shapes available (fig. 262), particularly the one that Price's Ultra High Frequency (UHF) television required. Its arrow form captured broadcast signals in the fringe area of the studio.[40] Eighteen years later, his design for a community center in Mineola, Texas, featured a suspended roof inspired by radio transmission towers, pointing to Goff's continued interest in the antenna as a symbolic feature.[41] Functionally and symbolically, the brass antenna pole was like a periscope, offering a view far beyond the Oklahoma prairie that surrounded Price's home. The antenna reached for the broad sky, capturing waves and signals and symbolizing the interior's broader connection to the world.

Goff's techno-totems continued inside the house, with a set of custom "TV sculptures" (fig. 263). Goff and Price were intrigued by signals and wiring and celebrated these invisible forces in a pair of Plexiglas objects that Goff designed to rest on top of the television and speaker cabinets. Each composed of two sets of vertical wings, the sculptures were identical except for their colors and varied adornment of plastic tiles and sequins. Golden lengths of wire woven into the backs of the sculptures linked them together and to the ceiling, illuminating and reflecting the functional rabbit-ear antennas that extended from the top and bottom.

Expressed both outside and inside the house, these sculpted brass and Plexiglas forms comprise one of the most fascinating parts of the Price design. Instead of hiding the technological apparatus of the television, Goff's practical and symbolic representations of invisible connectivity defined the boundaries of the space, representing the prosaic electrical wiring below.

FIG. 261 Goff. *Joe Price Studio, Bartlesville, Oklahoma, Elevation*, 1956. Graphite and colored pencil on tracing paper; 44.5 × 88.9 cm (17½₁₆ × 35 in.). The Art Institute of Chicago, gift of Shin'enKan, Inc., 1990.895.1.

38. On the Schumacher carpet, see Goff to Haskell Culwell Construction Co. (see n. 35).

39. Bruce Goff to Haskell Culwell Construction Co., Mar. 21, 1957, series II, box 8, folders 23–25, BGA, AIC. A list of features included a brass pole.

40. In a critical and perhaps cynical move, Robert Venturi poked fun at Goff's celebration of television signals by topping his design for the Guild House (1960–63) in Philadelphia with an overscaled gold-anodized television antenna.

41. De Long, *Bruce Goff*, 276–79. Many of his house designs in the late 1950s and early 1960s featured television antennas on their roofline, including the Cecil Alvie and Gervis V. Comer House, Dewey, Oklahoma (1957–58), and the unbuilt Louella and Owen H. Tolf House, Lake Koshkonong, Wisconsin (1958), and Geri and Sydney H. Rodin House, Libertyville, Illinois (1960–61).

FIG. 262 "One Antenna," *House and Home*, Sept. 1953, 161.

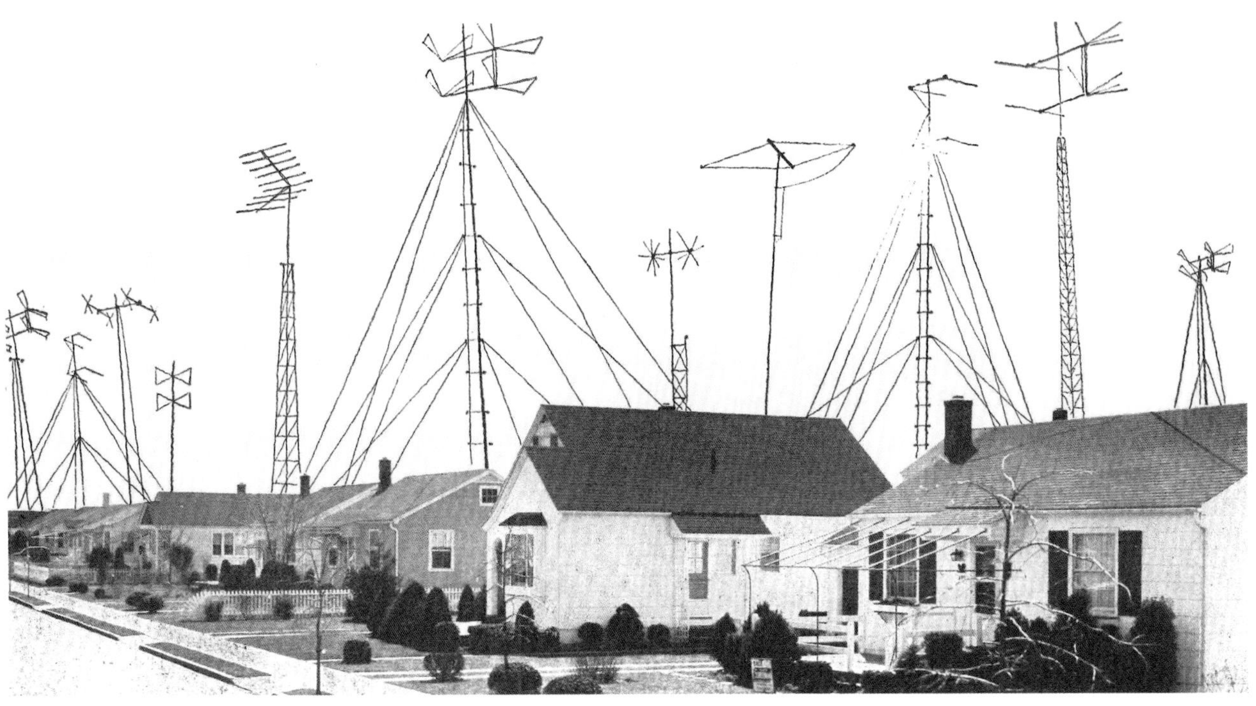

OPPOSITE, FIG. 263 Antenna sculpture in the Price studio, c. 1957. Photograph by Joe Price. Bruce A. Goff Archive.

CONCLUSION

In 1951 Deborah Allen, the editor of *Interiors* magazine, invited Bruce Goff to contribute sketches addressing a "specific problem of television use" for a special issue on television technology for interior and industrial design.[42] He had not dealt with television yet, and faced with a quick turnaround and little time to produce something new, Goff did not respond. By 1957, however, he proposed a solution to the problem of the television with the Price studio. In retrospect, Goff acknowledged the phenomenal impact of modern electronics on interior design. In 1963, he noted that a multifunctional "recreation room . . . designed as the central area of the home" had been normalized as a prototype for domestic interiors.[43] Even the kitchen was to be an alcove to the recreation room, combining all cooking and entertainment facilities in the same open space. The hearth and piano, once so dear to him, had been replaced by "television, radio, intercommunication, and movie projection."[44]

Goff also grappled with other emerging challenges in his houses in the late 1940s and 1950s. The concept of "home" shifted and changed to accommodate returning GIs and their families. The federal government, manufacturers, real estate agents, critics, photographers, and the editors of popular and professional magazines vied to define house and home.[45] The dominant domestic narrative idealized suburbanization, consumption, informality, traditional gender roles, racial discrimination, and the nuclear family.[46] Goff's clientele of artists, musicians, and teachers supported his designs, which became a hallmark of resistance to that model. In his collaboration with Joe Price in Bartlesville, Goff continued to shape a spatial and conceptual alternative to the family-oriented suburban ideal. Alongside and in dialogue with Hugh Hefner's 1956 designs for *Playboy*, Goff developed Price's bachelor pad as a sophisticated and highly designed lair: a permissive environment focused on pleasure and entertainment.[47] Price's white-shag-carpeted studio, complete with the latest electronics and a conversation pit, was not only a groundbreaking work of architecture—it also played a significant role in defining modern living in the postwar era.

42. Deborah Allen to Bruce Goff, May 2, 1951, series I, box 30, folder 17, BGA, AIC.
43. Bruce Goff and Douglas Harris to Briar Associates, Nov. 14, 1963, quoted in De Long, *Bruce Goff*, 214.
44. De Long, *Bruce Goff*, 214.
45. Elizabeth Gordon, the editor of *House Beautiful*, was as strong advocate for what she called the "station-wagon way-of-life." See Monica Penick, *Tastemaker: Elizabeth Gordon, House Beautiful, and the Postwar American Home* (Yale University Press, 2015).
46. On informality in postwar houses, see Jacobs, "Casual Living," 133–68.
47. Both versions of the American Dream required purchasing clothing, furnishings, and cars to establish one's identity. *Ebony* magazine, first published in 1945, adapted these narratives for African American readers. See Kristina Wilson, *Mid-Century Modernism and the American Body: Race, Gender and the Politics of Power in Design* (Princeton University Press, 2021).

FIG. 264 Goff and Larry Wayne Grantham (American, 1951–2002). *First National Bank of Independence, Independence, Missouri, Perspective* [unbuilt], 1970. Graphite on tracing paper; 86.4 × 57.1 cm (34 1/16 × 22 1/2 in.). The Art Institute of Chicago, gift of Shin'enKan, Inc., 1990.871.2.

Autofuturism: Architecture for This Thing That Is You

Penelope Dean

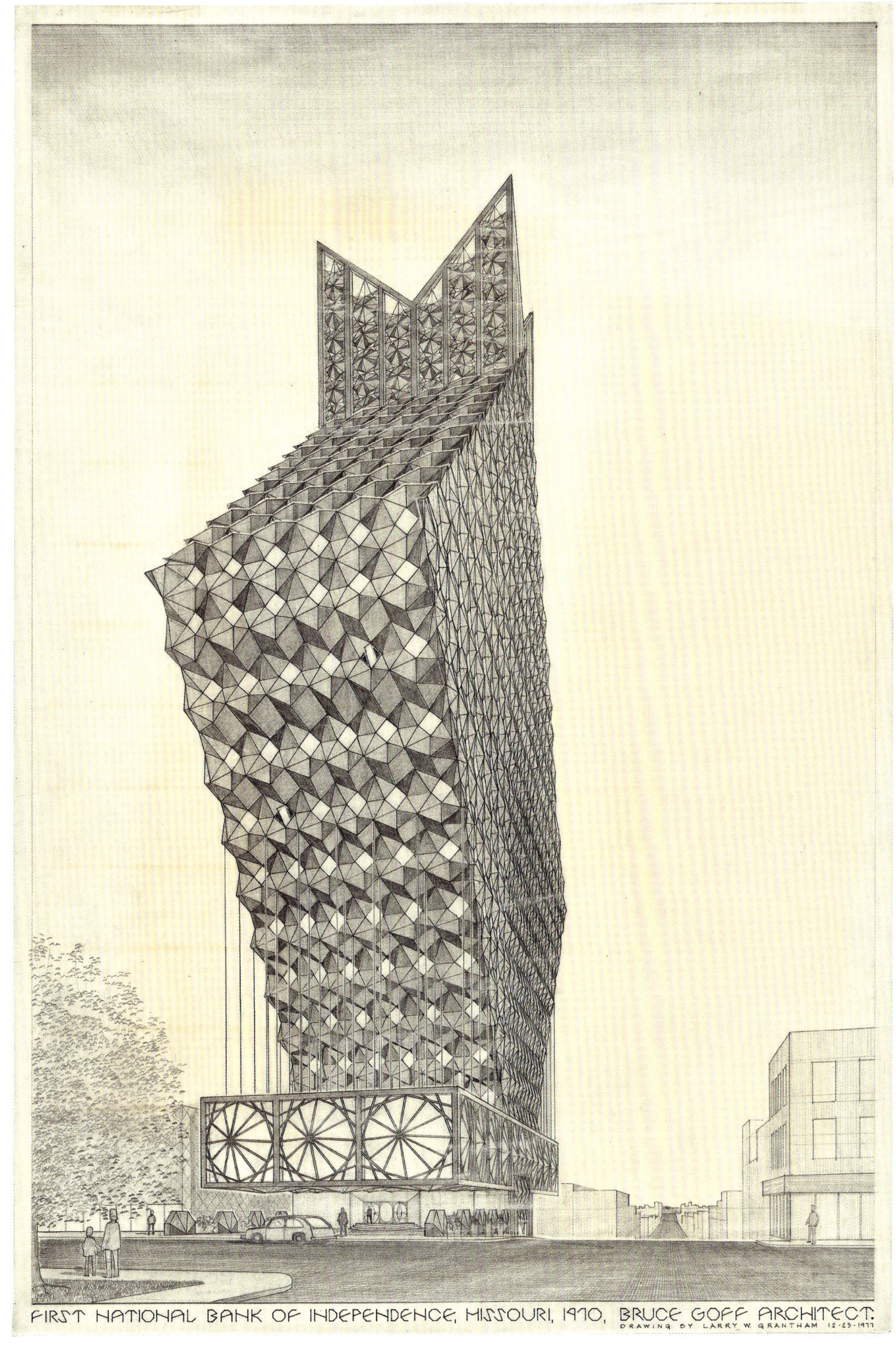

In his speech at the 1977 conference An American Architecture: Its Roots, Growth, and Horizons in Milwaukee, Bruce Goff credited *Harper's Bazar* illustrator Erté for his own long-held conviction that clients should serve as the starting point for design.[1] Erté's stunning magazine covers, ink drawings, and pithy texts—which Goff cut out and collected between 1919 and 1928—showcase women in striking outfits defined by geometric outlines, monochrome palettes, and intricate details such as glittering stars and exotic leaves (fig. 265). Each ensemble radiates from a woman's body in celebration of her own qualities and style. What Goff admired in these designs was the "divine spark of individuality," as Erté characterized it, and the idea that a woman's apparel could be designed "in accord with this thing that is *you*—this thing that is no one else in the whole wide world."[2] "Now why couldn't a house be that way?" Goff asked rhetorically.[3] Pronouncing architecture an expression of self, Goff shifted the stakes of design. If Erté's art nouveau was a way to naturalize the machine age, Goff's version was a way to personalize the space age.

FIG. 265 Erté (Romain de Tirtoff; French, born Russia, 1892–1990). Cover design for *Harper's Bazar*, Jan. 1922.

Delivered late in a career that produced a remarkable range of houses for "business men and women, religious groups, professionals, manufacturers, editors of newspapers and magazines, writers, artists, musicians, farmers, air-pilots, and even the U.S.N. Seabees!," Goff's revelation that expressive individualism derived from Erté's commercial art came at a pivotal moment.[4] Beginning in the late 1940s, Goff advocated for an "individual architecture for individuals" that went against the grain of prevailing architectural modernist ideologies and countered midcentury social conformism.[5] Yet by the late 1970s, individualism was about to come of age—sociopolitically, culturally, and economically. Embraced in political circles by British Prime Minister Margaret Thatcher and President Ronald Reagan soon after taking office (1979 and 1981, respectively), and by historicist postmodernists in architecture such as Charles Jencks, public intellectuals such as Tom Wolfe in "The 'Me' Decade" (1976), and economists Milton and Rose Friedman in *Free to Choose* (1980), a privileging of the self had entered the mainstream. Goff's client-centric approach presaged a future on the brink of arrival.

Goff's augury invites us to reconsider futurism, a concept that superficially applies to his architecture because characteristics of his work *look* futuristic: Many projects include spherical shapes and curvilinear geometries, and several drawings exude mysterious lights on black backgrounds and include streamlined cars and space age signage. But there are discrepancies between what you see (in Goff's forms and renderings) and what you read (in his writings about his built work). Goff did not envision the future—he offered ideas on how to deliver it. One of those contributions was challenging the widespread architectural assumption that conceptions of the future must be tied to yet-to-be-realized technological innovation.[6] Another was unlinking futurism from its collective (i.e., utopian or avant-garde) technological underpinnings in architectural culture and relinking it to broader midcentury notions of individualism and consumerism. This reorientation mirrored broader economic developments during the postwar period as business executives, economists, and motivation researchers, among others, pivoted away from a focus on selling products to understanding who was buying them. They realized they needed to understand consumer choices and desires before making future-looking products. Although Goff was likely unaware of these developments, his attention to clients and their individuality suggests his proximity to broader mainstream tendencies, opening the

1. Bruce Goff, speech, Milwaukee, Oct. 29, 1977, typescript, 12, series V, box 2, folder 1, Bruce A. Goff Archive, Ryerson and Burnham Archives, The Art Institute of Chicago (hereafter BGA, AIC). See also Bruce Goff, "Alcan Lectures on Architecture," 1981, typescript, 9, series V, box 2, folder 6, BGA, AIC. My argument concerning Goff's self-confessed client focus can be seen as a parallel to that made by Robin Evans regarding the eighteenth-century British architect Robert Adam. See Robin Evans, "The Developed Surface," in *Translations from Drawing to Building and Other Essays* (MIT Press, 1997), 197.

2. Erté quoted in "Erté Gives to Every Woman an Individuality," *Harper's Bazar*, Feb. 1919, 48, series VIII, box 3, folder 4, BGA, AIC. Goff referenced this article in his address to the conference An American Architecture, Milwaukee (see n. 1).

3. Goff, speech, Milwaukee, 13 (see n. 1).

4. Bruce Goff, *Forty-Four Architectural Realizations*, 1966, unpublished manuscript, 16, series V, box 1, folder 21, BGA, AIC.

5. In this regard, Goff's architectural individualization paralleled the individualization of postwar art at that moment.

6. My use of *futurism* throughout this essay does not pertain to Italian Futurism, the artistic and social movement that originated in Italy in 1909, but rather to futurism more broadly in architectural culture, which has largely (and narrowly) been linked to scientific and technological progress on the one hand, and utopian and visionary thinking on the other. For conceptualizations of futurism outside architecture, see Lawrence R. Samuel, *Future: A Recent History* (University of Texas Press, 2009). For portraits of individual futurologists across cultural history, race, and gender studies, among other fields, see Glen Adamson, *A Century of Tomorrows: How Imagining the Future Shapes the Present* (Bloomsbury Publishing, 2024).

FIG. 266 Goff. *Jerry Alex and Mary Blakeley House, First Design, Highland Park, Texas, Interior Perspective* [unbuilt], 1949. Colored pencil with graphite over diazo print on cream wove paper; diam.: 53.5 cm (21⅛ in.). The Art Institute of Chicago, gift of Shin'enKan, Inc., 1990.883.3.

possibility of an alternate futurism, a self-actualizing futurism of the now.

This essay argues that although Goff drew inspiration from the aesthetic of futuristic genres such as the atomic age, Googie architecture, machines, science fiction, and space travel, he abandoned the technoscientific ideologies of progress that accompanied them. In doing so, he created space for an ideology that prioritized personal expression over technological determinism—an *autofuturism*, a futurism modified by the Greek prefix *auto*, meaning self.[7] Tracing the ways Goff unlinked technological ideology from his visual representations—in the context of evolving popular definitions of futurism—and reflecting on Goff's interpretation of futurism as a liberating spirit of imagination, I look at his critique of regulatory design frameworks and speculate on the way he bridged from what he called the dangers of "commonism" to "autoism."[8]

The second half of the essay examines Goff's conceptual invention of the client at the intersection of broader social, cultural, and economic developments, revealing what appear to be contradictions in Goff's work: it was reactionary (socially), speculative (culturally), and conservative (economically). Although these stances seem logically inconsistent, they express the inevitable contradictions and idiosyncrasies of individual desire, both Goff's as a designer and that of his clients. Goff inadvertently channeled a socioeconomic future already in the making, one in which it was vital to not only understand but also satisfy consumer preferences. The result was a technical paradigm of customized specifications, drawing annotations, idiosyncratic details, and specific materials tailored to a diverse clientele, all of which embodied autofuturism, a futurism that did not need to be directed.

7. My definition of *autofuturism* is distinct from the contemporaneous "Afrofuturism," a term Mark Dery coined in 1994. Afrofuturism evolved out of jazz and art in the 1940s–60s and is largely understood as a broad aesthetic movement encompassing a diverse range of African American artists who addressed African American concerns about twentieth-century technoculture. Goff's autofuturism eschewed a faith in science and technology for client needs and preferences, a mode that aligned with postwar American consumerism.

8. For "commonism," see Goff quoted in Donald L. Hoffmann, "Cites [*sic*] Architectural Need in Designing of Houses," *Kansas City Times*, Dec. 7, 1963, n.p., series VII, box 3, folder 22, BGA, AIC.

NO FUTURE

Nowhere did Goff write about the future as a point of departure for his architecture.[9] His texts neither evoke terminology like *innovation* nor hint at visionary impulses. There are no mentions of spaceships in documented discussions with his clients. Yet many of his drawings and designs are infused with futuristic imagery from different time periods. From the pink and brown suspended celestial rings of the glowing Jerry Alex and Mary Blakeley House (fig. 266) to the cratered, otherworldly planets (or conjoined bubbles) that configure the unrealized Grace and Larry Abraham House (1967), his forms reflect an era when futurism emerged as a recognizable field in North America—technological, scientific, and fictional during the World War II years, and based in space travel, the atomic age, and information forecasting in the postwar years.[10] Although futurism exerted a *visual* influence on Goff's drawings and renderings, the architect often redirected, reduced, or even rejected its ideological foundations.[11]

FROM LEFT, FIG. 267 Goff. *Hypothetical Study*, 1926. Watercolor and graphite on cream wove paper; 25.4 × 18.5 cm (10 × 7¼ in.). The Art Institute of Chicago, gift of Shin'enKan, Inc., RX 18410/26.2. FIGS. 268A–B Designed by Hugh Ferriss (American, 1889–1962). Studies for Maximum Mass Permitted by the 1916 New York Zoning Law, Stages 2 and 3, 1922. Black crayon, stumped, and brush and black ink over photostat, varnish on illustration board; 66.8 × 51cm (26⁵⁄₁₆ × 20¹⁄₁₆ in.). Cooper Hewitt, gift of Mrs. Hugh Ferriss; 1969-137-2.

Such discrepancies between image and underlying principle are apparent in some of Goff's earliest studies. His hypothetical architectural drawings from the 1920s and 1930s showcase the aesthetics of German Expressionist and visionary American architecture while disregarding their triggering motivations. For example, Goff's 1931 perspective studies composed of thick, sweeping black linework emulate the dynamic India ink sketches Erich Mendelsohn created in 1914, but whereas Mendelsohn represented the dynamics of new materials made possible by the machine age, Goff was simply experimenting with "other ways of designing."[12] Similarly, Goff's emerald-green Alpine-like study from 1926 (fig. 267) appears directly indebted to the smoky, crystalline delineation of Hugh Ferriss's 1922 "Evolution of a City Building Under the Zoning Law" (figs. 268a–b). While Ferriss derived his pyramidal shapes from the form-giving principle of New York's zoning laws, Goff modestly altered Ferriss's depiction by changing the color palette (from black and white to green and blue) and perspectival view (from worm's-eye to bird's-eye view). Goff's pyramids and stalagmites did not derive from the current code but from the phenomena of either the natural or the archaic. As David G. De Long noted of the period, "It was the visual images rather than the underlying philosophy he found appealing."[13]

Between the mid-1940s and mid-1960s, when futuristic imagery entered what Reyner Banham called "the space of science and science fiction," Goff adopted a language of spheres, planetary rings, Sputniks, and discs on the one hand, and stylistic Googie architecture–like fins and fonts on the other.[14] Yet across the spaceforms and techno-features, Goff tempered his imagery with localisms—of client or site—that contradict the

9. Although the words *future* and *futuristic* occasionally appear in Goff's writings, this does not suggest Goff embraced the future as an initiating concept for his architecture. For example, his high school yearbook cites "Futuristic art" as his chief accomplishment in 1922, but there is no reference to architecture and the future is something already "accomplished." See Goff's 1922 Central High School yearbook, *Tom Tom*, 52.

10. Samuel, *Future*, 201.

11. In an unpublished housing report Goff prepared in 1933, he explicitly rejected the "future" and "Utopia of the future" as relevant for architecture. See Bruce Goff, "Thoughts on Housing as Architecture," 1933, unpublished manuscript prepared for Alfonso Iannelli and his associates, 1–2, series V, box 1, folder 3, BGA, AIC.

12. Quoted from a 1953 conversation with Philip B. Welch, which he cited in "Goff's Creative Growth and Design Philosophy," in *Goff on Goff: Conversations and Lectures*, ed. Philip B. Welch (University of Oklahoma Press, 1996), 22.

13. David G. De Long, *Bruce Goff: Toward Absolute Architecture* (Architectural History Foundation; MIT Press, 1988), 27 and see also 88.

14. Reyner Banham, "Space for Decoration: A Rejoinder," *Design*, no. 79 (July 1955): 24–25.

FIG. 269 Goff. *Evelyn and John Garvey House, First Design, Urbana, Illinois, Perspective* [unbuilt], 1952. Graphite on tracing paper; 71 × 90.6 cm (28 × 35 11/16 in.). The Art Institute of Chicago, gift of Shin'enKan, Inc., 1990.860.1.

otherworldly references. His 1952 perspective drawing for the Evelyn and John Garvey House (fig. 269) includes six aluminum spheres suspended in a circle at different levels. Accessed via a ramping corridor enclosed in a transparent tube, each globe contains either a bedroom, bathroom, kitchen, dining area, or study, providing intimate inner worlds for family life. Similarly, the perspective for the unrealized Venus Soft Drinks Bar (fig. 270)—a project Goff later regretted and wished he had kept out of sight[15]—depicts a large white capsule with a blue planetary ring alongside Sputniks touching down like spacecraft on a driveway. Despite the building's unearthly appearance, Goff's scrawled notes indicate an intimate, earthly environment inside: "drive in," "black top underneath," "ramp covered with carpet," "soft light," "padded bar," "gold rain," and "easy access."[16] In both the Garvey house and the Venus bar, otherworldly tropes disguise inner-world encounters.

Revealing similar contradictions, Goff's unbuilt Dominic Giacomo's Motor Lodge (fig. 271) showcases futuristic features assuaged by the archaic: industrial trimmings from the space age juxtaposed with the primitive materialism of the stone age. Bird's-eye perspectives depict red sandstone rocks stacked in cylindrical towers

15. De Long, *Bruce Goff*, 161.
16. Bruce Goff, handwritten notes, n.d., series II, box 14, folder 12, BGA, AIC.

FIG. 270 Goff. *Venus Soft Drinks Bar, Wichita, Kansas, Perspective* [unbuilt], 1959. Colored pencil and graphite over diazo print on cream wove paper; 62.4 × 107.5 cm (24⅝ × 42⅜ in.). The Art Institute of Chicago, gift of Shin'enKan, Inc., 1990.1101.

and embellished with steel fins, vertical signage, and streamlined vehicles à la Googie architecture. It is hard *not* to see the motor lodge's shotgun marriage of rubble and car culture as indebted to Bedrock, the town from the animated series *The Flintstones*, which launched a year earlier, and anticipating the sinewy accoutrements of Orbit City from *The Jetsons*, which aired the following year. Like Bedrock, the Giacomo project juxtaposes the past (rocks) with the present (cars), but whereas the cartoon dealt in irony, displacing modern life into a prehistoric setting, Goff used deadpan humor, merging "the nature boy and the popular mechanics" visual languages he identified in 1953 into a singular style—a retort to his question from the same year: "Why must it be all one or the other?"[17] Goff displayed a tolerance for inconsistency by having it all ways, preempting a return to unprocessed materials in the burgeoning age of the Anthropocene.

In each of these projects, Goff relied on popular futurism as a *context* for visual inspiration, drawing formal sensibilities from popular science fiction movies and television animations. Goff enjoyed "pseudo technical

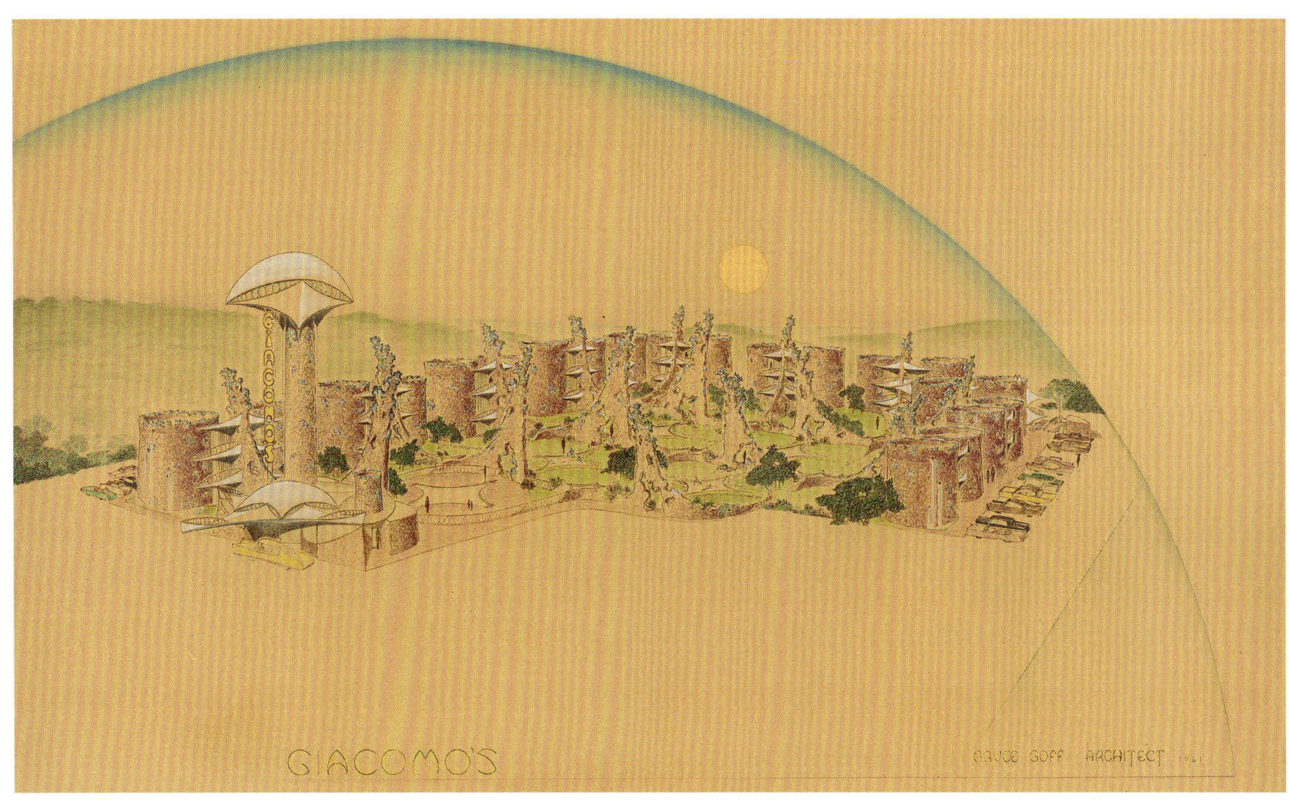

FIG. 271 Goff. *Dominic Giacomo's Motor Lodge, First Design, McAlester, Oklahoma, Perspective* [unbuilt], 1961. Colored pencil and graphite over diazo print on cream wove paper; 58.7 × 87.6 cm (23⅛ × 34½ in.). The Art Institute of Chicago, gift of Shin'enKan, Inc., 1990.1117.6.

17. Bruce Goff, lecture, University of Oklahoma School of Architecture, Oct. 28, 1953, in Welch, *Goff on Goff*, 91.

movies" such as *The War of the Worlds* (1953), highly regarded for its technicolor special effects at the time, and avidly watched the original *Star Trek* (1966–69) series (fig. 272), which transposed discussions of contemporary societal issues into a futuristic context.[18] For subsequent projects, Goff looked to magazines and books trafficking in futurology. He owned Alvin Toffler's *Future Shock* (1970), a bestseller concerned with the impact of rapid technological change on society, and he subscribed to *Omni* (fig. 273), a new-wave magazine published from 1978 to 1997 that brought together fiction, fact, science, and the paranormal in psychedelic color and fluid shapes.[19] It is easy to see the parallels between Goff's architectural forms, colors, and geometries, and the special effects of popular film, television shows, and magazines—transparent saucers, curvaceous spaceships, and the angular interior of the Starship Enterprise. Popular futurism was an intensely visual and central part of Goff's optical zeitgeist.

Publications like *Future Shock* and *Omni*, which emphasized the impact of change on individual lives, also exposed a deeply social underside to popular futurism. Goff had observed the disconnect between visual *representations* of popular futurism and its social *reception* in his early lectures and writings. He dissented from critics labeling his work futuristic, because the term implied "going too far" and "doing things for the 'future' rather than the present."[20] Many descriptions of Goff's aesthetic between 1947 and 1970—"out of this world," "space and saucer," "strange," "Martian esthetics," "Space-Camp"—were as much a product of popular futurism as Goff's work was visually indebted to it.[21] The problem for Goff was not their terminology per se, but the implication that his work was untimely because of its appearance. In response to such criticisms, which reflected society's uneasy relationship with technological transformation, Goff reframed the problem as one of reception.[22]

He questioned the received idea that the pace of societal change—futurism's social underside—was something to fear. "All of this may sound like Buck Rogers stuff or science fiction, but so would many of the things that we accept today as accomplished facts, that have been thought of just a few years ago," he wrote in 1967.[23] Goff recast the future as neither a liability nor—in Toffler's characterization—a "shock" but rather as the natural evolution of the "continuous present," an idea indebted to novelist and poet Gertrude Stein of no beginning and no end, only a middle.[24] By normalizing the future, Goff attempted to allay fears of its impact. As in Giacomo's Motor Lodge, he wanted to have it all ways: a third way between future and past.

In downplaying the future's lure, Goff's thinking aligned with sociologists in the late 1960s who had grown skeptical of the future as a theater of "technological virtuosity."[25] "We have become more conscious of the coming of the future and at the same time the shape of the future is more opaque or appalling," Edward Shils declared in 1967.[26] At the same time, Goff called for a change in values, claiming technological developments represented something else entirely—an imaginative spirit, freedom of thought, and an embrace of the unknown. That this unconventional thinking in the scientific sphere did not influence the sociocultural sphere perplexed him: "Even in these exciting days of discoveries here and in outer space there is, strangely, an ever-increasing fear of non-conformity and more and more refuge is being sought in conformity."[27] For Goff, ingenious discoveries were essential to social progress.

FIG. 272 Starship Enterprise interior, *Star Trek: The Original Series*. Still from season 1, episode 24, "This Side of Paradise," aired Mar. 2, 1967.

THE FUTURE IS YOU

Goff's conception of society was narrowly focused on the individual—that is a futurism of one, not of the collective—a *you*topia as opposed to utopia. Inspired by Erté, who inversely viewed fashion "like an architectural creation," he decided early on that his clients would serve as a point of departure.[28] Goff later described, "It seemed to me that I had to choose between being purely abstract in my approach or in trying to deal with people

18. See Welch, *Goff on Goff*, 92; and De Long, *Bruce Goff*, 308.
19. Kathy Bell, review of *Omni*, *The English Journal* 68, no. 7 (Oct. 1979): 84.
20. Bruce Goff, "Notes on Architecture," June 1957, unpublished typescript, 4, series V, box 1, folder 11, BGA, AIC.
21. For "out of this world," see Rose Spradlin, "Organic Architecture Shown in Most-Talked About House," *Norman Transcript*, Aug. 31, 1947, series VII, box 1, folder 35; for "space and saucer," see "Space and Saucer House: Oklahoma Family Lives in Suspension in a Unique New Structure," *Life*, Sept. 19, 1955, series VII, box 1, folder 40; for "strange" see Don Hoffmann, "What Shape Is Your House?," *Kansas City Star*, Jan. 20, 1963, n.p., series VII, box 3, folder 22; and for "Martian esthetics" and "Space-Camp," see Ada Louise Huxtable, "Peacock Feathers and Pink Plastic: A New Yorker Sees Bruce Goff," *New York Times*, Feb. 8, 1970, D25, series VII, box 3, folder 29, all in BGA, AIC.
22. Samuel, *Future*, 78 and 123.
23. Bruce Goff, "The Continuous Present in Architecture," Apr. 3, 1967, in Welch, *Goff on Goff*, 207.
24. See Goff, "Thoughts on Housing."
25. Edward Shils, "The Intellectuals and the Future," *The Intellectuals and the Powers and Other Essays* (University of Chicago Press, 1972), 216. First published in 1967.
26. Shils, *Intellectuals and the Powers*, 219.
27. Bruce Goff, "Individual Architecture by and for Individuals," *Palette '67* (Spring 1967): n.p., series VII, box 3, folder 26, BGA, AIC.
28. Erté, *Harper's Bazar*, Sept. 1920, 59. Goff's clipping is preserved in series VIII, box 3, folder 3, BGA, AIC.

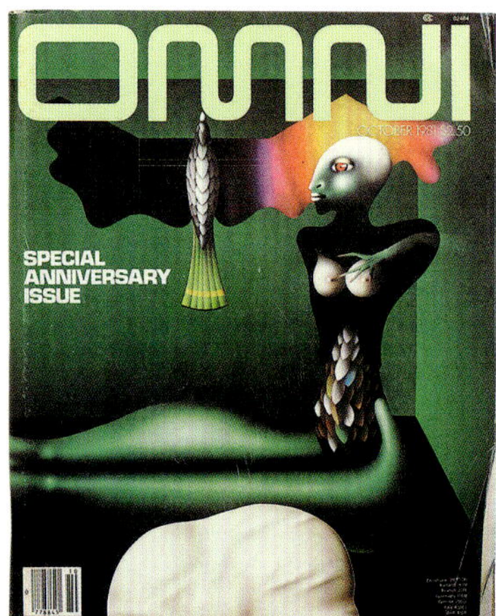

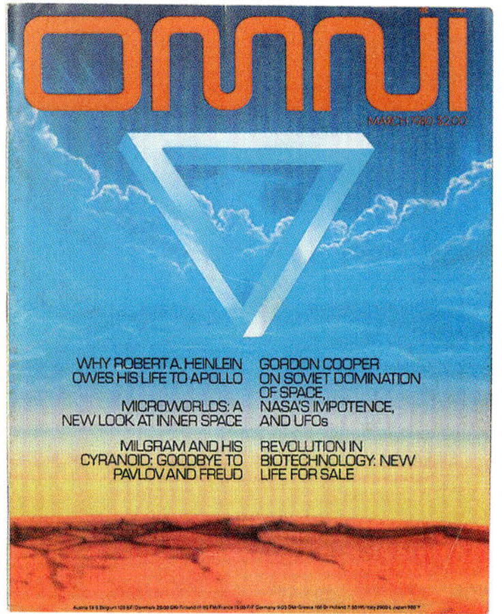

FIG. 273 Issues of *Omni* Goff owned, 1978–83. Private collection.

in a way they could understand if they wanted to. I chose the latter course."[29] He subsequently railed against notions of the "average man," recognizing each client as unique: "They ranged from shy, timid, quiet introverts to outgoing extroverts and exhibitionists, from hard-driven businessmen to sensitive idealists."[30] He advanced the modest idea of a house as "a portrait of the owners and their needs."[31] And Goff speculated that the commonality between his clients was them "realizing themselves as individuals" and appreciating his "efforts toward [creating] individual architecture for individuals."[32] Many clients affirmed his assessment. Al Dewlen wrote in the broadly circulating general interest magazine *Coronet* that Goff's design for his house was "among the finest representations of his theories for individualized architecture."[33] Elaine A. Gryder recalled, "We wanted a home that was different; something that would fit our personalities."[34] Eugene and Nancy Bavinger, meanwhile, acknowledged Goff's "ability to solve individual problems."[35] For Goff and his clients, American individualism was the first stronghold of architecture—it provided a new way forward. As the postwar economy enabled a greater number of individuals to enter the housing market, either by purchasing developer-built tract homes or buying land to construct custom-designed houses, many wanted the individual attention of a client-based service.

This wave of autofuturism ran parallel with North American businesses reconceiving citizens as consumers from the 1950s onwards. As Lawrence Samuel noted of the period, executives framed the future as "heavily domesticated" and imbued it "with consumer-based agendas to promote a particular industry, company or product."[36] The American home was a locale for much speculation and prediction, as popular journals such as *Ladies' Home Journal* and *House Beautiful* promoted houses of tomorrow, miracle kitchens, and houses of the future that were full of new appliances, electronics, and conveniences. Although Goff was skeptical of the "cliched" editorial policies of popular design magazines, his focus on the "'user' or 'consumer'" inadvertently mirrored a socioeconomic future of corporate capitalism already in the making.[37] Behind all the futuristic imagery was a conflicted social motivation that, on the one hand, reflected a more general turn in marketing culture toward fully comprehending the needs and wants of customers, while on the other hand, tapped into the declining social trait of inner-directedness as conformist society gave up its prohibition of expressionism.

Motivation research and merchandising took off during the 1940s and 1950s, as psychologists and sociologists sought to understand how people made buying decisions, using consumer surveys, focus groups, and paper questionnaires. These pseudoscientific studies, driven by market segmentation, reflected an economy that could no longer be sustained by companies merely imposing products on customers. Economist Theodore Levitt pithily summed up the corporate U-turn in 1960: "The view that an industry is a customer-satisfying process, not a goods-producing one, is vital for all businessmen to understand.... Given the customer's needs, the industry develops backwards, first concerning itself with the physical *delivery* of customer satisfactions."[38]

It is unlikely Goff was aware of this general reversal in marketing strategy, but he arrived at similar conclusions for architectural production—that one should not dictate a predetermined style but rather "first try to understand the people [one is] doing the house for."[39] This client-first model contrasted with the product-first model that drove modern architectural production and suburban tract development as architects embraced concepts of standardization for top-down aesthetics (e.g., Mies van der Rohe) and developers and builders offered standardized building components for consumers to choose from in catalogues. If modern architects saw no need to prioritize client preferences and American industry wanted to understand customers for financial gain, Goff embraced his clients as the conceptual context for an individual architecture: *his* individual architecture.

For Goff, an individualized architecture could only be achieved by rejecting conformity. The debilitating sociocultural conventionality of this period appalled him and his clients. "One of the biggest dangers today is not communism, but commonism," he declared in 1963, referencing Frank Lloyd Wright's earlier comments about "the common man" being "responsible for the drift toward conformity" and a "block to progress."[40] The tyranny of developer-driven suburban mediocrity, policing of roof materials and styles, Federal Housing Administration limitations, good taste committees and restrictive set-back regulations, and real-estate constraints that affected financing (you can't resell a weird house) and construction (who will build a weird house?) cramped his individual style.[41] And the managerial procedures of corporate futurism—"research planning," "teams," "complexes," "clusters," and "reports"—that had crept into architectural education and eroded the individuality of authorship infuriated him.[42] Across society,

29. Bruce Goff, lecture, University of Oklahoma School of Architecture, Mar. 11, 1953, in Welch, *Goff on Goff*, 34.
30. Goff, *Architectural Realizations*, 1.
31. Bruce Goff quoted in Loy Ferguson, "Bavinger House Resembles Medieval Castle," *The Oklahoman*, May 25, 1955, 1 and 4, series VII, box 1, folder 40, BGA, AIC. See also Hoffmann, "What Shape Is Your House?" (see n. 21).
32. Goff, *Architectural Realizations*, 17.
33. Al Dewlen, "Architecture's Unpredictable Artist," *Coronet*, Mar. 1958, 45, series VII, box 3, folder 16, BGA, AIC.
34. Elaine A. Gryder quoted in Susan Puckett, "Gryder Home Throws a Curve to Some Surprised Passersby," *Clarion Ledger*, Mar. 21, 1980, C1, series VII, box 2, folder 25, BGA, AIC.
35. NCARB application report, dated 1967, on the Eugene and Nancy Bavinger House, Norman, Oklahoma, series I, box 1, folder 10, BGA, AIC.
36. Samuel, *Future*, 64–65.
37. For "cliched," see Welch, *Goff on Goff*, 91. For "'user' or 'consumer,'" see Goff, *Architectural Realizations*, 45.
38. Theodore Levitt, "Marketing Myopia," *Harvard Business Review*, July–Aug. 1960, 20.
39. Goff, lecture, Mar. 11, 1953, in Welch, *Goff on Goff*, 34.
40. Goff quoted in Hoffmann, "Cites [*sic*] Architectural Need." For Frank Lloyd Wright's comments, see Mike Wallace, "Interview with Frank Lloyd Wright," Sept. 1, 1957, hrc.contentdm.oclc.org/digital/collection/p15878coll90/id/81/.
41. For comments on financing, see Goff, "Individual Architecture." For comments on the FHA and good taste committees, see Welch, *Goff on Goff*, 146 and 221–23; and Goff, *Architectural Realizations*, 12–13 and 55.
42. Bruce Goff, "A Young Architect's Protest for Architecture," *Perspecta* vol. 13/14 (1971): 330. See also H. H. Waechter, "The Architecture of Bruce Goff,"

bureaucracy, and the university, Goff saw conformity hindering the "individualism, personal growth, and self-expression" that intellectuals from Lewis Mumford to Aldous Huxley to George Orwell had advocated for and that Goff himself aspired to.

Goff's clients who shared the trait of "inner-directedness," as defined by David Riesman in *The Lonely Crowd*, also refused to adapt to such conformity.[43] They invited Goff to provide alternatives to "the usual box house of several little box rooms with rectangular holes cut in them for doors and windows" and imagine worlds "which would become an escape from business, from pressures of society, and from prying eyes of gossips."[44] Many clients were apathetic to criticism, most famously encapsulated in Ruth and Sam Ford's retort, "We don't like your house either" (fig. 118). If developers Levitt and Sons standardized the American suburban dream and made it accessible to the many, Goff customized the dream and made it exotic for the one (two, three, or four).

As clients looked to Goff to satisfy their unique design needs, Goff reciprocated by feeding into their desires for exceptionalism. He frequently characterized *their* houses as his best work yet, a personal favorite. Goff pronounced Eugene and Nancy Bavinger's House "not like any house in the world."[45] He informed Al and Jean Dewlen, meanwhile, that his unbuilt design for them was "my trump card that I save until last in showing my work and it always makes the biggest impression."[46] The approach was strategic: "Each of my clients can be sure he is getting an 'original' and that there has never been nor will there ever be another like it."[47] Moreover, Goff provided a service that was as personalized as his designs. He carefully tended to the tastes of his female clients, treating them as people, not passive consumers. He welcomed the ideas of Betty Nicol, who had "studied home publications, clipped plans on storage unit areas and adapted these to fit her own family needs," and complimented Elaine A. Gryder on the pink and purple fabric choices for her curtains and couch upholstery.[48] Just as Erté captured a woman's style on *Harper's* covers, Goff encapsulated his female clients' preferences inside their homes.

Goff's embrace of individualistic causes (consumerism) but rejection of group effects (conformism) provided the basis for an autofuturism that was entirely at odds with the futurity of midcentury modern architecture and Good-Life Modernism, which infused American suburbia and consumer goods with modernist aesthetics.[49] What Goff understood, unlike many, was that both modernisms—in their respective production (the good society) or reception (the good life)—were out of sync with the socioeconomic moment. They were fixed in an outdated intellectual framework derived from an era of mass production: product oriented, standardized, technological. Good-Life Modernism's attempt to package new kinds of lifestyles for a mass market remained entirely reliant on products, such as the house and its furniture. Indeed, given this prevalence of a product-oriented mindset, it is not surprising that critics invariably positioned Goff's work as an alternative (futuristic) *style* of product.[50] Yet Goff's significant, if largely overlooked, contribution to midcentury modernisms was not to offer one style over another, but rather to precisely locate architecture at the inflection point of changing economic and social conditions by imagining the possibility of the client as a concept. He inverted the product-client relationship so that the client, not the product, came first. As the art editor of *Horizons* put it in 1961, "Goff's houses deny the validity of standardization as a way of life and proclaim that each human being is an individual whose inner self is more important than the outer casing by which he meets his obligations as a social unit."[51] Goff replaced standardization with customization.

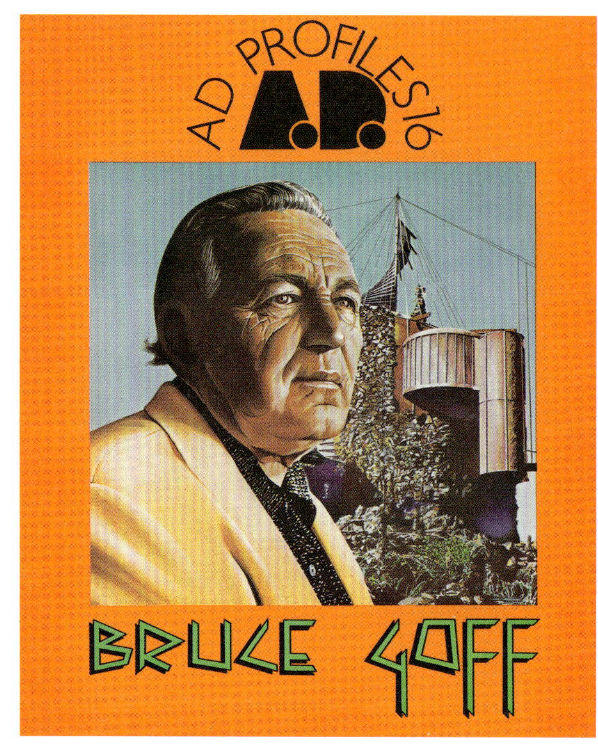

FIG. 274 *AD Profiles 16: Bruce Goff*, 1978. Special issue, *Architectural Design* 48, no. 10 (1978). Bruce A. Goff Archive.

AIA Journal 32 (Dec. 1959): 32–36, series VII, box 3, folder 17, BGA, AIC.

43. David Riesman with Nathan Glazer and Reuel Denney, *The Lonely Crowd: A Study of the Changing American Character*, rev. ed. (Yale University Press, 2001), 34. First published in 1950.

44. For "the usual box," see Bruce Goff, "Bavinger House and Price House," *Global Architecture*, no. 33 (1975), and for "an escape from business," see Joe D. Price, "Bruce Goff," *The Kentiku*, Mar. 1969, 39, both series VII, box 2, folder 12, BGA, AIC.

45. See Goff quoted in Loy Ferguson, "Bavinger House Resembles Medieval Castle," *Oklahoma Daily*, May 25, 1955, 4, series VII, box 1, folder 40, BGA, AIC.

46. Bruce Goff to Al and Jean Dewlen, Oct. 21, 1961, 1, series II, box 8, folder 10, BGA, AIC.

47. Goff, *Architectural Realizations*, 106.

48. See Elsye W. Allison, "'Quiet' House Comes Alive Through Vivid Interior Color," *Kansas City Star*, Nov. 5, 1967, 1D, series VII, box 2, folder 34, BGA, AIC; and Bruce Goff to Elaine A. Gryder, Mar. 13, 1963, series II, box 14, folder 20, BGA, AIC.

49. Mark Jarzombek, "'Good-Life Modernism' and Beyond: The American House in the 1950s and 1960s: A Commentary," *Cornell Journal of Architecture*, no. 4 (1991): 78.

50. See, for example, Elizabeth Gordon, "The Threat to the Next America," *House Beautiful*, Apr. 1953, 126–31 and 250–51; Jarzombek, "Good-Life Modernism and Beyond," 76–93; and Stephanie Pilat, "People, Place, Time, Materials, and Spirit," in *Renegades: Bruce Goff and the American School of Architecture*, ed. Luca Guido et al. (University of Oklahoma Press, 2020), 177–99.

51. John Canaday, "Pavilions on the Prairie," *Horizon*, Nov. 1961, 44, series VII, box 3, folder 19, BGA, AIC.

In all these ways, Goff's writings and lectures about individualism foretell a future in the making: a future where individuals precede objects, a future where individuals abandon conformism, a future where "each creative artist has the need and the right to be an individual," and a future where the architect becomes a consumer of surprising materials, textures, and colors.[52] In this context, the true imagery of autofuturism is not space age visuals, but the "individual expression of design to the smallest detail," as Goff foretold in 1942.[53] Ignited by that "divine spark of individuality," autofuturism relied on a technical paradigm of meticulous specifications and annotations. In other words, it lay in the particulars—in the individuality of materials, of solutions, of client wishes and decisions, and of architectural responses to client needs. All this was registered in written instructions and reactions between architect, client, and contractor: construction drawings, client–architect letters, contractor–architect exchanges, scrawled design notes, specific client requests. Through technical—as opposed to technological—means, Goff's architecture emerged as a manifestation of choice and tailoring. Particularism, not universalism, was the visual hallmark of his autofuturism.

Less experimental than adventurous, particularism is *everywhere* in Goff's documentation of his design processes. It appears in his pithy instructions to Irma Bartman's contractor: "All wood-grain vertical, not sandblasted. Paint inside of linen cabinet turquoise blue. Note new plant-shelf in monitor, above end of tub."[54] It occurs in the Gutmans' feedback to Goff's material selections (yes to white chips, dark blue trim, and fiberglass screens; no to Formica, high-pile carpeting, and grass cloth).[55] It arises in the Gryders' wish list for their architectural plan (a "kitchen—completely modern, with outstanding curved eating bar connecting family room").[56] And it is on display in Goff's drawing annotations for the Ford house's built-in furniture and the Garveys' driveway accessories. The "smallest details" reveal Goff's architecture for individuals evolving *with* the client, not for the client—less "participatory" and more bespoke.

THE SELF-GENERATION OF AUTOFUTURISM

In 1978, a year after Goff cited Erté as a source of inspiration for his client-first design process, *Architectural Design* put Goff's portrait on the cover of a special issue (fig. 274) devoted entirely to his work. The magazine included edited selections of responses to a questionnaire the guest editors sent to several of Goff's former clients. Unsurprisingly, their answers highlighted Goff's personalized approach in highly positive terms.[57] More significant, however, was the publication's reliance on a client survey in the first place. It demonstrates how fully client considerations had shifted from the periphery to the forefront as architectural culture realigned with its socioeconomic context. At the time of Goff's death in 1982, his calls for individual work and individual architecture were being fully realized, though in terms he likely never would have imagined, in part because the specific client he had worked so hard to construct had disappeared into merely a customer.

What Goff's autofuturism accomplished in built works, correspondence, drawings, lectures, and writings was a reshaping of the framework in which discussions around architecture, clients, and indeed futurism itself took place without the crutch of yet-to-be-realized technological innovations or utopian impulses. Alongside the emergence of customer-oriented discourses, Goff was surprisingly prophetic about individuality supplanting the collective. He prognosticated a society driven by distinctive tastes and preferences, self-expression, and self-determined design. He imagined the possibility for the client as a design context. And he reconceived architecture for "this thing that is *you*."

52. For "each creative artist," see Goff, "A Young Architect's Protest," 330.
53. Bruce Goff, "Aero House," unpublished manuscript, c. 1942, 3, series V, box 1, folder 5b, BGA, AIC.
54. Bruce Goff, "List for Jack to Check, Dec. 1941," typescript, series II, box 3, folder 19, BGA, AIC.
55. Emile and Charlotte Gutman to Bruce Goff, Aug. 5, 1958, series II, box 10, folder 28, BGA, AIC.
56. W. C. III and Elaine A. Gryder to Bruce Goff, Nov. 16, 1959, series II, box 14, folder 18, BGA, AIC.
57. John Sergeant and Stephen Mooring, eds., "AD Profiles 16: Bruce Goff," special issue, *Architectural Design* 48, no. 10 (1978).

California Trinity: The Al Struckus House

Janna Ireland

The pictures I found online did not prepare me for the reality of seeing Bruce Goff's Al Struckus House in person. You turn a corner and there it is—a grand extraterrestrial barrel, looking both like a structure from another world and like one that could exist only right here in Los Angeles, on that exact lot near the edge of the San Fernando Valley.

In Philadelphia, where I grew up, there is a tradition of trinity houses (also known as Father, Son, and Holy Ghost houses), which have three or four open levels, one room per floor, connected by a winding staircase. The Struckus house operates on the same basic principle, with an entry level, kitchen and dining area, bedroom, and living room stacked one on top of the other. Philadelphia trinity houses follow a staid townhouse format that blends in seamlessly with the brick-lined streets of Old City. Goff's house design exists in harmony with its surrounding landscape, too, only this landscape is one of boulders, trees, and California sunshine. With its exposed-wood beams, overlapping levels only nominally enclosed by netting, earthtones, and bug-eyed portholes, the Struckus house is one of a kind, a trinity reimagined via the space age and the *Swiss Family Robinson* treehouse.

It is always a challenge to convey the true essence of a place in pictures: Photographs flatten the three-dimensional world. The Struckus house, which seems to exist in four or more dimensions, poses additional challenges. Organic and singular in form, it is a shining example of Goff's design philosophy, moving forward through time unimpeded, always somehow in the "continuous present." I don't know whether my photographs can provide an accurate sense of its internal logic, but I hope they offer a sense of its magic.

4510

FEW
TENOCH
OAXACA
vtech

FIGS. 275–90 Goff. Al Struckus House, Woodland Hills, California, 1979–88. Photographs by Janna Ireland, 2024.

Selected Bibliography

BOOKS AND CHAPTERS

Cook, Jeffrey. *The Architecture of Bruce Goff.* Harper and Row, 1978.

De Long, David G. *The Architecture of Bruce Goff: Buildings and Projects, 1916–1974.* Garland, 1977.

De Long, David G. *Bruce Goff: Toward Absolute Architecture*. Foreword by Frank Gehry. Architectural History Foundation; MIT Press, 1988.

Futagawa, Yukio, ed. *Bavinger House, Norman, Oklahoma, 1950: Price House, Bartlesville, Oklahoma, 1957–1966*. A.D.A. EDITA Tokyo, 1975.

Guido, Luca, Stephanie Pilat, and Angela Person, eds. *Renegades: Bruce Goff and the American School of Architecture.* University of Oklahoma Press, 2020.

Henderson, Arn. *Bruce Goff: Architecture of Discipline in Freedom.* University of Oklahoma Press, 2017.

Mason, Carol. "Bruce Goff: How to Stop Enjoying and Learn to Fear Queer Art." In *Oklahomo: Lessons in Unqueering America*. State University of New York Press, 2015.

Meier, Allison C. "The Flamboyant Futurism of Bruce Goff." In *Midwest Architecture Journeys*, edited by Zach Mortice. Belt Publishing, 2019.

Mohri, Takenobu. *Bruce Goff, Architect.* Kenchiku Planning Center, 1970.

Perkins, Scott W., ed. *Bruce Goff: A Creative Mind*. Fred Jones Jr. Museum of Art, University of Oklahoma; Price Tower Arts Center, 2010.

Saliga, Pauline, and Mary Woolever, eds. *The Architecture of Bruce Goff, 1904–1982: Design for the Continuous Present*. Prestel; Art Institute of Chicago, 1995.

Sutton, Chris, ed. *Free Thought: The Art and Architecture of Bruce Goff*. Price Tower Arts Center, 2003.

Welch, Philip B., ed. *Goff on Goff: Conversations and Lectures*. University of Oklahoma Press, 1996.

PERIODICALS

Adams, Brooks. "The Delirious Palace." *Art in America* 77, no. 12 (Dec. 1989): 136–45.

Branch, Mark Alden. "A Breed Apart." *Progressive Architecture* 73, no. 6 (June 1992): 68–73.

"Bruce Goff, Visionary Architect." *Art in America* 53, no. 1 (1965): 82–87.

Casciani, Stefano, and Luigi Spinelli. "Bruce Goff: Punto e a capo per un'architettura totale" [Bruce Goff: A New Paragraph for Total Architecture]. *Domus* no. 903 (May 2007): 59–64.

Cobb, Russell. "Continuous Present: A Voyage into the Genius and Madness of Bruce Goff's Oklahoma." *This Land* 2, no. 16 (Nov. 15, 2011): 8–9.

"Consternation and Bewilderment in Oklahoma." *Life*, June 28, 1948, 71–74.

Dean, Penelope. "Ten Miles, Three Years, and Two Worlds Apart." *Flat Out*, Fall 2016, 3, and 62–64.

"Domus itinerario n. 121: Goff e gli Stati Uniti" [Domus Itinerary n. 121: Goff and the United States]. *Domus*, no. 780 (Mar. 1996): 87–94.

Fortini, Amanda. "The Man Who Made Wildly Imaginative, Gloriously Disobedient Buildings." *New York Times Style Magazine*, Sept. 10, 2018.

"Goff on Goff." *Progressive Architecture* 43 (Dec. 1962): 102–23.

Goldberger, Paul. "Tomorrowland, with a Dash of Fantasyland." *New York Times*, Dec. 4, 1988, 34.

Gordon, Alastair. "Back to the Future: Recalling One of the Dream-Weaving Architect's Earliest 'Unbuildable' Houses." *Architectural Digest* 66, no. 10 (Oct. 2009): 80, 85–86.

Hamburger, Bernard. "Bruce Goff." SADG: Bulletin de la Société des architectes diplômés par le gouvernement 162 (Dec. 1967): 2–8.

"Houses of Bruce Goff." *Architecture and Urbanism*, no. 134 (Nov. 1981): 3–16.

Huxtable, Ada Louise. "Peacock Feathers and Pink Plastic: A New Yorker Sees Bruce Goff." *New York Times*, Feb. 8, 1970, D25.

Iannelli, Alphonso [*sic*]. "The Boston Avenue Methodist Episcopal Church of Tulsa, Oklahoma." *Western Architect* 38 (Oct. 1929): 173–74, 190, pl. 147–52, fol. 192.

Jencks, Charles. "Bruce Goff: The Michelangelo of Kitsch." Ed. John Sergeant, and Stephen Mooring. Special issue, *Architectural Design* 48, no. 10 (1978): 10–14.

Kitnick, Alex. Review of *The Way He Always Wanted It II*, by Stephen Prina. *Journal of the Society of Architectural Historians* 68, no. 2 (June 2009): 281–83.

Knapp, Judith. "The Architecture of Romantic Whimsey: U.S. Architect Bruce Goff." *Architect and Builder* (South Africa) 15 (Nov. 1965): 30–32.

Kostka, Robert. "Bruce Goff and the New Tradition." *Prairie School Review* 7, no. 2 (1970): 1–2, 5–15, 23.

Lawford, Valentine. "Masterwork for Mr. and Mrs. Joe Price." *Vogue*, Feb. 1, 1972, 182–90.

Leigh, Betty. "Interview: 'I Do What Comes Naturally.'" *Inland Architect* 23, no. 8 (Dec. 1979): 18–23.

McCoy, Esther. "Retrospect: Bruce Goff." *Arts and Architecture* 2, no. 3 (1983): 44–47.

Molema, Jan. "De essentie van het Amerikanisme: De architectuur van Bruce Goff" [The Essence of Americanism: The Architecture of Bruce Goff]. *Archis*, no. 6 (June 1996): 18–29.

Morris, Robert. "The Hidden Sides of Architect Rebel Bruce Goff—A Rare Look at a Generous Genius." *PaperCity*, Jan. 26, 2019.

Norman, Carrie, and Thomas Kelley. "*Sic*. Building Syndrome." *Log* 51 (Winter/Spring 2021), 19–27.

Pillet, Michel. "L'insolite Monsieur Bruce Goff." *L'architecture d'aujourd'hui* 33, no. 102 (June 1962): 50–57.

"Pride of the Prairie: A High Priest of Individualism Is Designing in a Strikingly Regional Idiom for His Grass Roots Clients." *Architectural Forum* 88, no. 3 (Mar. 1948): 94–101, 190.

Prince, Bart. "Portrait: A Personal Memoir." *L'architecture d'aujourd'hui*, no. 227 (June 1983): 2–6.

Robinson, Sidney K. "Bruce Goff: Ford House, Aurora, Illinois, U.S.S., 1949–50." *GA Houses* 68 (2001): 64–79.

Rose, Steve. "'The Michelangelo of Kitsch': The Restoration of Outsider Architect Bruce Goff." *The Guardian*, Jan. 10, 2020.

"The Round House: Steel, Glass, Marbles, Copper, Rope and Coal Make a $64,000 Quonset-Hut Mansion." *Life*, Mar. 19, 1951, 70–75.

"Space and Saucer House: Oklahoma Family Lives in Suspension in a Unique New Structure." *Life*, Sept. 19, 1955, 155–56.

Webb, Michael. "Saving Bruce Goff." *Architectural Review* 217, no. 1300 (June 2005): 44.

Winters, Willis. "Bruce Goff in Texas: Renewed Visions at Lake Village." *Texas Architect* 39 (July 1989): 26–29.

Woods, Lebbeus. "The Inconsistent Hero." *Blueprint*, Oct. 1995, 51.

SPECIAL ISSUES

Alan, Howard, Betty Leigh, Hanni U. Janssen, and Jane Heron. "Bruce Goff, an Architectural Original." Special issue, *Inland Architect* 23, no. 8 (Dec. 1979).

"A Dialog of Difference: Reflections on Bruce Goff's Ford House." *MAS Context*, Jan. 25, 2021.

Friends of Kebyar (1983–present). Journal that focuses on Bruce Goff and organic architecture.

Leitl, Alfons, ed. "Bruce Goff." Special issue, *Baukunst und Werkform*, July 1953.

Sergeant, John, and Stephen Mooring, eds. "AD Profiles 16: Bruce Goff." Special issue, *Architectural Design* 48, no. 10 (1978).

Special issue, *Architecture and Urbanism*, no. 134 (Nov. 1981).

Special issue, *L'architecture d'aujourd'hui*, no. 227 (June 1983).

"Wege zu Goff" [Paths to Goff]. Special issue, *Bauwelt* 95, no. 37 (Oct. 1, 2004). German only.

DOCUMENTARY FILMS

Chabot, Charles, dir. *We Don't Like Your House Either: The Architecture of Bruce Goff*. BBC TV Production in association with the Shin'enKan Foundation, 1984. [51 min. 45 sec.].

Harris, Britni, dir. *Goff*. 2019. [91 min.]

Price, Joe D., dir. *The Artistry of Bruce Goff*. Thorne Films, Inc., 1965. [14 min.].

ARTIST FILMS

Emigholz, Heinz, dir. *Goff in the Desert*. Germany: Filmgalerie 451, 2003. [110 min. plus 50 min. extras].

Prina, Stephen, dir. *The Way He Always Wanted It II*. 2008. [27 min.].

Contributors

LAWRENCE CHUA is a historian of the modern Asian built environment. He is an associate professor in the School of Architecture at Syracuse University, New York and the author of *Bangkok Utopia: Modern Architecture and Buddhist Felicities, 1910–1973.* He has been a fellow at the Getty Research Institute, California; the Center for Southeast Asian Studies at Kyoto University, Japan; the Freiburg Institute of Advanced Studies, Germany; and the International Institute of Asian Studies at Leiden University, The Netherlands.

DAVID G. DE LONG is Professor Emeritus of Architecture at the University of Pennsylvania. His former and current affiliations include the Editorial Board of the Architectural History Foundation, Chairman of the Board of Directors of the Preservation Alliance for Greater Philadelphia, Western Pennsylvania Conservancy Advisory Committee, and Board of Directors of the Frank Lloyd Wright Building Conservancy.

PENELOPE DEAN is a professor in the University of Illinois at Chicago's School of Architecture. Dean has held fellowships at UIC's Institute for the Humanities and the Canadian Centre for Architecture at Montreal. Her work on the intersections of design, architecture, and business culture has appeared in publications ranging from *Harvard Design Magazine* to *Log* and been recognized through grants from the National Endowment for the Arts and the Graham Foundation. She is founding editor of the design magazine *Flat Out*.

ALISON FISHER is the Harold and Margot Schiff Curator of Architecture and Design at the Art Institute of Chicago. She specializes in alternative histories of modern architecture, design, and urbanism and has curated many exhibitions in these areas, including *Bertrand Goldberg: Architecture of Invention* (2011), *The City Lost and Found: Capturing New York, Chicago, and Los Angeles, 1960–1980* (2014), *Georg Jensen: Scandinavian Design for Living* (2018), *Bauhaus Chicago: Design in the City* (2019), and *Dan Friedman: Stay Radical* (2023).

SCOTT HERRING is Professor of American Studies and Women's, Gender, and Sexuality Studies at Yale University. He has authored and edited several books, including *Aging Moderns: Art, Literature, and the Experiment of Later Life* (Columbia University Press, 2022), *Another Country: Queer Anti-Urbanism* (New York University Press, 2010), and, with Lee Wallace, *Long Term: Essays on Queer Commitment* (Duke University Press, 2021).

JANNA IRELAND lives in Los Angeles, where she is an assistant professor in the Department of Art and Art History at Occidental College. Her photographic work is primarily concerned with the themes of family and domestic life, the built environment, and interactions between humans and the natural world. She authored *Regarding Paul R. Williams: A Photographer's View* (2020).

HADLEY JERMAN BRUSS is an independent scholar who researches, teaches, and writes about art, design, and photography of the American West. She earned a PhD in art history from the University of Oklahoma in 2020 and is the former Eugene B. Adkins Curator of the Fred Jones Jr. Museum of Art.

KELLY KEEGAN is a paintings conservator in Conservation and Science at the Art Institute of Chicago. Starting with her graduate internship at the Art Institute in 2005, she remained in Conservation under various fellowships and special projects positions, securing a permanent position in 2015. Her focus includes research and treatment of eighteenth- through twenty-first-century paintings, and contemporary analytical imaging techniques. Previous publications include technical studies of works by Jasper Johns, Auguste Renoir, Camille Pissarro, Gustave Caillebotte, and Ivan Albright.

CRAIG LEE is an assistant curator in Architecture and Design at the Art Institute of Chicago and the previous Daniel F. and Ada L. Rice Postdoctoral Fellow. He has held fellowships at Crystal Bridges Museum of American Art, Bentonville, Arkansas, and the Museum of the City of New York. Past projects have included work on Charles Moore and Helmut Jahn, in addition to writings on Denise Scott Brown, Edgar Miller, and the histories of outdoor advertising and commercial signage.

PAULA LUPKIN is an associate professor in the Department of Art History at the University of North Texas, Denton. She has authored and edited books and articles on diverse topics, including YMCA architecture, American interior design, and the relationship between beer, cannabis, and the design of Louis Sullivan's famous skyscraper, the Wainwright Building. Her most recent work includes "The Telegraphic Interior: Networking Space for Capital Flows in the 1920s," in *Interior Provocations* (Routledge, 2021).

NOLAN VALLIER serves as both a lecturer in musicology at the School of Music and a Clinical Assistant Professor and Assistant Archivist at the Sousa Archives and Center for American Music at the University of Illinois Urbana-Champaign. His work explores the musical lives of American architects, music about architects, and concerts that take place in unusual architectural spaces. He has presented nationally at American Musicological Society and Society for American Music conferences and locally at the Conference on Illinois History and at annual exhibitions held at the Sousa Archives.

Index

All buildings, unbuilt projects, and compositions are by Bruce Goff unless otherwise indicated. Page numbers in *italics* refer to illustrations.

Photo Credits

Unless otherwise noted, photographs of artworks in the collection of the Art Institute of Chicago are copyrighted by the Art Institute of Chicago. Photography by Aidan Fitzpatrick, Nathan Keay, Robert Lifson, Jonathan Mathias, Juan Molina Hernández, Craig Stillwell, and Joe Tallarico. Postproduction by Owen Conway, Kaitlyn Fultz-Campion, and Hayley Hinsberger. Preproduction and coordination by Elyse M. Allen.

Every effort has been made to identify, contact, and acknowledge copyright holders for all reproductions; additional rights holders are encouraged to contact the Art Institute of Chicago. The following credits apply to all images in this book for which separate acknowledgment is due.

FIG. 7: Mercedes-Benz Classic. FIGS. 10, 135, 212: © J. Paul Getty Trust. Getty Research Institute, Los Angeles (2004.R.10). FIG. 16: Eliot Elisofon / The LIFE Picture Collection/Shutterstock. FIGS. 29, 37, 38: Ernest Ellison Photograph Collection, The Filson Historical Society, Louisville, KY. FIG. 44: Wittelsbacher Ausgleichsfonds, München, inventory number B VIII 18. FIGS. 103, 115A–D: Photo by Joseph Mills. FIG. 161: Photo by E.G. Schempf. FIG. 137: Courtesy of Rago/Wright. FIG. 227: Image courtesy of Converso Modern, Chicago. FIG. 224: Photo by Natalja Kent. FIGS. 237, 239: Photo by Robert Reck. FIGS. 220, 225: Image courtesy of 20c Design. Photo by Joe Roldan. FIG. 193: © Elena Dorfman / Redux. FIGS. 222, 248: Photo by Horst P. Horst / Conde Nast via Getty Images. FIG. 226: © Alan Barley. FIGS. 242, 252: USC Digital Library. Wayne Thom Photography Collection. FIG. 244: Courtesy of Bronbeek Museum, Ministry of Defence, Netherlands. FIG. 245: Digital Image © 2025 Museum Associates / LACMA. Licensed by Art Resource, NY. FIG. 258: © Ezra Stoller / Esto. FIG. 260: Admiral: The clearest picture in television, 2014.277, Audiovisual Collections and Digital Initiatives Department, AVDJOPN2014_Admiral-TV-lady-2, Hagley Museum and Library, Wilmington, DE 19807. FIG. 272: Photo still courtesy of CBS Studios.

BRUCE GOFF ARCHIVE FILE NUMBERS, ALL PRECEDED BY 199001

P. 2: J27689. FIG. 1: J29055. FIG. 2: 100305-03-J27707. FIG. 3: J27699. FIG. 4: J27700. FIG. 6: J27693. FIG. 11: J27698. FIG. 15: J27675. FIG. 18: J4281. FIG. 19: J4002. FIG. 21: J4017. FIG. 22: J4010. FIG. 25: J4007. FIG. 26: BG_port3-J27678. FIG. 27: J6445. FIG. 28: J27679. FIG. 30: J29054. FIG. 31: J27661. FIG. 34: J27664. FIG. 35: J27687. FIG. 45: J27697. FIG. 52: J4014. FIG. 54: J26468. FIG. 60: J27692. FIG. 61: J27690. FIG. 69: J27695. FIG. 76: J27317. FIG. 77: J27654. FIG. 82: J27680. FIG. 85: J4538. FIG. 90: J25130. FIG. 93: J27656. FIG. 98: J27705. FIG. 100: J24848. FIG. 108: J27688. FIG. 109: J28002. FIG. 110: J4126. FIG. 111: J27685. FIG. 112: J27684. FIG. 113: J27691. FIG. 114: Riverside_1-J27696. FIG. 117: 27681. FIG. 122: J27665. FIG. 129: J4290. FIG. 130: 3999. FIG. 132: J27318. FIG. 139: J26444, J26453, J25476. FIG. 143A–D: J6449, J6443, J27710, J6447. FIG. 150: J27313. FIG. 158: J27701. FIG. 163: J27703. FIG. 164: J27702. FIG. 167: J27676. FIG. 168: J27674. FIG. 173: J27694. FIG. 174: J27704. FIG. 178: J27650. FIG. 184: J27720. FIG. 191: J27822. FIG. 215: J4282. FIG. 216: J4038. FIG. 217: J7605. FIG. 218: J4022. FIG. 226: J27673. FIG. 236: J5609. FIG. 246: J27717. FIG. 247: J27667. FIG. 253: J27708. FIG. 254: J27669. FIG. 255: J27670. FIG. 263: J27668. FIG. 274: J27652.

COVER: Rendering of Goff, *Structure Study*, 1943 (fig. 94), and Goff, *Untitled (Composition)*, 1932 (fig. 71).
BACK COVER: Rendering of Goff, *Untitled (Composition)*, 1933 (fig. 87), and Goff and Douglas Harris, *Irma Bartman House, Louisville, Kentucky, Interior Perspective* [unbuilt], 1957 (fig. 154).
FRONT ENDPAPERS: Bruce Goff at Chester Rant House during construction, Northfield, Illinois, 1938. Photographer unknown. Bruce A. Goff Archive.
FRONTISPIECE: Bruce Goff in office at University of Oklahoma, Norman, c. 1954. Photograph by Philip B. Welch. Bruce A. Goff Archive.
BACK ENDPAPERS: Bruce Goff working in his studio at Price Tower, Bartlesville, Oklahoma, 1962. Photograph by Douglas Harris. Bruce A. Goff Archive.

Bruce Goff: Material Worlds was published in conjunction with an exhibition of the same title organized by the Art Institute of Chicago, December 21, 2025–March 29, 2026.

Major support for *Bruce Goff: Material Worlds* is provided by Jack Butler and John VanderLinden, Margot Levin Schiff and the Harold Schiff Foundation, and Kathleen Nagle and Ralph Johnson.

Additional support is provided by the Graham Foundation for Advanced Studies in the Fine Arts and Dirk Denison and David Salkin.

Graham Foundation

Members of the Luminary Trust provide annual leadership support for the museum's operations, including exhibition development, conservation and collection care, and educational programming. The Luminary Trust includes an anonymous donor, Karen Gray-Krehbiel and John Krehbiel, Jr., Kenneth C. Griffin, the Harris Family Foundation in memory of Bette and Neison Harris, Josef and Margot Lakonishok, Liz and Eric Lefkofsky, Ann and Samuel M. Mencoff, Sylvia Neil and Dan Fischel, Cari and Michael J. Sacks, and the Earl and Brenda Shapiro Foundation.

FIRST EDITION
PRINTED IN ITALY

30 29 28 27 26 25   1 2 3 4 5

Authorized Representative in the EU: Easy Access System Europe, Mustamäe tee 50, 10621 Tallinn, Estonia, gpsr.requests@easproject.com

ISBN: 978-0-300-28407-2 (hardcover)

LIBRARY OF CONGRESS CONTROL NUMBER: 2025944498

PUBLISHED BY
The Art Institute of Chicago
111 South Michigan Avenue
Chicago, IL 60603-6404
artic.edu

DISTRIBUTED BY
Yale University Press
302 Temple Street
P. O. Box 209040
New Haven, CT 06520-9040
yalebooks.com/art

EDITED BY Sheila Majumdar
PRODUCTION BY Elizabeth Upenieks with Lauren Makholm
PHOTOGRAPHY RESEARCH BY Kristie Kahns
PROOFREADING BY Juliet Clark
INDEXING BY Theresa Duran
DESIGN AND TYPESETTING BY Content Object, Kimberly Varella with Gabrielle Pulgar
SEPARATIONS BY Professional Graphics, Rockford, Illinois
PRINTING AND BINDING BY Graphicom, Verona, Italy

PUBLISHING, THE ART INSTITUTE OF CHICAGO
Katie Reilly, Associate Vice President, Publishing
Lisa Meyerowitz, Editorial Director
Lauren Makholm, Director of Production

IMAGING, THE ART INSTITUTE OF CHICAGO
Bonnie Rosenberg, Director of Imaging
Nathan Keay, Associate Director, Photography
Elyse M. Allen, Associate Director, Production

This book was made using paper and materials certified by the Forest Stewardship Council, which ensures responsible forest management.

This book was set in Bau Pro (FontFont), Circular (Lineto), Fugue Mono (Radim Peško), PF Mellon (Parachute), and Platform (Commercial Type) and was printed on Munken Print, Fedrigoni Tatami, Garda Gloss, Wibalin Natural, and Imitlin Metal Neve.